THE TALENT SOLUTION

Aligning Strategy and People to Achieve Extraordinary Results

Edward L. Gubman

McGraw-Hill
New York • San Francisco • Washington, D.C. • Auckland
Bogotá • Caracas • Lisbon • London • Madrid • Mexico City
Milan • Montreal • New Delhi • San Juan • Singapore
Sydney • Tokyo • Toronto

Library of Congress Cataloging-in-Publication Data

Gubman, Edward L.
   The talent solution : aligning strategy & people to achieve
extraordinary results / Edward L. Gubman
      p.   cm.
   Includes bibliographical references
   ISBN 0-07-025161-4
   1. Manpower planning.   2. Organizational effectiveness.   3. Human
   capital.   4. Ability.   5. Industrial management.   I. Title.
HF5549.5.M3G8   1998
658.3—dc21   98-48679
                                                         CIP

McGraw-Hill

*A Division of The **McGraw·Hill** Companies*

      5 6 7 8 9 0 DOC/DOC 9 0 2 1 0 9

ISBN 0-07-025161-4

The sponsoring editor for this book was Jeffrey Krames and the production supervisor was
Suzanne W. B. Rapcavage. It was set in Palatino by Lisa M. King of Editorial and Production
Services.

Printed and bound by R. R. Donnelley & Sons Company.

This publication is designed to provide accurate and authoritative information in regard to
the subject matter covered. It is sold with the understanding that neither the author nor the
publisher is engaged in rendering legal, accounting, or other professional service. If legal
advice or other expert assistance is required, the services of a competent professional
person should be sought.

> —*From a Declaration of Principles jointly adopted by a Committee of the
> American Bar Association and a Committee of Publishers.*

McGraw-Hill books are available at special quantity discounts to use as premiums and sales
promotions, or for use in corporate training programs. For more information, please write
to the Director of Special Sales, McGraw-Hill, 11 West 19th Street, New York, N.Y. 10011. Or
contact your local bookstore.

 This book is printed on recycled, acid-free paper containing a minimum
of 50% recycled de-inked fiber.

To Rachel for her inspiration and advice,
to Mike and Charlie for their enthusiastic support,
and to Cassie for keeping me company while I wrote.

ACKNOWLEDGMENTS

Collaboration is one of our core values at Hewitt Associates, and this book is a direct result of many collaborative efforts and teamwork. It's a product of years of consulting and managing in a supportive, inclusive, team-oriented culture where no single person really accomplishes much, but together we regularly create miracles. I take full responsibility for what's said in these pages, but if there is credit to be given, it must be shared with many others.

I have been interested in how to align, engage, and measure people's performance for many years. These topics came into much sharper focus several years ago when we developed our *Improving Business Results With People* consulting model. This was a large-scale collaboration among several Hewitt consultants, including the practice leaders and consultants quoted in this book. Another set of insights came when I started working closely with the ideas expressed in *The Discipline of Market Leaders* by Michael Treacy and Fred Wiersema. I particularly appreciate Fred's openness and sharing of ideas.

There are several Hewitt people I want to thank publicly, though in doing so I know I will miss others whom I should mention as well. Christine Seltz provided early enthusiasm and assistance for this project. I could not have started without her. Dale Gifford, our CEO, generously allowed me some time away from other responsibilities to write and offered encouragement throughout the long process. My long-time associate and collaborator, Barbara Grala, typed and retyped the manuscript, kept me connected to the office but protected me from intrusions on writing time, and expressed so much excitement about the book that she was a great source of motivation. Danielle McDonald took on many additional management tasks so I could concentrate on writing, and Eddie Franco covered extra client assignments for me.

I also want to thank Diana Reace, who did much of the secondary research for the book. She was helped by our peerless Hewitt library and research staff. John Bausch, Lori Grubs, Peter Van Susteren, and Jenny Wich read the manuscript carefully and offered detailed and wise critiques. Pamela Filler worked diligently on creating and coordinating much of the Hewitt marketing support. Denise Clutts put in long hours revising the manuscript and graphics. Special thanks also go to Sandy Cook and my colleagues in the Organization Effectiveness Practice who offered constant ideas and encouragement, and to my Hewitt friends around the world for their advice and reassurance.

A big thank-you is due to the clients who allowed me to learn from them, interview them, and write about them. Their words and stories give life to the messages in this book. I hope I have done you justice in portraying many of the outstanding ways you are aligning strategy and people to achieve extraordinary results. The best part of consulting is the clients.

Finally, a huge thank-you goes to my family. Writing is a solitary task, and though I was home, I wasn't really present. My wife, Rachel, was never-ending in her support for this project and is a great advisor on issues large and small. My sons, Mike and Charlie, were more enthusiastic about this book than any other work project I ever tackled. Thanks, guys.

CONTENTS

PART FOUR

IMPLEMENT   277

INTRODUCTION

AWAKE AT NIGHT

Recently I listened to a brilliant presentation on a company's new business strategy. The person leading it was the company's head strategist—very smart guy with an MBA from a great business school. He took the group I was in through a detailed and elegant explanation of the process the company used to create the new approach. Then he introduced the strategy in a very easy-to-understand way. We covered customer needs, business capabilities, the new operating model, and the integrated activities the company would follow to ensure uniqueness and advantage.

There was only one thing missing. He never mentioned people, the one element the company really needed to address so it could change the way it did business and adopt the new strategy. This was even more noticeable because at the time of the presentation the company had several high-level searches going on for talent absolutely essential to implementing the new direction.

I see this all the time, and it mystifies me. When I talk to executives, most of them define their strategies with great clarity and confidence. Then I'll ask, "What keeps you awake at night?" All over the world they get a very serious expression on their faces and tell me the same thing, and it's not the business strategy: "Talent—I don't know how I am going to get and keep the talent I need to build my business." Yet there's rarely a strategy or plan to address the cause of their insomnia.

Consider this:

- Within a three-month span, four high-profile corporations—Apple, AT&T, Waste Management, and Walt Disney—all fired their newly hired CEOs or presidents because they couldn't perform to expectations.

- Michigan and Ohio began expensive national advertising campaigns to lure new skilled workers because unemployment levels were at record lows, despite employers raising

1

salaries and expanding benefits. "There are $50,000 to $100,000 jobs going unfilled," said a director for the Michigan Jobs Commission.

- In China, a high-ranking ministry official responsible for helping state-owned enterprises privatize said the reform movement is struggling because the planned economy raised a generation of "lazy boys" who don't know how to work.

- The *Far Eastern Economic Review* reports that Southeast Asia needs at least 3 million more managers, double the current number, to catch up with the developed world. As a result, competition is fierce and wages are soaring for qualified people.

- Back in the U.S., the CEO of a well-known global consumer products company says the company's growth is not limited by money or technology, but by its inability to double the number of managers who can work around the world.

IN SHORT SUPPLY

If any of these situations feel a little familiar, take some comfort in knowing you're not alone. In the U.S. and growing economies worldwide, the issue is the same: how to attract, retain, and deploy talented people who can help you grow your business when these people are in short supply.

This was not such a big problem a few years ago. There appeared to be more than enough skilled people, and companies acted like talent was abundant. Global business had not yet started to boom. The U.S. was deep in the throes of reengineering and downsizing, so the rush was to get people out the door.

Now the tide has turned. Unemployment in the U.S. is at a 20-year low. In Britain and in other countries that have restructured their economies, unemployment is falling quickly. In the new boom spots of the world, places like China and India, skilled help is at a premium. It's hard to find, and it's expensive.

Finding talent will be difficult and costly throughout the world for the next several years. The workforce isn't shrinking, but it's not growing skilled talent fast enough to keep up with global demand and opportunities. In the U.S., we will see this problem till at least 2002 and probably beyond.

> **Finding talent will be difficult and costly throughout the world for the next several years.**

In 1997, American economists, including Federal Reserve Chairman Alan Greenspan, were amazed the nation wasn't experiencing wage inflation from the tight labor market. They attributed it to productivity improvements, worker insecurities, the increasing use of part-time and contingent workers, and the return of older people to the workforce. However, they may not have been looking closely enough.

The national economic data didn't show it, but local and specialized surveys and anecdotal data began to report huge jumps in pay levels for people holding specialist talents, particularly in knowledge industries or skilled manufacturing. A survey of Chicago-area employers showed the same overall results as national trends, average pay increases of 3.5 to 5 percent. Yet digging deeper, average raises for the 20 hottest job categories ranged from 10 to 21 percent. Moreover, it took longer to find these people. The head of the Illinois Manufacturing Association, when asked to comment on the increase in the minimum wage, said, "The issue isn't the $5.15, the problem is finding the people to pay."

Everywhere companies keep saying the same things: There are people looking for work, but filling critical positions that need top-flight talent means long, expensive searches and big raises, if you can find someone. Once you have the people you need, then you get to worry about losing them to the large numbers of tempting and lucrative job opportunities. This is a seller's market for talented people.

BETTER MANAGEMENT WINS

If talent is scarce and valuable, companies win when they are smarter than the competition in creating an attractive work environment, picking the right people, and getting the most out of them. Why would skilled people go to work in a lackluster workplace when they have a choice of many appealing employers? Why would they stay if they feel the work isn't challenging or their skills aren't being fully used and developed? There are plenty of good jobs available. There aren't that many good places to work. In many of the world's fast-growing economies, it may be easier to access money and technology than good people. This means competitive advantage belongs to companies that know how to attract, select, deploy, and develop talent.

Managing talent now is the "make or break" skill in the information economy. In the old days, how you managed people was important, but your access and control over physical resources and money probably determined final success or failure. During the last 25 years, first in the U.S. and now in other high-value economies, your abilities to create information or service, or to add knowledge to basic manufacturing, processing, and logistics decide winning and losing. Since the ultimate source of all information, service, and knowledge-added is people, the only way to be successful is to manage people effectively. This is a lot harder than managing hard assets and finances.

Getting the most out of your talent is the talent solution. This book will help you answer your biggest question—how to attract, use, and keep the people you need to grow your business. It will tell you how to manage people to build long-term, extraordinary results. It won't explain how to find employees, but it will tell you how to become a more attractive employer so it's easier to hire. You will see how to build a lasting competitive advantage by understanding your customer strategy and using it to select, develop, and deploy talent. You will learn how to engage people and measure their contribution in meaningful ways. This is what I call *aligning strategy and people*. This talent solution can help you sleep a little better at night.

EXECUTIVE ATTENTION IS ON THE SHORT-TERM

In my experience, managing talent is not where many executives focus their attention. Executives usually address talent issues only when they are involved in a high-profile search for an important position or a retention battle to keep a critical employee. Otherwise, most of them leave selection, development, deployment, and retention to others.

Recently I heard Anthony Rucci, Senior Vice President of Administration at Sears, declare, "Nine out of ten American companies don't pay enough attention to employees and customers." I agree. Most executives instead seem to think like Harold Geneen, former Chairman of ITT, who said, "All business problems are people problems." These problems usually are addressed only when it's no longer possible to avoid them.

Executive focus still seems to be mostly on short-term financial goals or operational improvements. The most extreme example of this in recent years is "Chainsaw" Al Dunlap. Dunlap took over Scott Paper and greatly increased shareholder value—after all, he had become a big shareholder—but in the end there was no more independent Scott Paper. He cut costs down to the nub and laid off tens of thousands of employees. After he squeezed out all those costs, he couldn't grow Scott again. Too much talent was gone, and the people who survived wouldn't follow him. Instead, he sold Scott to Kimberly-Clark, and that was the end of a once great, autonomous company. Dunlap and the management team he brought in got rich and went on to their next ventures.

This may have been a great short-term move for Scott's shareholders, but it didn't build any long-term value. Maybe Dunlap and others like him should get paid a lot if all boards of directors want is short-term profits because they produce a lot of it. But so what? Short-term actions are the easy way to do things.

It's not difficult to pick out the parts of a business that aren't making enough money, sell them, spin them off, close them, move production overseas, fire people—all the while claiming things will be far worse if you don't. Almost anybody who can read a balance sheet can do that. Running a company for long-term growth and value is what's hard. The Dunlap approach suggests short-term maximization and liquidation is the only alternative when a company is in bad shape. How would he or people like him know without trying to turn the whole company around—without trying to build for the long-term?

To me it's about the same as buying an old house, fixing it up quickly to make it look good without paying much attention to structural or systems improvement, and selling it off for a fast profit. People do it every day, and they find ready buyers who don't look below the surface. Still, the people who redecorated the house didn't make it a home. The house becomes a home when a buyer is willing to put down roots and put time into really correcting the basic systems structure, just like trying to rebuild a company.

Above all, long-term value creation demands focusing on people. You have to build an organization where people want to satisfy customers every day, every year. This takes a long time, requires responding to a lot of diverse needs, and can be as frustrating as it is rewarding.

> **Long-term value creation demands focusing on people.**

Unfortunately, I have become convinced most executives would prefer to talk about and deal with any topic other than people. People drive them crazy, people have feelings, they're fickle, they often think and do the opposite of what you expect them to do, they make mistakes, they exceed expectations, they disappoint, they delight, they keep changing; and as they do, they keep changing their demands. Just when you think you have your employees figured out, they will want something different. No wonder rational executives prefer dealing with machines, ideas, or money.

BAD ADVICE, BAD FADS

Maybe it's the advice executives get. Take a look at most of the articles and books on corporate strategy. Employees rarely get mentioned. It's as if the strategies companies develop to advance customer and shareholder interests have nothing to do with the people who actually execute them. Very few companies think strategically about people, or have a written workforce strategy.

On the other hand, advice about how to manage people usually is strategy-free. Management practices are prescribed without any tie to what business the company is in and what it is doing to provide customer value. Speakers and writers describe goal-setting, empowerment, teamwork, or other approaches as ends, not means, that are positive almost by their very definition. Rarely is much evidence shown for how practices lead to increased business results. No wonder executives don't pay much attention.

I suspect this executive preference to focus on anything else besides people is what's behind most management fads. If you can promise executives their companies can become more profitable by starting an initiative on productivity improvement, quality circles, total quality, reengineering, shareholder value—anything else but people—you can get them to buy it. The last 20 years offer ample proof.

The reality is no strategy is ever implemented, and no change is ever created, unless and until you can get people to change. Every improvement to your company rests on people deciding to do something differently and better. When you can get people to want to, and know how to, change, then you can implement your strategy and accomplish your goals.

For example, consider the productivity improvement campaigns of the late 1970s and early 1980s. They turned into employee suggestion systems, performance appraisal programs, and incentive plans, because management couldn't improve productivity without some employee participation, short of laying people off.

> **Every improvement to your company rests on people deciding to do something differently and better.**

Quality circles in the early 1980s lacked real focus or accountability and were replaced by engineering-oriented statistical process controls. But that didn't work by itself either. The total quality management (TQM) movement, at least in North America, struggled until employee involvement techniques were added. The most successful total quality companies combined process controls and measurement with involvement and often had a good, long run. Companies that were really good at TQM incorporated it into day-to-day people management, while others saw their efforts fade.

Even the people who originated and profited from these changes now attest that they ultimately depended on employees. Studies have shown that 70–80% of reengineering efforts in the 1990s didn't accomplish their most important objectives, or simply devolved into downsizing. Michael Hammer and Jim Champy—the acknowledged founders of the reengineering movement—admitted their revolution failed because they underestimated the power managers and employees have over changing work processes. In later books, they both asked for a second chance with a greater emphasis on people.

The current emphasis on creating and improving shareholder value likewise is doomed without getting employees at all levels to make decisions differently. Fortunately, there is some evidence at least a few smart companies realize this. For example, Herman Miller, the office furniture and systems designer and manufacturer, is adopting shareholder value measures for both its executive and employee incentive plans and is training all employees about how to make decisions that drive value. If others follow Miller's lead, then shareholder value can be increased, and employees will gain too.

ALIGNING STRATEGY AND PEOPLE IS THE TALENT SOLUTION

Connecting people to strategy to serve customers will build extraordinary results and long-term value. This is the talent solution that will enable you to get the most out of your people, even when talent is in short supply. It also will help you attract and retain valuable people because you will be a highly successful company that takes wonderful care of its customers and is able to reward both shareholders and employees. Unless employees feel valued, they will not satisfy customers—and satisfied customers are essential for profits, cash flow, and happy shareholders.

To start managing talent effectively, you first must recognize that the things you have to do to make your business a long-term success are the same things employees need you to do so they can feel successful. Employees are not separate from the business, they are the business. While shareholders are focused on financial rewards, employees have a much broader set of needs. Many employee needs are linked to being part of a winning business. Helping employees meet these needs not only helps you find and keep skilled people, it's a way to get employees to delight customers and shareholders too.

Let me explain what I mean with an example. Some of my consulting over the years has involved employee attitude surveys. In many, if not most, of these surveys, the number-one problem cited by employees is always the same—communication. In fact, it comes up so often I sometimes wonder why we even conduct the surveys. The usefulness of an attitude survey comes when you break down the results into smaller pieces. Then you find out employees want to know four things:

1.   Where are we going as a company?
2.   What are we doing to get there?
3.   What can I do to contribute?
4.   What's in it for me when I do?

These are the big four communication needs on employees' minds. Fortunately, these are exactly the things you should hope they want to know. What company—large or small—regardless of industry, wouldn't benefit from being clear to employees about its:

- Strategy and goals
- Plans and processes
- Team and individual accountabilities
- Rewards

That's what employees want. Don't customers want informed employees who understand what they're supposed to do? Won't shareholders benefit when your people are aligned to what you want to accomplish?

Another quick story: Many years ago, I was consulting to a hospital in the Midwest about creating an incentive plan for its managers. The CEO had just completed working on a strategic plan with a big-name strategy consultant. When I suggested we share these plans with managers so they could use them to set goals for performance measures and incentives, the CEO quickly refused. He said, "We can't share our strategy, that's our secret!" Luckily, he later left the organization to become a lawyer—a profession maybe better suited to his penchant for nondisclosure.

This book is about why it's essential to connect strategy and people to manage talent, and more importantly, how to do it. It rests on three key concepts: alignment, engagement, and measurement. *Alignment* means pointing people in the right direction. *Engagement* means fostering commitment to your basic purpose and direction. *Measurement* means providing connected and balanced ways for your company and employees to keep score about how you are doing. When you do all three things, you will be managing your talent and company to achieve extraordinary results.

As you can see, these three things bring us right back to what employees keep telling us they need to know so they can succeed in your business—where you're going, what you're doing to get there, how they can help, and what's in it for them when they do. When they get this from you, they will be able to satisfy your customers, reward your shareholders, and create real long-term value.

ORGANIZATION AND CONTENT OF THIS BOOK

To guide you in your reading, here is a brief description of how this book is organized and what it contains.

- The first section of the book, Chapters 1–8, deals with alignment. Starting with your business strategy, you will learn how to align your work environment, talent, management practices, and business interactions to your company's strategic style.
- The next section, Chapters 9–11, explains engagement— what it is and the things you can do to more fully engage employees in executing your business strategy and delivering value to customers.
- Measurement is the next big topic, covered in Chapters 12–14. You will see how to begin with business performance measurement and push it through to individual performance management to help ensure you get the results you need.
- Chapter 15 is about getting started with strategy implementation. It helps you understand how to put alignment, engagement, and measurement processes into operation.
- Each chapter starts with a bulleted list that highlights its content and ends with some questions for you to consider so you can create a talent solution for your company.
- Additionally, the appendix addresses the specific issue of whether talent management practices actually make a difference to the bottom-line financial results of your business. I review a broad range of studies done in the last decade that show a strong relationship between good talent management practices and financial performance.

PART ONE

ALIGN

1

Strategy Implementation Through People

Some companies manage talent much better than others. In this chapter you'll see why that's true and how they do it, including:

- Examples of smart companies that know how to manage talent
- Why strategy implementation takes place through people and why you have to view your workforce strategically to accomplish this
- How the align–engage–measure cycle enables you to connect talent to strategy
- The value of knowing your strategic style and how it affects your talent solution

SMART COMPANIES

Late in 1994, a new executive team came aboard to rescue Continental Airlines from Chapter 11 bankruptcy and probable extinction. This was not the first turnaround team to take over the struggling carrier. Several had tried already and lost.

This new team, headed by Gordon Bethune, had a very simple recipe for success. Run a "good, on-time airline," one that business customers would find dependable and pleasant to fly, employees would feel is an enjoyable place to work, and shareholders would see as a good investment. The new team had to fix everything at once—finances, operations, and people, especially people whom it saw as the key to turning things around.

Getting crews to run an on-time airline with good service became priority number one. Bethune's management team did several things at once. It eliminated policies that got in the way of serving customers and teamwork and began communicating business plans and operating activities regularly to all levels of employees. It spent much of its time on the tarmacs and at ticket counters with employees to understand how to make things better. It installed an incentive plan that paid $65 to each employee every month the airline ranked in the top five of the Department of Transportation (DOT) on-time performance rankings.

By the end of 1995, Continental had paid the bonus nine times... and provided a total return to shareholders of 370 percent. In 1996, Continental reported record operating profits of $556 million and hit a "grand slam" by finishing in the top three on all four DOT customer service rankings. It experienced the biggest upward movement of any company on *Fortune's* most-admired list and was ranked the number-one airline in customer satisfaction for flights over 500 miles by J.D. Power and Associates.

Meanwhile, in a very different industry, from 1989–1994 Whirlpool Corporation enjoyed an amazing run of success. It became the world's largest manufacturer and marketer of major appliances, posted record earnings several times, saw its stock price hit its highest levels ever, and was called the best example of how to globalize in the business press.

In 1995, things slowed down. Despite reporting its third highest earnings ever, the company failed to hit its very aggressive stretch targets for financial performance and only made partial incentive payments to most of its employees. The recession in Europe and high start-up costs in China and India affected operations and results. The company lost some of its momentum, and Whirlpoolers became concerned that they could not continue their mission of turning Whirlpool into a global growth company.

Chairman Dave Whitwam responded. In 1996, he made some tough financial decisions and restructured certain operations. More than any of these efforts, however, he set to work on enhancing Whirlpool's culture and management practices. He reasoned that the company could not hit his stretch goals for growth and globalization without more attention to the people side of the business—and he was not about to give up on his goals. He led a reexamination of Whirlpool values, initiated educational efforts to build a new, higher performing global culture, and realigned pay, performance measures, and organization to reinforce the new values. Implementation was just beginning in early 1997, but the early returns looked very good.

What do these stories tell us about Continental and Whirlpool—tough companies in tight, mature markets? These two companies have figured out a very critical lesson: no strategy works and no success happens without aligning, engaging, and measuring the performance of your people to make it happen. This is how you get the most from the talent you have and how you become a workplace that attracts new talent. It's remarkable how many people have ignored this fundamental lesson or taken other paths.

For example, the old Continental, like many other companies, tried for many years under many other executives to do it the other way—grind people down, cut back on salaries, lay people off, communicate only under duress. Labor strife and other problems got so bad under former Chairman Frank Lorenzo that the DOT will no longer certify him to reenter the airline business. A string of his successors had new ideas for marketing, finances, and route structures, but lost their jobs for poor performance, while cutting people and costs relentlessly.

Gordon Bethune wouldn't have it that way, though. When he took over, he immediately started to communicate with people. He even reinstated some previous salary cutbacks as a way of building employee goodwill and motivation before the airline turned profitable.

Dave Whitwam had other choices in 1996 too—especially to move manufacturing from the U.S. to cheaper locations or do a massive layoff. Instead, he decided to do what he did when he took over in 1988, only better. At that time he introduced new performance measures to emphasize shareholder value and aligned employee performance management and incentives to support it. This time, he upgraded performance measures to increase and balance value creation for shareholders, customers, and employees, and revised the performance and pay practices that flow from them. In 1988, he reorganized into business units to focus on different market segments. This time, he began to build an integrated, global organization, established on a foundation of shared values.

A STRATEGIC VIEW OF PEOPLE

What I am describing here is strategy implementation through people—how to make your business plans a reality through your workforce. It has been said before that strategy development is hard work, but strategy implementation is even harder. If "the devil is in the details," then strategy implementation is full of demons.

When they think about it, most executives regard getting their workforces to carry out their plans as the most challenging part of enacting strategy. This is because they don't know how to do it. They are more knowledgeable and confident spending money or cutting costs, adding technology or buying a new product line, changing organizations or closing down a plant. However, it always comes back to how well your talent executes. It's why I keep hearing executives ask, "How do I get people to do what I want them to do?"

Since managing talent seems so difficult, executives naturally turn to other issues first. They look at their hard assets and resources, new technologies, innovations, and cycle time as ways to achieve their strategies before looking to their workforces. All of these elements may be necessary, but they are not sufficient. Your workforce is the only thing that is both necessary and sufficient to execute strategy.

Physical assets—land, precious minerals, manufacturing plants, and equipment—certainly are of great value. Yet in a world dominated by information, they aren't the source of wealth they used to be. Check *Forbes'* annual list of the most profitable companies. You will see it's dominated by service companies or companies that add some particular information to make a manufactured or processed product more valuable.

When physical resources no longer are the sure source of value creation, it suggests turning to money, technology, and information. However, these aren't very unique. Once you have money, you have access to most of the same technology and information everyone else does. Unless, and sometimes when, you're completely broke, you can borrow money to buy what you need. After a while, there goes uniqueness. How many large companies today are installing the same management information systems so they can get a competitive advantage? In the end, all they will be doing is keeping up with their competitors.

There are other powerful forces operating against your ability to maintain your unique value proposition. The free flow of information across companies, the business press, benchmarking, and the rapid movement of employees all suggest your competitors know what you're doing and how you're doing it shortly after you start. Continental's $65 on-time incentive was in the press the first time it was awarded, available for anyone to copy. Whirlpool's global strategies were written about widely. Some companies, General Electric is a good example, seem to trumpet their best practices and innovations as loudly as they can. Every company could copy GE's workout process if they were able.

Getting faster by reducing cycle time also is available to everyone, so it's not particular. It's also very hard to do. Have you ever really seen a fast systems change? Even loading new software on your home PC takes too much time. Big systems changes at work appear to take forever. Changing work processes sometimes goes faster—you can mandate some small changes right away. Large-scale process redesign usually drags on much too long.

With all of these issues, the real strategic opportunities for becoming a singular success, achieving uniqueness, and moving quickly lies in your most unique and potentially most powerful resource—your workforce. No one else has the talent you do. No one else employs people with the particular collection of knowledge, skills, abilities, leadership, motivations, aspirations, and concerns. Moreover, most of the people who are with you now will stay with you as long as you are a viable business and treat them right. Or as Continental's long-suffering employees showed, as long as they think you might get it right someday.

Your workforce also is the most dynamic resource you have. Nothing else you have offers the possibility of being able to change so quickly. Yes, lasting cultural change takes years. But if you ask people to do something useful, explain to them why it's useful, and help them understand how to do it, they can start right away and move a lot faster than most technology or work process changes. Witness Continental's rapid ascent in on-time performance. Or consider how quickly IBM turned things around under Lou Gerstner as he refocused people on creating total solutions for their customers.

What has been missing in most companies is a strategic view of employees.

What has been missing in most companies is a strategic view of employees and a systematic way to approach implementing strategy through them. Executives typically think if they just take care of the business, then the organization and workforce will take care of themselves. They introduce new plans and initiatives without considering whether they have the talent to make them happen or whether the people and practices are aligned to what needs to be done.

A big reason why companies don't take a strategic view of their workforce is because for years they assumed that enough people with appropriate skills would be available. They didn't consider that talent could become a scarce resource. Companies acted as if skilled workers were plentiful, so they could make whatever business plans they wanted and fire or lay off as they chose. There always would be ready replacements. Today we know that isn't true.

There are some exceptions—some companies do consider these things carefully. They build strategic workforces.

Amoco

When Amoco executives went off-site to begin planning a long-term renewal of their company in the late 1980s, they did something unusual. They focused on people first. They understood that if the world market essentially sets the price for oil, to beat the competition the company would have to be quicker, more efficient, and more innovative. Above all, this required employee attitudes, behaviors, and competencies to change, in addition to realigning organizational structures, performance measures, and work processes.

Amoco began to introduce initiatives to change people's behaviors, corporate direction, and business results. In 1992, it tied these activities and subsequent efforts together under a renewal model that includes strategic direction, structure, processes, rewards, and people. This model states explicitly that people are as crucial as strategy and structure. According to CEO Larry Fuller, "We must engage all the talents and energies of the entire workforce, which is at the heart of our renewal effort. In a word, the key is people."

Amoco's annual and long-term planning processes consider people issues, along with goals for return on equity and net income; environmental, health, and safety; and operational improvements. Current longer-term people strategies include:

- Improving the organization's capabilities to think and act quickly
- Identifying, building, and using critical competencies
- Improving the return on investment in people

These make sense for a capital-intensive engineering and marketing company that deploys huge amounts of capital per employee. Every year Amoco establishes annual objectives that align with these long-term strategies, and with the particular people issues the company is facing.

Marriott Corporation

At the other end of the capital-intensity scale is Marriott Corporation, which also gets high marks for thinking and acting strategically about people. Marriott's challenge is completely different than Amoco's. It has to build a workforce mostly out of low-wage employees, a very large percentage of whom are recent immigrants who struggle with the English language, American culture, and our approach to work. Today, the availability of these workers is getting tighter and tighter, but the economics of the hotel business continue to impose real market constraints on how much Marriott can afford to pay. Offering dramatic wage increases to attract higher-skilled employees would have an immediate impact on room rates, something Marriott can't do in the competitive business hotel market. Even if the hotelier could afford it, those workers aren't readily available in a growing U.S. economy, with declining unemployment.

Instead of just increasing wages, Marriott has analyzed the social situations of its workers and is attempting to meet their needs. It understands that low-income employees have a host of personal and domestic issues that have to be addressed for them to be able to come to work and serve guests. Depending on the local market and employee population, often heavily influenced by national origin and ethnicity, Marriott offers a variety of programs and informal activities that provide value to employees, help build employee loyalty, and encourage employee attitudes and behaviors that promote guest service. These include English language classes, daycare, welfare-to-work training, stock options, social service referrals, and cultural sensitivity training. There is some evidence that these solutions are more effective than higher wages in reducing turnover, absenteeism, and tardiness, factors that have a huge effect on productivity with this type of workforce.

What Amoco and Marriott are doing, like Continental and Whirlpool, is taking a strategic view of their workforces. They are leveraging their business strategies through people in the particular ways that build unique value for their customers and reward employees and shareholders. For Amoco, this means quicker decision-making and ongoing quality improvements. For Marriott, this increases labor productivity and guest service. At Continental, this brings on-time, dependable service. At Whirlpool, this continues the globalization and growth strategies it started. These actions and outcomes are their talent solutions. They have created strategic workforces that know their customers and how they want to serve them, have the right skills and motivations, and provide outstanding service or build terrific products.

HOW TO DO IT: ALIGN, ENGAGE, AND MEASURE

How can your company learn to take a strategic view of your workforce and follow a logical approach to implementing strategy through your people?

There is a very straightforward and practical way to do this. I have developed it over the years working with companies like Amoco and Whirlpool and watching others go through similar processes. It will enable you to deploy, develop, and retain your talent to increase your business results and deliver long-term value. You can tailor it to meet your specific situations.

I am confident about this framework for two reasons. First, I have used it or seen it used with a large number of companies in different industries to improve results. Whenever I present it to an audience, a significant number take it back to their companies and try it out themselves. When I hear back from people, they tell me this approach has increased their business results by making their workforce and management practices more connected to their strategies, and thus more effective.

Second, we are dealing with people, and this approach speaks directly to their needs. Though the pace of life and change has accelerated, human needs and nature remain fairly constant. People want the same things from work they always have: respect, trust, control over what they do, the opportunity to do a good job, pleasant interactions with coworkers and others, fair treatment, the chance to make a reasonable living, pride in what they do and their accomplishments, and the prospect of learning. They also want to know what your directions are and how they can affect them and be rewarded.

Meeting these needs enables people to connect to their work on emotional, social, and intellectual levels, and depending on the work, sometimes on a physical level too. It helps them feel complete and take meaning from what they do.

People want the same things from work they always have.

People have different levels of needs. That's what makes them different and makes life challenging for you as an executive or manager. Following this framework makes it possible for you to address these issues directly as you get your workforce to implement your business strategies successfully.

Here's the first part of the framework. To manage your talent to create outstanding results, you need to do three things:

- **Align your talent to your business strategy**. Make sure people know where you are going as a business, what you are doing to get there, how they can contribute to what you want to achieve, and what's in it for them when they do. These are the things people keep telling you they want to know. They also are the things that lead to higher productivity.

- **Engage your people in what you are trying to achieve.** Aligning them tells them what to do and enables them to understand the reasons why they should do it. Engaging them gets them excited about doing it. It helps them experience their jobs or assignments with more commitment and emotion. Excited employees should be a business result you try to achieve because even if the work is repetitive, enthusiastic employees give you extra effort and help customers feel like they are buying from the right company. They also create a great work environment that's the key to attracting and retaining other talented people.

- **Measure what your workforce is trying to do and give them feedback about it.** A psychology professor of mine used to say that doing something without knowing how you're doing just makes you tired. People want to know how they are doing. Otherwise they get frustrated, discouraged, or just don't improve. Measurement helps them understand their level of contribution and how to get better. In particular, they want to be able to keep score themselves because this gives them control over their situations and behaviors. You have to provide some useful measures to give them this control.

Though I have listed this as a three-step framework, it's not a linear process. Rather it's an ongoing cycle of three interrelated outcomes that you should be working to achieve. It enables you to look at your talent at any point in time and determine how well you are using it to leverage results. The cycle is illustrated in Figure 1-1.

As you can see, there's no starting point or preconditions for beginning. For instance, it's incorrect to assume that you cannot engage people until they are fully aligned. You can engage them in trying to help you help them become more aligned. Similarly, you can begin to measure even if your measurements aren't perfect or people are not heavily aligned or engaged. Appropriate measurement can help them become more aligned and engaged.

FIGURE 1-1

Talent Management Framework

Carl Marinacci, a vice president at Amoco, said it best. In a meeting we were attending, Carl responded to a manager who didn't want to make any changes to a compensation plan until a new business strategy was fully crafted, widely communicated, and broadly understood. Carl noted that if they waited that long, they would never have a plan. He went on to add that, "Business is like golf, you have to play it as it lays."

This is a good analogy for this using this framework. Think of alignment, engagement, and measurement as three different parts of your golf game, like driving, hitting irons, and putting. You can work on any of these aspects at any time, depending on your priorities. It's more difficult to work on all three at the same time, but it can be done. Also, you can never really stop, because everyone can improve. When you get better in one area, it has implications for the other areas. For instance, if you improve your driving and get longer off the tee, you will find yourself hitting different, shorter irons to get to the pin. This will make you want to improve that part of your game.

It's the same with aligning, engaging, and measuring your workforce. As you get better in each part, you will want to improve the other parts of your talent management practices. For instance, the more closely you align people to strategy, the more accurately you should be able to measure their contributions.

MANAGE TALENT TO YOUR STRATEGIC STYLE

Here is the second part of my framework. You should manage your talent according to the strategic style of your business. There are three different strategic business styles. Each gives you a clear and unique road map for how to align, engage, and measure talent to achieve big results.

Your strategic style is the characteristic way your company strategizes, operates, goes to market, and treats employees—your strategic personality, if you like. It's who you are as a company. Like people, companies have these personalities. They can grow and improve, but the basic character doesn't change easily.

As market demands increase, successful companies improve their capabilities and talent to meet them, but they do it within the

context of their strategic styles. People do this too. A person might improve an eating or shopping habit to fit a new situation, without really making a major change in behavior. That requires a significant life experience—a birth, death, marriage, divorce, and so forth. Similarly, every once in a great while some truly major event or crisis, usually a financial one, comes along that really forces a company to change its basic strategic style. These are the rare historical occurrences in the lives of companies that are so big they are widely noticed.

There's precedent for looking at companies this way. In the 1980s Michael Porter coined the term "generic strategies" to refer to alternative strategic positions in an industry. In a very popular approach to strategy, he suggested that companies could compete in one of three ways:

- Cost leadership—being the low-cost producer
- Differentiation—having a unique product or service
- Focus—concentrating special services or products on a specific market niche

According to Porter, competitive advantage comes from setting up unique value-creating activities to deliver on your particular kind of strategy. This allows you to erect barriers to entry by your competitors.

A more recent approach to describing strategic styles that updates and elaborates on Porter comes from Michael Treacy and Fred Wiersema in *The Discipline of Market Leaders*. This book received some heavy criticism for the aggressive way it was marketed and sold, but as *The Economist* pointed out, the criticism obscured some very useful ideas.

Briefly, the authors classify companies by the types of value the customer receives. Customers look for one of three sources of value from a company:

- Operational excellence—low-cost, reliable, and easy-to-use products or services
- Product leadership—leading-edge products
- Customer intimacy—highly customized solutions and services

The authors call these types "value disciplines" because market-leading companies organize their operations in disciplined ways to deliver their particular type of value to customers.

You can see that the Porter and Treacy and Wiersema approaches are very similar. Their notions of three kinds of companies and ideas about value chains and activity systems (Porter) and value disciplines (Treacy and Wiersema) explain business success in comparable ways. If you studied these approaches in depth, you would find some differences to consider if you were creating your company's strategy. However, they aren't as meaningful for our purposes in discussing talent management.

To describe talent management, I am assuming you have a business strategy and that you can classify it into one of these three types. In my consulting, clients find this very easy to do. My idea of strategic styles starts with these three types of business strategies and extends them deep into company capabilities, characters, and cultures to illustrate how they treat employees.

For leading companies who are very clear about what they offer their customers and who think strategically about their workforces and talent management practices, their strategic styles also explain the different ways they make decisions and behave toward employees. Your strategic style describes who you are and how you behave as a company, both to your customers and your employees.

> **Successful companies show their strategic styles by creating an experience of working there that parallels the experience of being a customer.**

Vicki Chvala, vice president of American Family Mutual Insurance, puts it this way, "We want our employees to think of us the same way our customers do—an operationally excellent company that is strong, growing, and friendly. This governs how we treat customers, and we also have used it to review our employee programs to change them to reflect these principles."

Like American Family, successful companies show their strategic styles by creating an experience of working there that parallels the experience of being a customer. At McDonald's, being on a lunch crew is somewhat like eating there. Everything is laid out pretty clearly for both the employee and customer so both can move quickly to deliver or receive consistent quality and value. Employees are treated in a fair and standardized manner and don't have a lot of choice about what to do and how to do it. This is like the customers who are encouraged to order by number and accept the choices McDonald's offers them.

Motorola is a much different company, but the idea of a parallel experience is the same. An engineer gets his or her greatest rewards from developing leading-edge products, but also is paid and treated very well. The Motorola consumer, who probably purchases from a distributor instead of the company, realizes value from the technical excellence of the product and often pays a premium for it because of quality and technology.

Another way to understand this is to consider it from the standpoint of a company's brand. In a recent *Fortune* article, John Costello, Sears' head of marketing, described the value of a brand. According to Costello, a strong brand signifies a company's relationship with its customers, most valuable asset, main differentiator, best defense against competition, and key to customer loyalty. Now if you go back and reread that sentence and substitute character or culture for brand and employee for customer, you see what I mean by parallel experience.

Strategic styles are illustrated in Figure 1-2.

You can use this approach to understand and decide how to manage your talent in different ways, depending on your strategic

FIGURE 1-2

Strategic Styles

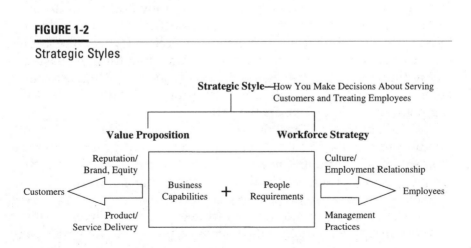

style. The three different styles tell you how to align and engage people, and how to measure your business and workforce success. Using your style to manage talent will create a work environment consistent with your customer environment. This will give employees a better sense of who you are and what you want them to do. It will become easier for you to attract, motivate, and retain people. This will increase productivity and business results.

Successful companies' strategic styles reside deep in their core and influence everything they do. They describe habitual ways of doing things. That's why I compare them to individual personality traits that also don't change much over time. Both the Porter and Treacy and Wiersema labels do a nice job of describing the three types. I have gotten a lot of value from the Treacy and Wiersema work and prefer to simplify their labels by using "Operations," "Products," and "Customers" to name the styles.

A TALE OF THREE COMPANIES

You can understand the three strategic styles and how they affect talent management by looking at three very different companies.

Cargill Incorporated

Cargill is the world's largest processor, merchandiser, and distributor of agricultural commodities and related products. It's a tightly focused operations company in very slim margin businesses. It concentrates on delivering high-volume, low-cost, basic products. From the strategic to the tactical, and from its products to its people, Cargill stresses operational efficiency and cost. Almost nothing is wasted, and nothing is very extravagant at Cargill, one of the biggest companies in the world. Quality and service are maintained at highly competitive levels, but cost is the driver.

Cargill pushes cost responsibility out to its many business units. The business units, in turn, keep pressure on staff groups to keep their services focused and useful and their costs low. Before launching any project, Cargill wants to know what financial results it will deliver.

Cargill uses its workforce in a strategic way to deliver against this cost discipline. It defines its business capabilities and employee competencies to conduct processes and operate facilities with low cost and high quality. It builds a culture and hires people who have this mindset. It trains people to look at the financial paybacks of almost everything they do. It organizes into business units to keep profit accountability at lower levels, but uses a matrix of the business units with regions or worldwide product lines to share information for continuous improvement. It engages people through inspiring them to help raise the world's standard of living by providing basic commodities at reasonable prices. Cargill measures operating and budget performance to drive business decisions and holds people accountable for operating success.

Glaxo Wellcome Inc.

Glaxo Wellcome is a much different, though equally successful, company, and a strong contrast to Cargill. It is a product-driven company that focuses on creating and marketing prescription drugs. Since it has unique, leading-edge ethical drugs, it can command a price premium for what it creates and sells.

This means that cost is not a driver; the driver is the need to invent new drugs. The company hires scientists and others who are good at participating in, managing, or supporting the research and development process. Since discovering and bringing each new drug to market takes so much time, money, people, and other resources, it has some need to be efficient, but nothing like Cargill.

Glaxo Wellcome will start projects not knowing where they will lead, as opposed to demanding a projection of bottom-line return. Its culture is focused on creating the big breakthrough that will cure a disease, not the efficient provision of basic products. Its people think big-picture, not incremental improvement. The organization is full of large, functional groups where like-minded or similarly tasked people can come together within and across disciplines to create. Cost control and business measurements are kept at fairly high organizational levels where most employees don't have to spend a lot of time on them.

You can see the huge differences in strategic styles in these companies. Yet each provides products that its customers want at prices they are willing to pay, is considered a leader in its industry, offers strong financial returns to shareholders, and is a wonderful place to work for the right (but very different) people. Each has a compelling vision and set of values, wonderful people, and great results, but they are as different as night and day.

Gold Medal Cleaners

This description of strategic styles applies not only to large, rich companies but to small businesses as well. One of the most successful small businesses I know is Gold Medal Cleaners of Wilmette, Illinois. Gold Medal has been in business more than 70 years in the Chicago area and now is run by the third generation of family members.

Gold Medal is a customers company that sells service and cleanliness. Its 15 full-time employees know that their first priorities are to take care of the customer at the counter and provide the highest quality in laundry and dry cleaning. The company backs them up with the best machinery, purest cleaning chemicals, and most careful training it can. Gold Medal may be the most expensive cleaner in an area with dozens of competitors, yet customers bypass the others and pay the premium to use it. Even people who have moved away will drive for miles because of the service and quality.

What the Gold Medal staff understands is that in this type of company, you must treat the customer with absolute respect every time and do whatever it takes to keep them, including redoing work without complaint. The owners understand this attitude starts with hiring people who are enthusiastic and service-minded and treating them with the same respect they want employees to show to customers.

A STRATEGIC APPROACH TO MANAGING TALENT

These three companies show you how to manage talent. The key is to manage your people strategically in very different ways depending on how you want to deliver value to your customers. If your basis for competing and winning is cost and value, you hire a particular kind of people and do one set of things with your workforce. If the basis is products, you do things differently. If it's service, you manage in a third way.

Once you identify the strategic style of your company, you can enter the cycle of aligning, engaging, and measuring. This will cause you to identify the specific business capabilities that make the most sense for your strategy and detail the cultural values, employee competencies, and employment conditions you need to have. You will be able to create a workforce strategy about how you should acquire, use, and develop talent. This will help you select which management practices make the most sense for you, given the way you want to compete and serve your customers. Finally, you can learn the appropriate ways to engage and measure, depending on your style.

When you really begin to align, engage, and measure your talent based on your strategic style, you will be creating a group of interrelated, consistent messages and practices that establish and deploy a particular type of workforce in a unique way. You will choose to do certain things because they fit your strategic style, not because they are current or best practices. You also will choose to not do certain things. Even though they may be great ideas, certain practices just won't fit. Actually, this will make your company a very attractive and comfortable place to work for exactly the kinds of people you need and give you a big advantage in recruiting and retaining talent.

Executives have wanted this type of strategic approach to talent management for years. Not having it may be one big reason why so many of them haven't been knowledgeable or comfortable managing talent. With this approach, they can see a straight line from who their company is, to the types of people they need, to how to manage and develop them.

Additionally, the inability of many human resource (HR) departments to deliver a strategy-based approach to talent management has cost them dearly in organizational respect and effectiveness. I don't think this is the sole responsibility of the HR department, because strategic talent management should be a line management activity.

Still, the HR department in most companies is the owner of these practices. When it is unable to deliver a strategic rationale for adopting new practices, it gets ignored, criticized, or, at best, faces a tremendous struggle for acceptance. Additionally, when practices are unrelated to their strategic context, there's a much greater chance that they won't work at all or won't deliver what their sponsors said they would. One client I consulted to recently on these issues chartered a study team to create a workforce strategy and didn't include anyone from HR, a sure sign that its department offers little business value.

Until now the suggestions of most academics, consultants, and writers have not linked management practices to the strategic style of a company. Their recommendations generally have been context-free, suggesting these approaches could work for anyone. However, the best practice for a company of one style is largely irrelevant to a company of a different style. You need to connect your practices to your strategic style or don't waste your time.

A good case in point is the push for pay-for-performance. People have been prescribing this for years for every situation, first in the form of merit pay and then as incentive compensation. Conversely, critics of pay-for-performance, like the late quality leader, W. Edwards Deming, blasted it in all situations. However, neither of these positions is adequate. Pay-for-performance works very well in some situations, depending on the strategic style of the company, and doesn't work very well in other situations, depending on the strategic style. For example, it is very difficult for many product companies to do pay-for-performance in a highly leveraged way, and most would be better off not trying it.

Kurt Lewin, the distinguished social psychologist, once said, "Nothing is so practical as a good theory." I would amend his words slightly to say nothing is so practical as a good framework. By starting with your strategic style to identify the talent you need and then aligning, engaging, and measuring, you will arrive at a practical and effective way to manage talent and create amazing results.

CREATING THE TALENT SOLUTION

1. Do you think of your workforce as your essential vehicle for implementing business strategy? What would it take for your company to start thinking and acting strategically about people?

2. How well are you doing at aligning, engaging, and measuring today? What are your biggest opportunities for improvement?

3. What's your strategic style? Is this widely recognized by your executives? Managers? Employees?

CHAPTER **2**

Align to Business Results and Strategy

Over the next several chapters, you'll go through a detailed approach to aligning strategy to talent. This chapter will start the journey and explain:

- What alignment is and looks like
- How alignment starts with balanced business results
- The advantages and limitations of using strategic styles to align people and strategy

There is an old saying in real estate that "The three most important things are: Location, location, location." Get that right and most everything else takes care of itself.

Similarly, in managing talent, the three most important things are: Alignment, alignment, alignment. Get it right, and most everything else will work. *Alignment* means pointing your people in the right direction to do the right things. This makes it much easier to engage and measure.

IMPROVING BUSINESS RESULTS WITH PEOPLE

Alignment starts by telling employees what game you're playing and how you plan to win. This helps them understand your strategic style and how you are executing it. Any of the three strategic styles gives you the opportunity to win. From there, how you execute makes you successful. It's absolutely essential that your employees know who you are and what you intend to do to succeed. Then they can execute for you and your customers.

This communication is incredibly meaningful to both you and your employees. They want to know just as much as you want them to—maybe more. People want to excel and win. They associate winning with having a plan—knowing how you want to win. Putting things into alignment and communicating about it helps them understand that you have a plan, what you are asking them to do, and why.

You also should understand that alignment is extremely difficult to do and maintain. I can use a golf analogy again because, like golf, you are dealing with many variables at the same time. In golf, you have to pull everything together at the same time—your ball's lie, target, club selection, posture, how hard to swing, distance, wind, and so forth—to produce one beautiful outcome.

Likewise, aligning people means simultaneously paying attention to several different practices and variables—who you select, how you train them, how they are organized, what you tell them, how you reward them, as well as what they are doing and how they are feeling about it, their customers, you, and themselves. When you align your talent and practices to your strategy, you produce a terrific business result. Just like a great golf shot, doing it once doesn't mean you will be able to do it again. Still, the harder you work at it, the more accomplished you will become—and the more often you will align and win.

At Hewitt, our consultants use an alignment model called "Improving Business Results with People" (IBR). Using the model is a lot like developing a good golf swing. If you keep using it, it turns into one of those repetitive, enduring, and effective skills that helps you be successful in almost every talent management situation.

The IBR model is designed to ensure you line up all the critical elements in talent management. If you pay attention to these pieces and execute them right, you will create alignment that enables you to achieve extraordinary business results. The alignment model is illustrated in Figure 2-1.

I will highlight the model quickly now to set the stage for going through it in more detail throughout the book.

Business Results and Strategies describe the outcomes you are trying to achieve as a company and the strategies you are using to get there. Business performance measurement is how you express the results you want. Strategic style is the context for alignment.

FIGURE 2-1

Improving Business Results with People (IBR) Model

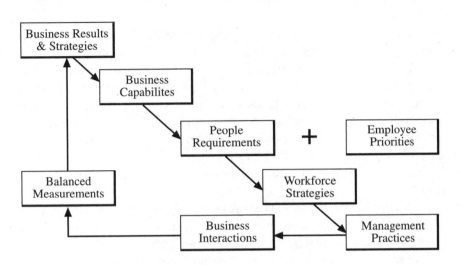

Business Capabilities refer to your distinctive abilities as an organization to use money, technology, information, people, and other resources to create a competitive advantage. The successful organization knows its capabilities in the context of its strategy and continually exploits them in its marketplaces. It also knows its limitations and tries to avoid situations where it will be tough to win. This is different than trying to overcome limitations, which can be a losing game. New capabilities can be developed, but once established, they tend to be enduring and not easily changed.

People Requirements are the things you demand from people to exercise your capabilities—what you need from them to be successful. I describe requirements as three things: culture—the shared norms and values you want to shape behavior and decision-making; competencies—your individual and collective employee talents; and contract—the psychological and social agreements you need from your employees about how hard they should work, how long they can expect to work for you, work/life balance issues, and so forth. People requirements are a "top-down" look at what you need from employees to be successful, but it's only part of the equation.

Employee Priorities are the "bottom-up" of the equation. My Hewitt colleague Jack Bruner, practice leader for employee benefits, describes these as "needs, fears, and goals." These as what employees want today, what keeps them awake at night about their work lives and careers, and what they want for their lives and careers for the long-term. Your company needs to balance top-down people requirements with bottom-up employee priorities to manage talent for long-term value.

Workforce Strategies are the distinctive plans you have for acquiring, developing, deploying, and retaining your people for competitive advantage. Many companies still don't have explicit workforce strategies, leaving things implicit or doing things by chance. Why anyone would leave their most distinctive resource to chance is always a mystery to me. I will wager that most organizations manage their workforce primarily by using the "squeaky wheel gets the grease" approach. They lurch from problem to problem or fad to fad without a rationale, plan, or measurement of how they are doing.

Management Practices describe the ways you enact your workforce strategies. There are five main talent management practices: staffing, organizing, learning, performing, and rewarding. These need to be aligned with your workforce strategies and integrated with each other to make alignment work and shape the kinds of business interactions you want.

Business Interactions are where all business results occur. Interactions describe how employees deal with customers, with each other, and with leadership. Interactions involve serving customers, teaming, taking direction, leading, developing products, marketing, selling, reducing costs—all the things that make business happen. If you've done it right, your management practices will shape and measure the interactions you need.

Balanced Measurements are both the business and individual measurements that gauge how well you and your employees are doing. Measures need to balance the objectives of shareholders, customers, and employees because this equilibrium is what enables you to succeed for the long-term.

WHAT ALIGNMENT LOOKS LIKE

What does real alignment look like? It's like the old adage, "you'll know it when you see it," because everything works together beautifully. Its distinguishing characteristic is a clear line of sight from strategy to people.

Whirlpool Corporation

Whirlpool Corporation, the leading worldwide manufacturer and marketer of major household appliances, created tremendous workforce alignment and outstanding business success in the period from 1989 to 1994. In 1988, Whirlpool recognized the need to become the leading global manufacturer and marketer of appliances if it wanted to transcend a slow-growth domestic marketplace, defeat its rapidly consolidating domestic and foreign competitors, and return greater value to its shareholders. Whirlpool restructured, expanded by acquiring foreign companies, and above all, challenged its employees to "raise the bar on performance."

In the old Whirlpool, mass manufacturing, shared responsibility, and undifferentiated marketing were reinforced by an old employment relationship of almost guaranteed employment and treating and compensating everybody about the same. The company didn't give much honest performance feedback, frequently promoted people because of seniority, and rarely confronted performance problems. In other words, it was like a lot of other North American companies that managed to do just fine in the growing economy of the 1950s, '60s and '70s, but started to struggle in the tougher '80s. Holding everything together from the employee perspective was a cash profit-sharing plan for salaried employees with a 30-year history of payouts averaging 25 percent of pay to everyone, regardless of performance.

In the new Whirlpool, the company required employees to listen more closely to customers and vendors to really hear their needs, collaborate to improve and differentiate product quality, and learn to work globally. The company insisted on higher individual and team accountability and made compensation much more dependent on performance. This alignment communicated that if employees helped implement the new strategies and returned more to shareholders, they would learn more, earn more, and have far greater opportunities in the new global company.

The result was a company that, for six years—an eon in today's business climate—went from worrying about its domestic survival to occupying the number-one position in its industry in the world. It saw its stock price soar and was labeled the best and fastest example of successful globalization to date in the new world economy. Employees received greater pay, big new opportunities for learning and advancement, and the pride associated with being with Number One.

BALANCED BUSINESS RESULTS

My definition of strong business results is:

- Great value for customers
- Rewarding work situations for employees—including psychological, social, and financial rewards
- High returns for shareholders

Business history shows that you need all three to be a highly successful, enduring company. Companies that repeatedly favor one group over the other two generally don't last, even if they have a good run for a few years. Companies that are out of balance have a hard time managing talent, even when the balance favors employees.

> Companies that are out of balance have a hard time managing talent.

People Express was an airline founded in the 1980s on the concept of being a great place to work. Employees loved it, and for a few years it grew very quickly and was the darling of management professors and business writers. Yet it was out of balance and didn't provide the returns to fund the reliable service customers need from an airline. Soon it was out of business and had no talent to manage.

Even with the need for balance, it's reality to recognize that 1) every business goes through cycles—there's no avoiding that, and 2) things get out of balance sometimes when trying to meet the different needs and demands of customers, employees, and shareholders.

Yet I find that when confronting down cycles in their businesses, smart companies turn it around faster than do others. Companies like Cargill, Glaxo Wellcome, Lincoln Electric, Whirlpool, and others move more quickly than competitors to counteract problems and downturns.

There are many reasons for this, but a big part is that they manage their talent better so they are more able to engage people to make necessary changes. This is no easy task. Still, if you have people aligned with a good sense of who you are and what you are trying to do, they will be faster and more receptive to move in new directions. They will have greater confidence in your abilities to make and execute plans and a stronger sense of why you are doing things.

Though balanced results suggest a state of equilibrium, remember achieving balance actually requires considerable movement to equalize things. Also, balance is dynamic. Pieces go in and out of sync and need to be recalibrated. One constituency may start to get too much at the expense of others. Smart companies recognize this and work at maintaining balance. Most importantly, they manage and communicate this long-term balanced perspective with their people; talk about what, how, and why things have to change to restore balance; and then do it.

Getting Back Into Balance

The Whirlpool renewal started in 1988 when Dave Whitwam saw things were out of balance. Employees were getting more than their fair share of returns and shareholders were getting too little. The company had grown to about $3 billion in sales. Yet absolute profits had not grown much from when the company had about $1 billion in revenues, costs had increased, and the profit-sharing plan kept paying employees at historic levels.

Whitwam challenged the company to improve its net income, return on equity, and total return to shareholders through hard driving, cost reductions, and productivity improvement. Yet he also told employees that if they created "a bigger pie," their pieces would continue to be large and even grow. For the next several years, both shareholders and employees gained as return on equity and stock price grew, as did annual employee incentives. Meanwhile, customers continued to pay incredibly low prices for major appliances. Adjusted for inflation, appliances in the U.S. cost about what they did 20 years ago.

Kellogg Company faced an imbalance of a different sort in 1996. Its competitor, Post, lowered cereal prices 20 percent across the board. Kellogg had already begun a long-term program of price reductions, but was forced to rapidly accelerate in response to Post. Some of the business press criticized Kellogg and predicted it was on the way to long-term ruin, but the company recovered quickly.

Though 1996 was not a good year, Kellogg leaders took the time to aggressively reduce costs, revisit business strategy, and create global workforce strategies. They communicated these issues to employees and started taking steps toward implementing new, higher-value approaches through operations, product development, and people.

By early 1997, the company recovered the market share it lost when Post cut prices, made a key acquisition in Lender's Bagels, started some new ventures, and looked forward to growth. The cereal price reductions created a better balance for consumers—about $1 billion was returned to them in the U.S.—and Kellogg was able to use this as an opportunity to become even stronger. According to Senior Vice President Bob Creviston, "We'll take our brand equities and build them into multi-product lines, with better consumer understanding, improved research and development, and a new emphasis on nutrition driving us."

STRATEGIC STYLES

A Shorthand for Strategy

These kinds of balanced results are achieved by specific strategies and focused implementations. These specifics will differ from company to company and be different for each company at various times. This variation is fascinating, but it's not useful to help draw lessons about how to manage talent across situations. For that, it's more instructive to look at the big similarities among types of companies.

Using strategic styles to describe these similarities enables you to see the power of alignment in managing talent. The styles are a good proxy for more particular strategies because they start with your approach to customers, consider your capabilities in delivering value, and extend into managing organization culture and talent.

There are vivid examples of the three strategic styles. W.L. Gore and NIKE are product companies. Gore's creation and continuing expansion of uses for Gore-Tex have built its presence in products as diverse as space suits, computer cables, dental floss, and outerwear. NIKE's high-impact designs for athletic footwear and clothing have made it larger than all its competitors combined. These companies have built organizations and treat employees in ways that enable them to create leading-edge products. Cargill, Southwest Airlines, and Whirlpool are operations leaders because their employees deliver standardized products or services with great cost/value relationships for consumers. IBM, Nordstrom, and USAA are customers companies where employees provide customized solutions to meet unique customer needs or terrific service that goes well beyond competitive offerings.

What's clear is that these companies focus on doing the things they know best and don't try to be all things to all people. They are true to their styles. In personality terms, I would call them *integrated* or *authentic*. They know that not everyone wants to pay a premium for genuine Gore-Tex fabric, get to the airport early to board an airplane by number on Southwest, or depend on one company like IBM for a broad range of computer solutions. They know who they are, what they offer their customers, and what they need to be good at doing. They don't try to serve other types of customers with other offerings.

Fred Wiersema says that the most frequent comment he gets when explaining his concept of value disciplines to audiences is, "Our goal as a business is to be the leader in products, cost, and customer service. What does it take to be world-class at all three?" His research results are clear. No company in the world is a leader in all three disciplines.

Fred says it's critical to be world-class in your chosen discipline and very competitive in the other two. So an operations company must try to be the best in its industry at speed, convenience, reliability, and value, and needs to be on a par with others in offering advanced products or flexible service. It doesn't have to, and probably cannot, offer the most advanced products or customized services and keep costs low. Products and customers companies have similar requirements.

Your inability to sustain your discipline and style and to drive that focus through your organization will cause your company to fail. All your systems and practices need to be aligned to provide your kind of value. That way customers will understand what to expect from you and how to buy so they'll be pleased. Just as vital, your employees will know who you are and how they need to interact with customers and each other.

When a company attempts to change its style, customers become confused because their expectations are not matched, and employees don't know how to deliver value. This is a bad recipe. People don't walk into Sears expecting to see Bloomingdale's high fashions and prices. Nor do they check into a Marriott Hotel to get the self-service, basic room, and low price they should get at a Super 8 Motel.

Limitations of Describing Strategies as Styles

Though I use it as a shorthand for strategy, a company's business strategy is far more complicated, unique, and dynamic than can be conveyed by the concept of strategic style. You need to understand and go beyond the limitations of describing styles to use them productively. As my Hewitt colleague, Neville Osrin, says, "A framework is useful only as long as it reveals more than it obscures."

An analogy to personal styles can be helpful here. You may know people who have a "driving" personal style to get things done or an "analytic" style to study things. This helps you predict some things about them and hopefully work with them more effectively. However, everyone is unique, and to really get to know them, you would have to learn a lot more about their life experiences, attitudes, and behaviors.

For example, McDonald's is an operations company, but to understand the company better, you need to know its vision of feeding a bigger part of the world's population, its plans for global expansion, what criteria it uses to go into a new country or location, why it uses many more franchises than company-owned stores, how it targets children as its main customers, how it intends to compete in the oversaturated U.S. market, and so forth. Knowing McDonald's style only enables you to realize it competes primarily on cost, convenience, speed, and standardization. You need to dig deeper to understand how that happens.

Additionally, classifying by style can lead to stereotyping. For instance, there may be a tendency to think that an operations focus means poor customer service. That's not the case at all.

Operations companies can offer great service when certain conditions are met. If the product or service offering is complex or needs some slight tailoring, then the target market has to be carefully limited so the customer can be qualified, understand the offering, and make decisions quickly and easily. GEICO offers low-cost home, auto, and life insurance over the phone with fast and helpful service but only to people who meet its precise criteria for driving records, credit risks, income, and other factors. A bad driving record or health history makes it very hard to get coverage from GEICO.

If the audience cannot be carefully targeted, then the offering has to be far more standardized for the level of service to be consistently good. This is how Continental Airlines rose to first place in rankings of customer service for long-haul carriers. It changed procedures, trained, communicated, and offered incentives to raise the level and consistency of its service.

The other limitation of describing styles is they can seem static and unchanging when the overwhelming condition of business today is change. Styles, like personality, are quite enduring. Like a person, occasionally a company will change its style in the face of devastating necessity. Shell Oil is an example of this, attempting a major makeover from a products to an operations style. However, most companies try to master the impacts of change while relying on their basic styles.

In those situations, knowing your style and using it to your advantage can help your company turn things around quickly. This is because your customers, or former customers, know you best that way. Your task is to assess whether there are enough customers out there who want your value offering and then improve its worth to them. You can recover quickly if you are able to do this, because you are reducing the uncertainty of your customers and making it easier for them to buy from you. They don't have to change. Sears and IBM are powerful examples of major transformations who got there by sharpening their focus on their styles—Sears as an operations company and IBM as a customers company.

> **Knowing your style and using it to your advantage can help your company turn things around quickly.**

You may be most vulnerable to competitive attack by a company with a different style. What was world-class in customer service yesterday probably is being achieved by some operations company today with better target marketing and service through technology and process improvement. U.S. Bancorp's retail business lines are operations focused, but their new retail customer information system enables them to deliver faster and more personalized service than some of their customers companies competitors. It has raised the bar on competitors who will have to find a new world-class level of customer service to survive.

These occasional breakthroughs reshape the entire competitive landscape. Creating them or responding to them is more than just doing better within your style. Still, knowing the strengths and limitations of your style and your competitors gives you a clear road map for knowing how and where to counterattack.

When Post launched its price attack on Kellogg, Kellogg had to respond with reductions, but it went further. Kellogg also renewed its products focus of offering a "better breakfast." It revitalized its research and marketing, sought out acquisitions, and committed to new product development and line extensions. Its launch of Cocoa Frosted Flakes was one of the biggest new cereal introductions in years and increased market share dramatically.

The Value of Strategic Styles

Given these limitations, does this framework "reveal more than it obscures?" I think it does because it leads you to the old and very correct Shakespearean wisdom, "To thine own self be true." As a starting point, not a total understanding of strategy, it explains a lot more than it clouds.

Above all, it provides you a focal point for making strategic choices. Most of the strategic progress you will make in your company will involve focusing ever more sharply on what you already do well—building more advanced products, offering more spectacular service, or doing things faster or more reliably, and executing better. This is how most breakthroughs come about, advancing strengths you already have beyond the point anyone thought you could. They don't occur because you move away from your strengths—that has always been a slippery slope to disaster.

Knowing your strategic style also provides a framework for understanding your strengths and limitations versus those of your competitors. It can guide you to expand your strengths by deepening them or becoming more versatile, while avoiding situations where you are at a competitive disadvantage. It leads you to think about your core capabilities as a company—which are world-class, which need upgrading, and what you probably should stop doing because you can't get to world-class. This gives you a way to manage change, whether it is incremental change, major transformation, or competitive attack.

THREE KINDS OF PEOPLE

There's one more reason why I favor using strategic styles. It enables you to align directly from strategy to talent. Your style represents your typical habits of making decisions and managing people. It also tells you what kinds of people you should be hiring.

There are lots of ways to characterize people. A long time ago, back in a college sociology class, I learned a simple one from the professor. It has stuck with me ever since because it's direct, intuitive, and valid. I see it played out all the time in managing associates and working with clients, as well as in personal relationships. The professor said there are three types of people in the world: people who like things, people who like ideas, and people who like people.

People who like things are good at making things happen. They like action, methods, and concrete results. People who like ideas love invention, visions of the future, free-form debate, and pursuit of the new and different. People who like people value relationships, understand motivation, and enjoy satisfying others.

Admittedly this is a simple view of the world, but it corresponds exactly to the three types of companies I have been describing. You can see this in Figure 2-2.

FIGURE 2-2

Alignment Between Personal and Strategic Styles

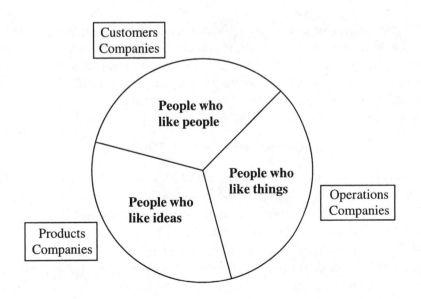

This simple model describes the predominant orientation of companies and people, where their strengths and preferences are, and how they can align with each other. It's an advantage if your personal style as a leader aligns closely with the strategic style of your company. A customers company is better off if it's run by someone who likes people. A person who likes and is most comfortable with things or ideas is not likely to have the deep insight into people it takes to deliver superior, customized service. These mismatches can occur in the other types of styles too.

It also will be much easier for your employees to fit in if they share your company's predominant style. How you think and act toward customers and toward other employees will be much more comfortable and obvious. Conversely, both your organization and your employees will have to work harder to make the fit if the alignment between styles is missing.

These aren't the only kinds of people each type of company should hire. Companies aren't pure types, and neither are people. Products companies also have customer and operational aspects to them. People who like ideas also relate to people and things. Every organization needs diversity of thought and differences in background, experience, and thinking. This adds richness and enables companies to understand other types of customers, business partners, and employees.

Still, this clear link between company style and individual style is the final reason why I use strategic styles as a brief way to describe strategies. They enlighten the whole alignment model and make it easier to grasp and put into action. They provide the context for all of the things you need to do to manage talent.

CREATING THE TALENT SOLUTION

1. Looking at the IBR model of alignment, how well are the elements aligned at your company?

2. Are you pursuing balanced business results? If not, what's most out of balance?

3. How does your strategic style show itself in the way you serve customers, battle your competition, and manage your talent?

CHAPTER **3**

Build Capabilities to Deliver Results

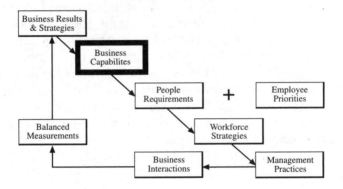

The next step in the IBR alignment model requires you to consider your business capabilities. Business capabilities are a huge factor in how you manage talent. Here you'll see:

- What business capabilities are and how they help provide competitive advantage
- How strategic styles and business capabilities match up
- How to understand your capabilities and your limitations
- The need to decentralize if you are going to serve different kinds of customers

BUSINESS CAPABILITIES

Business capabilities are the structures, processes, and systems your company builds that enable you to implement your business strategy. Your goal in developing these capabilities is to build unique abilities that competitors have difficulty copying so you have the advantage. From another perspective, your capabilities are the tools and methods your employees will use to implement your strategy.

Business capabilities will be as individual as your company. ARCO, the West Coast oil giant, is renowned for its capability as a marketer. It has captured substantial market share up and down the West Coast by limiting its stations to that geographical area and being first to introduce customer-friendly retail innovations to the service station business, including convenience markets, fast foods, cash-only lower pricing, and debit cards. MBNA is one of the largest issuers and processors of credit cards. It markets exclusively to affinity groups (i.e., college alumni associations, the Audubon Society, Minnesota Twin fans, and so forth) and has grown rapidly because of its targeted group marketing and its speed in customer service. Its back door neighbor is W.L. Gore who is famous for its capability in developing new applications for its microfiber, Gore-Tex. Retail marketing, target marketing, customer service, product development, and line extension are just a few examples of business capabilities that can bring strategic advantage.

CORE CAPABILITIES

As you move through the IBR model and look at aligning business results and strategies to business capabilities, you can see very quickly that different strategic styles demand different core capabilities. Your core capabilities are your company's essential abilities, the ones that stand out above all the rest to create advantage and value. What do you do that is absolutely the best in the world? You had better have something, and it must enable you to win against your competition.

> Different strategic styles demand different core capabilities.

The operations style demands consistent application. At McDonald's that means consistent quality, service, cleanliness, and value, or QSCV as they call it. This is not just a slogan. It's the way the company has built its value offering to customers, reputation, and success. Standardized delivery of those four elements must be a core capability if a McDonald's store is going to make it.

For the customers style, highly individualized, "whatever it takes" service and relationship building with customers is the core capability Nordstrom uses to distinguish itself from other department stores. Nordstrom was the first department store to pay all employees on commission, probably reflecting its shoe store roots. This pay plan encourages Nordstrom employees to give more attention more quickly to customers than the traditional hourly or salary pay plans many of its competitors use.

The core capability of products companies is constant innovation. That's their lifeblood. 3M even uses the word *innovation* in its ads. 3M is known for assessing its progress in innovation by measuring the amount of revenues it gets every year from new products.

Long-term, successful businesses will turn to these core capabilities time and time again to sustain leading performance, to enter new markets, to create change, and to rescue themselves from potential problems or miscalculations (see Table 3-1). From a company perspective, these are the abilities that most maintain the strategic style. A customer who has had the pleasure of dealing with a leading company probably has experienced these core capabilities, been delighted by them, and returns to repeat the experience whenever possible.

TABLE 3–1

Strategic Styles and Business Capabilities

Strategic Styles	Companies	Core Capabilities
Products	Bloomingdale's, Glaxo Wellcome, Kellogg Company, 3M, Motorola, NIKE, W.L. Gore	Constant innovation
Operations	American Airlines, Cargill, Lincoln Electric, McDonald's, Shell Oil, Southwest Airlines, Target Stores, Whirlpool	Consistent application
Customers	Hewitt, Home Depot, IBM, Johnson Controls, Nordstrom, USAA	In-depth relationship building

Innovation, application, and relationship building are general ways to refer to a set of core capabilities. Particular companies will practice these differently and have unique ways to describe them. I have highlighted each of these sets of capabilities because they match up best with the strategic styles. Once you go beyond them, capabilities will be specific to each company.

Specific Capabilities

For example, within the set of capabilities labeled relationship building, USAA is great at segmenting its market, in this case military personnel and families, targeting specific customers to pursue with particular services, delivering value added services to those targets, treating customers extremely well on the telephone and in correspondence, and measuring market and customer share. It also is very good at internal service capability—treating their own employees like customers—because that's a crucial way customers companies manage talent and get employees to serve customers well.

An operations company like Whirlpool has a whole set of capabilities within its application core. Whirlpool is world-class at applying manufacturing processes, logistics, distribution, inventory management, and parts and service support. It also measures and manages costs with extreme precision. All of these capabilities are necessary to implement its strategy fully.

Individual companies will execute these capabilities very differently, even within the same style. Among customers companies, Johnson Controls, the automotive seat manufacturer, does it by having its designers work hand-in-hand over the long-term with Chrysler designers to customize car seat design and manufacturing. Johnson Controls builds both the minivan bench that includes the infant car seat and the ergonomic racing cradle that holds the Dodge Viper driver. On the other hand, a customer service representative at Hewitt's Benefit Center will deal with hundreds of different people in a week. The representative can provide unique service to each caller thanks to technology that accesses complete participant records instantly.

Product innovation spans a wide range of products and services, from Glaxo Wellcome's life saving AIDS drug "cocktails" to 3M's micro-coating techniques, and NIKE's high-fashion designs. Sometimes a key innovation is incremental, an extension beyond what was done previously. However many times it's an absolute breakthrough, a new way of seeing and doing things. The stream of constant innovation includes both.

Capabilities can't be static in the face of business changes. In its transformation, Shell Oil is changing from its traditional products style to an operations focus. Part of this is getting better at doing things much more efficiently in finding, producing, transporting, and marketing gasoline.

Shell also has decided that it cannot do all of these things alone and has entered into partnerships with Amoco and other oil companies. This means a new capability for Shell is managing joint ventures. According to Gaurdie Banister, President of Shell Continental Companies, "We'll do some things with others when that makes the most sense, and some things by ourselves when that's the best decision. But we need to learn how to move quickly into these relationships, integrate them smoothly, and look for other opportunities as they come up."

KNOWING YOUR CAPABILITIES... AND YOUR LIMITATIONS

Just as important as knowing your capabilities is knowing your limitations—what you don't do well. An easy example of this is to understand what would happen if an operations company that offers standardized products, say Whirlpool's washing machines, tried to customize products every time customers asked. Imagine if you can, how long Whirlpool would take to change its manufacturing and assembly processes for a customer who wanted push buttons instead of knobs. The company would have to become a "job shop" instead of a mass manufacturer.

This is a key point about business capabilities—not trying to overcome your limitations, but knowing them and avoiding situations where you are vulnerable. Southwest Airlines is a master of this. It stays away from the bigger airport hubs and longer routes where travelers demand meals, reserved seats, a first class section, movies, and other amenities. Rather than try to meet that form of competition, Southwest knows it's a lot smarter to avoid it and compete by improving its costs, speed, and limited, standardized offerings.

At the other extreme, watching a customer-intimate organization try to go to market with a standardized offering is painful. At

Hewitt we are a customers company. Our limitation is that almost every time we try to build what we hope will be a new, standardized service, it quickly turns into a family of services tailored for different types of clients or an approach that is completely customized for specific clients.

We always start with the best of intentions to create something that can be repeated over and over. Then one client wants the service one way, while another needs it delivered differently. The next thing we know, every client asks for something unique. True to our style, we are delighted to customize and can't say no. When we are done, we will have launched a new service area that many of our clients will want tailored to their own situations instead of a standardized offering.

What does this tell us at Hewitt about our limitations? Clearly we shouldn't invest a lot of time trying to build standardized offerings. Customers companies just don't manage the product development process the way products companies do. Its runs counter to who they are.

Going through the process of identifying your capabilities—which are core, how do they support your strategic style, and how do they fit with each other, which ones need to improve, what capabilities could better be done by someone else, etc.—and then doing something about them is at the heart of strategy formulation and implementation. Talent management issues enter as you assess your capabilities because capabilities demand particular kinds of people and certain things from them. Upgrading, adding, or changing capabilities require that you determine whether your people can perform to your desired new abilities.

A manufacturing company with a products style found itself having greater and greater difficulty commanding premium prices because of copycat competitors. The company carefully considered moving to an operations focused style and playing the price game. Then it looked closely at its capabilities and its people.

The company decided that it had a much greater chance of success reviving its research and product development functions, which until recently had been world-class, than it did building completely new capabilities in highly standardized manufacturing, distribution, and sales. In particular it believed it would need a 60 percent change in its workforce, and that seemed highly unrealistic given a tight labor market in its locations. Recommitting to a products focus was also a way to renew the historic traditions of the company and re-energize its staff. Two years into this new/old strategy, financial results were at their highest in five years.

In the IBR model, business capabilities derive straight from your desired business results and strategy. As you can see, your capabilities are a big part of your strategic style and pose major implications for talent management because your people are the ones who execute your capabilities. Attempting to switch styles requires massive changes by your workforce. Shell is one of the few companies I know of who has attempted to do this in recent years.

CENTRALIZATION/DECENTRALIZATION

This again raises the issue of whether you can possess two or three different styles in the same company. Can you offer different things to different customers, complete with different business strategies, capabilities, and talent? How can you manage such complexity?

There does seem to be one way for you to "have your cake and eat it too." It's possible for one company to master two or three styles and their related capabilities and talent issues—but you have to be willing to decentralize to do it. You have to be willing to establish separate, independent business units serving different customers in different markets with different capabilities, people requirements, and workforce strategies and practices.

This is an extraordinarily complex challenge because it demands true decentralization. It is so difficult that there aren't many truly decentralized companies. Many companies have what I call "operational autonomy" but label themselves decentralized.

In an operationally autonomous company, business units have lots of control over their decisions, but they still are involved in basically the same types of businesses with the same value offerings, strategic styles, and workforces. Products companies are famous for this type of organization. They provide operating units lots of freedom to create and serve markets but the same or nearly identical people and policies across units. True decentralization comes when you realize you have to manage your customers and employees differently in each unit.

Companies struggle with this all the time. Walt Disney is an example. For years it tried to use the same strategic style and management practices across most of the company. Gradually Disney realized it was in several different businesses with distinct strategic styles. Its imagineering business is a products company that has created some of the most beloved cartoon and movie figures in the world. This business has to be managed for innovation. Disney's theme parks may be the best examples of operations companies you can imagine. They apply what the imagineers create to provide consistently delightful experiences for park visitors. The need to decentralize became clearer for Disney as it broadened into other businesses like retailing and residential land development.

3M also dealt with this when it spun off Imation, a $2.8 billion part of its business. Imation was created out of a collection of products that needed to compete on price. This required an operations style, including new workforce strategies and practices, that products focused 3M was not well-suited to execute.

This may sound easy, and it's not difficult to set up different units. What is really hard is when you try to create separate workforces. Most of the companies I see try to have a high level of consistency in the way they manage people. They do this in the name of fairness. Ultimately, this gets in the way of creating successful business units with different strategies and capabilities. It can take years for even the most effective companies to realize they need to align to separate strategies. Then it can take several more years to actually establish different cultures, workforce strategies, and management practices.

U.S. Bancorp

U.S. Bancorp was born from the merger of First Bank System and U.S. Bancorp. It is a super-regional bank extending from Chicago to the Pacific Ocean. The bank derives about 50 percent of its income from its operations-style retail bank and 50 percent from its customers-style relationship bank business.

U.S. Bancorp has found that it currently needs almost completely different alignment approaches in the two sides of the bank. Speed and standardization don't mesh well with personalized service and individually tailored solutions. There are opportunities for integration, but they mostly are around technology, customer information, and handing off the right customers from retail to relationship bank. U.S. Bancorp has created a business unit structure that enables both sides to separate from each other and focus on unique capabilities.

What's striking about U.S. Bancorp is that it moved so quickly to create the separation rather than agonizing about it for years. It started with a decentralized mindset, and the leaders of each side of the bank saw they had to go in separate directions. Early on this extended to the types of people each hires and the ways they manage talent. Wendy Bloom, a manager at U.S. Bancorp, says, "Even before the merger, when we were still First Bank System, we realized that we were in two different businesses. Our tight focus on costs and accountability helped us figure out fast that our businesses need flexibility to meet their bottom-line goals. You can't get there with 'one size fits all'."

The bank created its decentralized structure by recognizing the differences in its two types of customers and what it needed to offer them. The retail bank offers "any time, anywhere" convenience banking for its customers, while the relationship bank provides highly personalized banking for "ultra-affluent" customers. These can be charted as shown in Table 3-2.

The bank's supporting systems and practices to grow and maintain these capabilities look similar within each part of the bank but increasingly different across the parts. An example is the talent alignment process used in the commercial part of the relationship bank.

The commercial bank recognized that complex clients need solutions developed and delivered in teams. Even in striving for highly individualized solutions, the bank knew that with the huge variety of products available and the expected levels of turnover, it would take a team of people to maintain a long-term relationship with a customer.

It created a team alignment process around five key values that support intensive collaboration: integrity, initiative, accountability, teamwork, and innovation. It changed its hiring profile to bring in internal and external hires who could live the values. Employees learned about the values and expected behaviors through workshops, self-development processes, and peer feedback. Performance and pay systems to reinforce these behaviors also were created.

None of this was done in the retail bank because the approach to customers is structured so completely differently. Yet I know of many companies that can't let go of consistency to this degree. These others would feel they were doing something wrong to the retail bank staff by not including them, rather than responding to their specific needs with other practices and tools.

TABLE 3-2

Decentralization of U.S. Bancorp

	Retail Bank	Private Bank
Customer	Broad, retail marketplace	"Ultra-affluent' within marketplace and middle-market companies
Value Offering	Anytime, anywhere banking	Highly personalized banking relationship
Strategic Style	Operations	Customers
Capabilities	• Standardized product offerings • Full line of retail products • Low prices, low costs • Centralized operations and transactions • 24-hour customer access through technology • Consistent, accurate, fast, and predictable service • Customer information system for cross-selling • Rigorous profit planning for low-margin transactions • Convenient access from multiple locations, including home and telephone banking	• Highly individual-ized banking solutions • Full-line of retail products • Personal trust services • Investment services • Financing, 401(k), and cash management • Ready availability • Relationship skills: listening, probing, and understanding • Deep client knowledge • Discrete, long-term relationships main-tained by teams • Deep knowledge of bank resources and ability to bring them together to solve problems

W.W. Grainger is a $4 billion distributor of industrial products and supplies that is letting go of consistency as it builds a new business. The company was founded on a speed and convenience business of catalogues and distribution centers for its industrial and commercial customers. In recent years it has been growing a new integrated supply consulting business for big customers. This business puts Grainger consultants on-site at clients to manage purchasing and inventory. This is a customers business that requires intense familiarity with the host company, adaptation to its culture and business practices, and the ability to find unique solutions to lower its supply costs while improving availability.

Gary Goberville, vice president at Grainger, says to support the emergence of the new business, the company is going from being highly centralized to "centralized decentralization." Gary explains this as benefiting from common values, similar quality processes whenever possible, and open exchange of information, but very different delivery mechanisms, support processes, people practices, and employees. Learning to manage in this new environment has been an intensive focus for Grainger's leadership development efforts because it requires major changes.

CREATING THE TALENT SOLUTION

1. Which capabilities does your organization possess that enable you to win in the marketplace?
2. Which ones do you need to develop that you don't have now?
3. How well do these capabilities match your desired business results and strategies? Are they aligned with your strategic style?
4. What are the limitations of your capabilities? Where does it make sense to not compete?
5. Are you appropriately centralized/decentralized in your talent management practices?

Define What People Need to Do

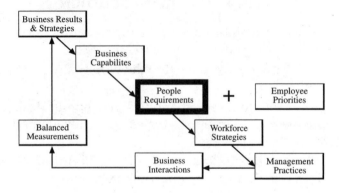

Managing talent means being clear about what kinds of people you need and what you expect them to do. In this chapter, you will:

- Learn a framework for defining people requirements
- Understand how culture impacts high performance, values alignment, selection, and change
- See how to use competencies to define necessary behaviors
- Get a perspective on the psychological contract between you and your employees

PEOPLE REQUIREMENTS

Each strategic style and related business capabilities demand different requirements from your people. In fact, these are so different that Fred Wiersema suggests that someone who works for Wal Mart would be a lot happier working for Federal Express, similar operations environments, than working for a different kind of retailer like Nordstrom or Bloomingdale's. The style and environment of the delivery company will seem a lot more familiar to the person than would the customers or products environments of the two other stores.

I describe these people requirements as the Three Cs: culture, competencies, and contract. These three are interrelated so it's hard to separate them completely. Together they spell out the things you need from your workforce to align and deliver results (see Figure 4-1).

CULTURE: HOW TO BUILD IT

Everyone has his or her own definition of culture. Earlier, I said it was the shared values and norms that shape behavior and decision-making in your company. Another way to think about it is the business beliefs and values you espouse, and the individual beliefs and values you want people to hold so they treat customers, each other, and your company in a particular way.

FIGURE 4-1

The Three Cs

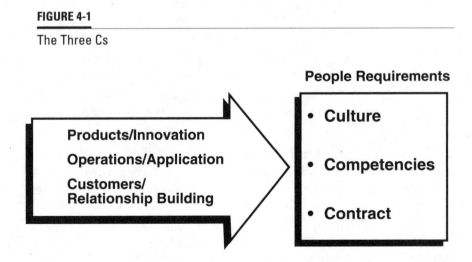

People Requirements

Products/Innovation
Operations/Application
Customers/Relationship Building

- Culture
- Competencies
- Contract

Culture comes mostly from two places—the company's history of how people have behaved and been treated by management, and what the current CEO believes and how he or she behaves. Sometimes these two elements are in sync. Sometimes they're not. When a company wants to "change its culture," it's usually because the CEO has a different set of beliefs or thinks the changing marketplace requires them and wants people to adopt new behaviors.

Many books have been written about culture. To be brief, I'll focus on the few things you should consider in building a culture to manage talent and implement strategy. These are what goes into a high performance culture; culture as the "glue" that ties people together; how to use culture as the key to fit and selection; and how to create an adaptive culture.

HIGH-PERFORMING CULTURES

What kinds of values and beliefs must you promote to produce extraordinary results year after year? All high-performing cultures have four key values and beliefs in common. You must repeat them constantly and back them up with your actions so people know they have consequences.

> All high-performing cultures have four key values and beliefs in common.

The beliefs are:

- Customer—We do whatever it takes for the customer.
- Excellence—We want to be the best at what we do all the time.
- Group—We want to treat each other fairly and with respect. In other words, we show caring for each other.
- Individual—We respect individual dignity and make work satisfying, either because it's enjoyable or the challenges posed by it are motivating.

That's it. Everything else is elaboration. When you strip away the fads and the fancy ideas about high-performance cultures, this is what you notice across different types of companies with different strategic styles.

What will vary given the three strategic styles is how the customer gets served, how the "whatever it takes" part looks. At Whirlpool this means doing what's necessary to build a highly dependable washer or dryer that will deliver reliable service for a long time. At Glaxo Wellcome it's working as long and as hard as possible to find the next compound to treat AIDS. At Hewitt it may mean traveling to China with a client for several weeks to help figure out how to hire people for a start-up venture. So the definition of "whatever it takes" will differ, but a similar value and spirit will be there. Meanwhile, the other three beliefs need to be the same, regardless of strategy.

I have seen many companies try to get much more complicated in describing their desired cultures, but simplicity is best. High-performing cultures really come from focusing people on doing the absolute best they can on the work itself and establishing enjoyable work relationships that bring everyday emotional satisfaction. That's where you should start.

This is exactly why Ford Motor Company's "Quality is Job 1" is so compelling to employees. It focuses people on building high-quality cars. Building your culture around advancing one's profession or making a contribution to society or the environment also can be useful in some cases, but too many organizations go way beyond that and confuse the issue.

In his book on the early days of the U.S. space program, *The Right Stuff,* Tom Wolfe tells a great story that makes this point. Gus Grissom, one of the original astronauts, was part of a group visiting the Convair plant in San Diego where the Atlas rocket was being built. Grissom was a quiet man who was uncomfortable speaking to crowds.

Grissom was asked to address the workers making the rocket he would ride into space, but he became nervous and tongue-tied. All he could think to say was, "Well... do good work!" After a minute to absorb this deep wisdom, Convair employees went wild with enthusiasm at Gus' simple comments. "Do Good Work" became the plant's slogan, appearing on banners and posters—a simple mission for a very complex business.

A few years ago, I took a group of high-level managers from Shell Oil to visit the reservations center at Avis Rental Car. The Shell people were interested in finding out about different types of workforces and recognition strategies. The Shell managers, used to working on complex problems with lots of resources and long time frames, saw row after row of people dealing with a constant current of simple problems over the telephone.

The Shell team was amazed at how the Avis reservationists could keep it up, handling the same nitty-gritty issues hour after hour with enthusiasm and grace. At the debriefing we concluded that Avis people had all of the characteristics of a high-performing culture. They wanted to help their customers as much as they possibly could; they wanted to provide excellent service, better than Hertz, National, and the others; they treated each other with respect and affection; and they genuinely seemed to enjoy helping as many people as possible rent cars to take care of business or go on vacation. They were focused on the work, the customer, and each other.

GLUE: VALUES THAT BIND

The second part of culture is "glue," the values that bind people together in a company. This is absolutely critical to aligning strategy and talent, but it's also the "squishiest" part of culture. This is the "I can feel it, but I can't measure it" part.

When I think about culture as glue, I always remember a brilliant presentation I once heard from a labor economist on how to increase the value of human assets in business. During the question-and-answer session at the end, someone asked him about the role of culture in developing talent. Even though he was a warm, affable, and smart fellow, the economist said, "It can't play any role. As an economist, I can't quantify culture, so I don't believe in it." The reaction from the audience was unkind.

Most of us do believe in culture, and many CEOs and other leaders spend enormous amounts of time and resources to mold, maintain, and enhance the cultures of their companies. They're convinced it has a direct, if hard to measure, impact on people's behavior. If they want to be successful, they first need to install the four beliefs of a high-performance culture so people know how to behave. Next, they need to "bind" people to it so they have the desire to get it done.

This is where the "glue" comes in, or "identification," if you prefer a more sophisticated term. To deliver on your strategies, you have to get people to identify with your company's values and beliefs. Your people have to feel that your values are their values so they can take to heart what you are trying to do. When people care about what you're trying to do, they'll have the motivation to do it. You'll also have a great working environment. Think what this will do for your productivity and retention.

One of our foremost authorities on winning, Chicago Bulls Coach Phil Jackson, writes in his book, *Sacred Hoops*, that "the most effective way to forge a winning team is to call on the players' needs to connect with something larger than themselves." Jackson calls this a "spiritual act" because you have to give up some of your self-interest for the greater good. Jackson says, and I agree, this is true for any kind of team—sports, work, volunteer activities, or other endeavors. An executive in a chemical research and development facility in Europe told me almost the same thing recently.

> Identification occurs most powerfully through values alignment— matching company values with personal values.

Identification occurs most powerfully through values alignment—matching company values with personal values. Usually companies attempt to do this by stating their values and asking, or demanding, that people line up with them. This causes companies to write down their values.

Mission Statements

Many people criticize mission and values statements created by companies as not worth the paper, and a lot of the ones I have seen aren't very clear, stimulating, or realistic. Some don't even reflect how the company really behaves. Still, how will someone know what you value unless you tell them? Word-of-mouth may be a more powerful communicator, but it's not as reliable or consistent. Part of building culture is providing the workforce with a common language to discuss how it should behave.

The power of these statements come from their directness and simplicity. They're better when they're brief, straightforward, and human. You also want to make them somewhat aspirational since many people do look for inspiration in their work.

The real power of these kinds of statements derives from their accountability. For the most part that accountability is your responsibility as the leader. Once you put it on paper, people will expect to see you "walk the talk" by living up to your values and beliefs. Be prepared for plenty of scrutiny and skepticism until you pass muster.

Cargill communicates its culture in a particularly powerful way. Its vision is to "raise living standards around the world by delivering increased value to producers and consumers." This is a noble aspiration, but it's delivered simply. The mission statement that follows is a brief account of how Cargill will be the best in its chosen businesses by balancing and meeting the needs of customers, employees, and shareholders.

Cargill then lists the brief, basic beliefs that are the foundation of the relationships it builds with all its constituencies. These do an exceptional job of reflecting the unique character of the corporation through the definitions used for some relatively common corporate values: integrity, excellence, growth, teamwork, long-term view, and desire to compete. Within the same communication, Cargill lists its five core competencies and strategic directions.

This communication enables Cargill to provide its employees with deep insight into its essential direction and values. People can make the identification they need, as well as get a clear way to think about how to treat each other. Nancy Siska, Cargill vice president, says the company needs this information because its operations are so far-reaching. "What holds us together, despite our vast geographies and different lines of business, are our common financial processes, HR practices, and most importantly, our cultural values."

Once you've clarified your values, you have to help people understand how they and the company both will benefit from them. This takes lots of persuasion, examples, and persistence. Phil Jackson turns to "Zen Christianity" and Sioux folklore and ritual for inspiration and techniques. Or you can travel the world like James Burke, former CEO of Johnson & Johnson, patiently explaining the company's values to employees and getting their acceptance. Many companies like Amoco or Whirlpool use a "cascade down" communication stream to successive groups of employees. Whatever you do will require a great amount of selling.

After you've started to make the sale, you'll need consistency and consequences. In low-trust environments or companies that haven't focused on values, employees look for inconsistencies. They'll jump on anything they perceive to be an inconsistency to show you're not sincere in your values. You have to be unyielding in upholding your values and explaining why your actions match your values.

You'll also need to take actions and build management practices that demonstrate consequences for values-based actions. This is particularly true when you're rewarding behavior through pay, promotions, and recognition. Are you rewarding what you say you value? Many national surveys of employee attitudes suggest employees don't think their employers do this.

No matter how you do it, you have to achieve identification if you are going to build the culture you want. With identification comes motivation, and even more powerfully, trust. You'll have nothing to fear or hide from your employees, and they'll have nothing to fear or hide from you because your values and interests are the same.

SELECT FOR FIT

This is the third part of culture—selection for fit. Companies with strong cultures pick people who fit their cultures. They recognize that technical, interpersonal, and problem-solving skills are not enough for a successful hire. People have to fit the values. People who don't fit need to find employment elsewhere.

This is an absolutely essential part of strong talent management, but it makes hiring processes more difficult, subjective, and time-consuming. It's much easier to screen for intelligence, aptitude, technical, and even interpersonal or presentation skills. These characteristics are closer to the surface and more assessable through testing and interviewing.

It's much harder to probe for values and beliefs, because they are closer to the core of a person's personality. They are deeper and harder to bring out through conversation. Just because a person tells you how he or she behaves in certain situations doesn't mean the behavior will actually occur. For that, you need to find out what values and beliefs are driving the behavior. The only way to do this is to have a number of different people ask the same questions in a variety of ways.

You also have to try to assess someone else's values through the perspective of your own, so your value filters may be editing what you hear. Facing these obstacles, most companies who screen for values will increase the number of interviews and sometimes use outside evaluators, so more people can make an assessment. In the end it's a very subjective call, so it's better to get a consensus from more people.

One company that takes values in hiring very seriously is Herman Miller, the designer and manufacturer of advanced-design office furniture and systems. Vice President Rod McCowan says Miller looks for employees who embody their five values—contribution to customers, community and participation, change, integrity, and economic value. Above all, Miller executives must possess the value of "servant leadership," dedicating themselves to serving Miller's customers, employees, and communities, ahead of their own personal interests. The only way to really assess that is through many conversations with a large number of interviewers.

When you select for fit with values, you go a long way to ensuring values alignment and a strong culture. These employees will come into your organization predisposed to hear what you have to say and buy into what you are trying to do. There will be less suspicion and cynicism because you are starting with a closer match. For example, Miller is a participative place, and if it made a mistake and picked an executive with a strong authoritarian approach, it could have a corrosive effect on Miller's culture.

ADAPTATION: BALANCING STAKEHOLDER NEEDS

This leads us to the last aspect of culture—adaptation. In *Corporate Culture and Performance*, John Kotter and James Heskett show that a strong culture alone isn't enough. You must build a strong and adaptive culture, one that is capable of changing. Kotter and Heskett argue the best way to do that is to ensure you are balancing the needs of your three key stakeholders—customers, employees, and shareholders. If you are listening and trying to meet and balance the needs of all three groups, then you will be externally focused and quicker to change.

From this perspective, the two most important groups to listen to are customers and employees. Shareholders are pretty consistent in what they want—high returns. It's customers and employees who keep changing. Listening to them will help you stay current with your markets, especially if employees are dedicated to meeting customer needs.

Your strategic style, core capabilities and values are the foundations of what you do and who you are. They can be adapted to new conditions, but they don't lend themselves easily to radical makeover without tremendous efforts at transformation. Most of these fall short.

If you have created an adaptive culture and are listening and responding, then you shouldn't need major transformation, just on-going, market-based change. General Motors, IBM, and Sears are well-known examples of three companies that stopped adapting and needed transformation. As I write this, IBM and Sears are succeeding with massive changes. GM is still a work-in-progress.

Transformation is a pretty rare occurrence. More often companies try to sharpen their focus and fine-tune what they do on an ongoing basis. This requires changing some attitudes and behaviors, while preserving strategic style, core capabilities, and enduring values. This is cultural adaptation.

At Hewitt we have spent more time adapting and shaping our culture in the last five years than we did in the previous 20. Client demands, competitive pressures, the mix of our work, and the changing profile of our associates have required us to do this. Since we have been proud of our traditional culture, our efforts at adaptation have tried to balance continuity and change.

Even this type of adaptation can be extremely difficult. Like other companies, we're constantly asking associates to do things better, cheaper, and faster for our clients. At times this means cutting back on some "nice to have" things, or asking people to be more self-sufficient. Some of our associates object to any attempts to change our work environment and exaggerate these to claims that we are destroying the culture. As our Chief Executive Dale Gifford points out, "People confuse traditions with culture."

Adaptation occurs when you are listening to your customers and employees and changing your behaviors and practices based on what they tell you. If you have instilled the values of a high-performance culture, aligned business and personal values, and selected for fit, then there should be close congruence between what both groups are saying. That's because employees will be listening to your customers and will want to do whatever it takes to serve them. Even though some people will object to change, the majority should be willing to go along with you because they will see the opportunity to create more value.

NECESSARY COMPETENCIES

The second part of people requirements are competencies. Competencies tell people what they must be good at if they and the company are going to succeed. In research I helped conduct for the American Compensation Association (ACA), we defined *competencies* as "individual performance behaviors that are observable, measurable, and critical to successful individual or corporate performance."

People sometimes confuse competencies and culture since both manifest themselves in behaviors. One difference is that most competencies imply skill or learning, where value-oriented behaviors, like showing respect or taking initiative, are more like personal characteristics. Not all of the value-oriented behaviors that make up a culture are critical for performance or can be learned. Some are more related to fit.

Another golf analogy may help explain this. You are asked to play at a very exclusive country club, one where you are expected to dress and act in a very genteel manner. This has nothing to do with how good a golfer—how competent— you are. Perhaps you play a terrific round of golf, shooting in the low 70s. But you dress in loud, obnoxious shorts, topped by a raggedy-looking shirt, and you have a frequent habit of screaming when you hit a great shot and cursing loudly when you don't. How you dress is not critical to your successful round, but odds are quite good that people's perceptions of your round will be influenced by your appearance and characteristics, in addition to your performance. This certainly could affect whether you can play that course again. Some might conclude that you are very competent but not a good fit culturally.

To build talent you must have both strong, adaptable cultural values and high-performance competencies.

You may say this distinction is valuable only to consultants and psychologists. Still, to build talent you must have both strong, adaptable cultural values and high-performance competencies. These both should come from, and align with, your strategic style and business capabilities. Most importantly you should tell employees clearly what your culture and competencies need to be. Put another way, talent comes from fit and skills. If you want to win, you will develop these carefully and your people will know what they are so they act accordingly.

Here's where the distinction between culture and competencies—fit and skills—matters: fit is mostly a matter of selection. You can try to change some behaviors, but if you don't have basic values alignment and the right characteristics, you won't be able to change enough behaviors to get fit. Values run deep in people and don't change much over time.

On the other hand, competencies are mostly a matter of experience and learning. You can select for some of them, but the way work and jobs are changing today, you'll never be able to predict all of the skills you will need tomorrow. To keep creating value, you will need to educate and develop people continuously so they keep growing the competencies they need.

You can see this overlap in Figure 4-2.

This close relationship between culture and competencies was demonstrated in the research we did for the ACA. We collected data from 217 North American companies that had described the employee competencies they needed for successful performance and were using these descriptions to manage people. We found that companies were using competencies in two ways:

- To "raise the bar" on employee performance so people increased their skills and became more successful
- To focus on core values and culture so they could ensure employee fit and build a culture for competitive advantage

FIGURE 4-2

Culture and Competencies

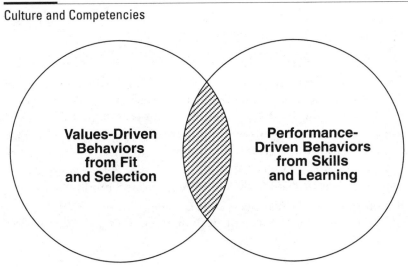

Values-Driven Behaviors from Fit and Selection

Performance-Driven Behaviors from Skills and Learning

Companies had developed their lists of competencies by reviewing their strategic plans, talking to senior managers, and asking high performers and functional experts what they did that made them so successful.

A food and beverage company created a list of leadership competencies they used for executive and management training, development, and evaluation. Once these groups became comfortable with them, the company modified them and extended them to all salaried employees. The competencies are:

Problem-Solving Skills	Interpersonal Influence	Personal Orientation
Analytical thinking	Leadership skills	Drive for results
Intellectual curiosity	Interpersonal effectiveness	Customer impact
Innovation and creativity	Respect for others	Technical knowledge
	Business impact	Self-management

Each of these had specific behavioral definitions appropriate to either the executive and management or salaried groups so people could understand how to act. Are these all competencies or are some of them values? As I said before, I am not sure it matters as long as people understand what they need to do. Companies also can get much more specific and describe technical skills in depth. This usually is a cumbersome process but can be effective for training if you are taking in large numbers of new people.

Here's an example of the technical competency project/program management for a consulting engineer.

Project/program management—The ability to create, conduct, and deliver a project or program from start to finish that meets or exceeds customer specifications and is successful for the company.

- Develops and communicates reasonable expectations that result in win/win situations for the customer and the company.

- Leads project activities and team members to achieve on-time quality deliverables, high customer value, and profitable results.

- Recognizes priorities, dependencies, and critical paths that are important to the sequencing of project activities and manages to successful resolution.

- Analyzes and specifies the staffing needs for a project or program—doesn't under- or overstaff.
- Anticipates issues that will need to be addressed as the project progresses, prevents problems from occurring to the greatest extent possible.
- Solves problems quickly, effectively, and cost-efficiently.

Now imagine you were a new consulting engineer. Wouldn't you appreciate that kind of detail about what's expected from you? Wouldn't it be powerful if your company communicated this information to you, trained you on what you didn't know, and evaluated you on whether you got it done? That's the potential power of competencies.

This discussion is not about how to develop competencies, but is to help you understand the crucial role competencies can play in managing your talent and aligning it to strategy. They do this by specifying people requirements—clarifying to your workforce what's expected.

Fortunately our strategic styles framework (Table 4-1) gives you a very useful way to identify general competencies. Each style tells you what kind of work environment you are going to need and what key competencies will be required from employees to win. You can modify these lists to fit your company.

These aren't the only competencies you will need in your company, just the more general ones that will enable you to achieve great results. Some of these can be used in selection. All of them should be used for development. Hiring and developing people for these competencies will bring your talent closer to your strategy.

CONTRACT: YOUR TERMS

The third and last aspect of people requirements is what I call contract. These are the work commitments you need from your employees. This usually isn't a legal contract, but the word implies both parties agree to it. Employee needs, fears, and goals are covered in a later chapter, so think of contract here as your company's expectations or terms.

TABLE 4-1

Strategic Styles Framework

Strategic Style	Work Environment	Employee Competencies
Customers	Values-driven, dynamic, changing, informal, collegial, conversational, few policies, service-oriented, qualitative, bottoms-up, employee as customer, "whatever it takes"	Relationship-building, listening, rapid problem-solving, independent action, initiative, collaboration, quality-focused, understands motivation
Operations	Stable, predictable, measurable, hierarchical, cost-conscious, team-based, formal, compliant, "if it ain't broke, break it bit by bit"	Process control, continuous improvement, teamwork, analysis, financial/operational understanding, group facilitation, attention to detail, drive for results
Products	Exciting, experimental, learning-focused, technical, informal, fast-paced, resource-rich, comfortable, constantly changing, speed to market, "if we build it, they will come"	Life-long learning, information sharing, curiosity, creativity, group problem-solving, breakthrough thinking, artistic, visionary

From this perspective, *contract* is the dedication or drive your employees need to show for your company to succeed. This is based on the efforts, hours, and results you expect from people. It also reflects the length of tenure you expect from employees and the balance between work and family life you will offer. It may even address how often you expect them to relocate and what happens if they don't move.

Professor Denise Rousseau of Carnegie Mellon University has written extensively on the psychological contract between companies and employees. She describes it as a continuum of contract terms stretching from the *transactional contract,* defined as "what have you done for me lately," to the *relational contract,* which calls for a longer-term, more complex relationship. Contract terms may be written or informal.

Transactional contracts really are distinguished by being more explicit, economic, results-driven, and performance-contingent. Once set, they are not much open to change regarding duties, learning, or location, and have to be renegotiated if a change is desired. Transactional jobs include commission salespeople, professional athletes, actors, stock and bond traders, and investment bankers. These contracts have the advantage of promoting high performance/high rewards but with a great risk to job security.

Relational contracts are much longer-term in nature and may be less specific or demanding about performance. Though they lose something in results, they gain the advantages of experience, learning, and more flexible deployment of people. Many large, older companies continue to have relational contracts with their employees, even though these have declined in recent years. These companies offer long-term employment and investment in people in return for the ability to train and move people as needed.

The most powerful way to think about the differences in these contracts is on the dimension of employment tenure. Tenure, or job security, clearly has been the biggest workplace issue discussed in the U.S. in the last 10–15 years. We can depict this contract dimension as shown in Figure 4-3.

Employment security, or career employment, is what most large U.S. companies used to offer employees. According to the popular press it no longer exists in the U.S. and is fading in some European countries. However, to paraphrase Mark Twain, the reports of its death are highly exaggerated. Many companies, especially technical ones, like Motorola, Hewlett-Packard, and Procter & Gamble, still offer career employment to the majority of their employees.

Gaurdie Banister, President of Shell Continental Company, the on-shore production division of Shell Oil USA, recognizes this. "In a long-term function like exploration and production, we aren't interested in training people to go somewhere else." Still, after the downsizing of recent years, many companies are moving more to the left on the scale, towards employability. This still equates to longer-term, though perhaps not career, employment.

There are some large companies that focus on portability— "come work hard for us for several years, earn a lot, learn a lot, and then move on." Apple Computer, PepsiCo, and, increasingly, General Electric, after hundreds of thousands of layoffs, are examples of this.

Contingent employment means assignment, project, or temporary work. Contingent work is growing, but the size of the contingent workforce depends on how you define it. The most conservative definition covers only employees who have short-term or temporary employment relationships and includes about 10 percent of the U.S. workforce. The broadest definition includes service firms, independent contractors, and part-time workers and may be as large as 35 percent of the workforce. That's up from about 25 percent five years ago.

It's too early to tell what impact the tightening labor market will have on the number of contingent workers. It could be that many of them become permanent employees to fill shortages. Or it could be that companies will continue to hire on assignment or project work to maintain a more flexible workforce.

The writer and consultant William Bridges thinks contingent work will become a way of life at companies for all but a modest size core of internal workers. Bridges believes fixed jobs cannot keep up with the global and technological changes affecting business. He sees more jobs evolving into assignments, and careers becoming a series of assignments at various companies. Employees will move based on their skills and attitudes and employers' needs to get tasks done.

Wayne Anderson, Senior Vice President at Amoco, agrees that Bridges' job shift is occurring, but not yet at the magnitude Bill sees. According to Anderson, today Amoco may be 85 percent core, 15 percent contingent employees. In the future, Amoco could shift to as much as 50/50.

The issue for your company is alignment with strategy. What types of contract terms make sense for your strategic style, business capabilities, culture, and competencies? Again, you can use your strategic style to provide a reference for general contract terms (see Table 4-2).

FIGURE 4-3

Employment Tenure

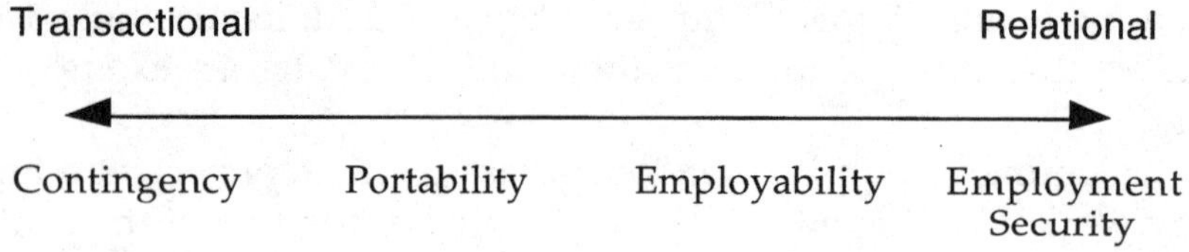

Transactional   Relational

Contingency   Portability   Employability   Employment
                                                            Security

TABLE 4-2

Using Strategic Style to Set Contract Terms

Strategic Style	Contract Terms
Customers	More likely to be relational contracts; longer-term careers to build longer-term customer relationships despite unpredictable work experiences, workplaces, and career paths; customer needs come before employee needs; long hours dictated by the customer and based on meeting customer needs; close identification with organization values, especially service.
Operations	Likely to vary between transactional and relational contracts; careers can vary from short-term to long-term depending on the processes used to deliver value; predictable career paths and work experiences; work within a more fixed structure; follow rules laid down by hierarchy, work processes, or standard operating procedures; hours vary, dictated by what it takes to produce results or fulfill shifts; process or policy needs before employee needs; identification with jobs or functions and levels.
Products	More likely to be relational contracts; medium- to long-term careers based on organization's ability at discovery or product development; long hours based on discovery; flat career paths or dual career ladders; flexible organization and career structures; employee needs often come first so discovery can take place without distracting identification with profession.

You now have gone through three stages in the IBR alignment model and have completed the review of business results and strategies, business capabilities, and people requirements. Before moving on to workforce strategies, try answering the following questions.

CREATING THE TALENT SOLUTION

1. How closely does your company resemble the characteristics of a high-performance culture?

2. Look at your mission or values statement. What could you do to improve it so it really captures what you are trying to do for customers and who you are as a company, and so it has more appeal to employees regarding their work?

3.   Do you select for fit? If not, what do you select for? What do you do to make sure a candidate fits your culture and values?

4.   Have you defined competencies for key positions or groups of employees? Do you provide training and development so they can grow the skills and competencies you need to be successful and they need to stay current?

5.   Are you clear in your own mind about your contract terms for employees? Have you laid it out for them?

CHAPTER **5**

Build a Workforce Strategy

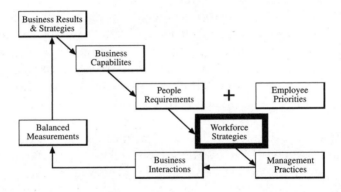

Smart companies build plans for their workforces just like they build plans for the other parts of their businesses. In this chapter, you'll learn:

- What a workforce strategy is and why you need one
- What's in a workforce strategy
- How workforce strategies differ for each strategic style

WHY YOU NEED A WORKFORCE STRATEGY

You have a workforce strategy when you take a planned approach to acquiring, deploying, developing, and retaining talent. A strategy is fundamental to aligning and managing people, yet not enough companies do it. They may plan how they recruit, or they may create a process for developing certain key types of people. Rarely do they take a thoughtful, coordinated, and planned approach to hiring, utilizing, growing, and keeping their people.

Some years ago I worked with a large pharmaceutical company on fleshing out their business strategy. A key part of the strategy called for replenishing a very dry pipeline of new compounds and products with an intensive, five-year campaign of spending and growth in research and development. This was before they started thinking about a workforce strategy.

After we began developing the workforce strategy, it became clear that the market supply of new Ph.D. chemists would never match this company's needs and plans, let alone the demands of the industry. There just weren't enough graduate students in chemistry. The company had to revisit its business strategy and find a more realistic path, focusing on acquisitions and licensing, as well as discovery.

This same thing happened to McDonald's many years ago. After looking at its workforce strategically, it realized that at its hoped-for rate of growth and usual rate of turnover, 50 percent of all of the teenagers in America would need to work for the company at one time or another. Since this didn't seem likely, the company began to look at retention, development strategies, and working conditions to reduce turnover and recruit other members of the population, especially senior citizens.

Perhaps your company could have gotten by without a workforce strategy when there was an abundance of employees, but that has changed today. Skilled help (from tradespeople to technicians, managers, and executives) now is in tight supply. This is true in the U.S. and in growing economies around the world. Unemployment may be high in some stagnating, restructuring, or yet-to-be-developed economies, but in the growing economies of North America, Latin America, and Asia, good help is very hard to find.

Part of this shortage is demographic—the generational cohort entering the workforce now is small, at least in the U.S. and other developed countries. It will stay this way in the U.S. until about 2002–

2004, when the children of the large, middle group of baby boomers hits the workforce.

Another part of this is driven by education and skill—many people don't have the knowledge and talents required to be successful in this global economy. Projections by some futurists suggest one-half to three-quarters of all new jobs in the U.S. will require some college-level education by early in the next century. This compares with less than one-quarter of new jobs now. Not coincidentally, about 25 percent of American adults have some college education as of the mid-1990s.

Additionally, education requirements are going up all over the world as economic conditions improve and technology proliferates. Today, because of their growing economies, education systems, and talented workforces, India, Ireland, and Israel are three hot spots for software development. In the near future, newer and less developed countries will emerge to compete with them.

Finally, and I am speculating about this, some people in the U.S. at least may be turned off at the prospect of joining large companies or following more traditional career paths. There's some evidence among younger people coming out of college now and among those downsized in the massive layoffs of the late 1980s and early 1990s that they would prefer never to enter or reenter the corporate world. Early baby boomers, who entered the workforce between 1965 and 1970 and worked for large- or medium-sized firms, will have endured at least three periods of recession, downsizing, or reengineering that affected them, their family members, or close friends. Their 20-something child has watched them worry through it.

Demographic projections can be made with some certainty, but no one can be certain about education or attitude. Education standards and levels generally are going up around the world. There are renewed efforts to raise them in the U.S. after they have deteriorated for quite some time. There is no way to tell when they will start to turn around in the U.S. and when the effect will be felt. It's clear they must improve, and it will take a long time.

While Americans tend to have more years of education than most other countries, test scores of American students in math, science, geography, and other key subjects tend to lag well behind students in South Korea, Japan, Singapore, and Hong Kong. What classes do American college students take that leave them behind students from other countries? About 30 percent of them have to take at least one remedial course in reading, writing, or math. The number is increasing, indicating learning didn't take place in high school. People not going to college often receive remedial education at work. It's going to be hard to out-think the rest of the world in an information economy when we are playing catch up in education.

A recent survey of the National Association of Manufacturers showed two-thirds of its members said a significant number of entry-level employees lack necessary skills. The Association's president was quoted in early 1997 as saying, "I used to think I was in the manufacturing business, but more and more I think I'm in the education business."

Moreover, attitudes seem to be completely unpredictable. I could argue with very few facts about Generation X values and attitudes toward work, but one thing does seem clear; with the societal and business upheavals and the incredible pace of technological change they've seen, Gen Xers don't put much stock in permanence, including long-term employment relationships. Who knows what will happen as this group gets older? Will they become more traditional and achievement-oriented, or will they insist on a new approach to work different from our customary practices and institutions? You will only know as it happens.

WHAT'S IN A WORKFORCE STRATEGY?

This shortage means you need to think strategically about talent issues so you can be positioned to achieve your business plans. If you have a plan and set out to create a strong organization that provides value for shareholders, customers, and employees, you will be seen as a better place to work and be capable of attracting smarter and more desirable employees.

A workforce strategy can consist of several elements. These may include:

- Your people requirements—the cultural values, competencies, and contract terms, as I've already described them, that you've decided you need from your workforce to deliver your value offering and execute your strategy
- Employees' needs, fears, and goals—what's on your employees' minds and in their hearts

- The resulting employment relationship—what you get when you combine your requirements and your employees' needs
- Organization design—the broader accountabilities and behaviors, staffing issues, and structures that enable people to work together to serve your customers
- Your priorities for change—based on these four areas, the initiatives you will pursue to implement and leverage your strategy

When some people think of organization design, they think only of the boxes on the organization chart—who reports to whom, and how to make your box as big as possible. That's not what I mean here. Organization design means your broader thinking about how you are going to bring people into your company and keep them, what results and behaviors you expect from them, and how you are going to structure things so they can achieve those in the best way possible.

The workforce strategies I have seen or helped develop start with a broad and complex range of issues. Often you need to cover societal, demographic, global economic, marketplace, and technological issues, in addition to people and business directions. Generally you need to keep working them until a coherent plan evolves.

The process to develop a strategy will vary from company to company, but it's vital to get information from as many constituencies as possible. Strategies developed in isolation will fail. A Hewitt survey on the topic a few years ago found that the most successful strategies were:

- Created with broad executive and employee input
- Written down
- Communicated after they were developed

Like all strategy work, there will be tradeoffs, hard choices, things that cannot be done given different constraints, directions that may need to be deferred, and the need to integrate the various elements. Problems in one part might disrupt the entire strategy, so issues need to be dealt with until they fit together logically. Since your people are involved, there may be more uniqueness and variability than you face creating business strategy. Big changes on the workforce side will guarantee at least the same level of havoc as if you tried to radically restructure your business.

The outcome should be a written depiction of the talent you need to carry out your business strategy and the means to secure that workforce. Without a workforce strategy, how will you know whether you will be able to deliver the value your customers and shareholders want?

The final strategy document shouldn't be very long; maybe a few pages, certainly no more than ten. It should be directional and actionable—it needs to tell your company what to do about people to make the business work. It can be a strategy statement, a description of the desired employment relationship, or a list of plans and programs that fit together to produce some specific outcomes. In other words, it can be as varied as different companies' business strategies. The two things I am sure about are:

- When you read the business strategy and the workforce strategy, you should see an immediate and obvious fit. The workforce strategy ought to make perfect sense as the way to get the business strategy done. Some companies even will make it part of the business strategy.
- If it's too long and involved, it will end up on your shelf, just like all of those other three-ring binders full of business strategies that never get looked at or used, much less shared with your workforce.

The three strategic styles lead to three distinct kinds of workforce strategies. There are real, meaningful differences between styles and many similarities within them. Setting up your workforce strategies to execute your business strategy and align to your style will enable you to plan and manage your talent to optimal effect.

Here are the workforce strategies of each strategic style in detail and a sampling or excerpt from each kind of company's strategy.

OPERATIONS COMPANIES

All employees in an operations company need to focus on delivering the best cost/value they can to customers. Many of these companies are dealing in commodities or near-commodities, and the margins associated with most of the products and services are small. They cannot command the premiums that custom service or new technologies bring. Some of these industries are partially or fully regulated.

This requires a highly standardized approach to serving customers. Usually this means a more *top-down* management style than in other companies, with more directions and prescribed processes.

This doesn't mean that employee participation should be ignored. It means that participation and involvement should be done within a more structured environment and a demand for tangible results, probably with specific goals or parameters. It would be unreasonable to offer employees much autonomy in companies that have to demand conformity to procedures or regulations as a business necessity.

Hard Cultures

I often find these companies have what I call "hard" cultures. This doesn't mean they are bad places. On the contrary, many operations companies are terrific places to work, like Cargill, Grainger, and Shell. A hard culture demands tangible, concrete results all the time. If you can't show a result that will benefit this kind of company, rethink or shelve the project you are considering. An MBA student interviewing with one of these companies told me her interviewer demanded to know what results she had produced in her graduate program, and that grades weren't enough of a bottom-line.

Hard cultures even get demanding when they talk about soft stuff, like people and relationships. EDS, the technology services and outsourcing giant, began a change effort to get its huge workforce to pay more attention to customer needs through training on empathetic listening and becoming more aware of their own feelings and values. In true hard culture fashion, this became a mandated change for EDS' workforce—everyone had to attend. There will be no stragglers on the road to understanding personal feelings at EDS.

The workforce challenge in this strategic style is how to get people to thrive in this type of environment so they can satisfy customers. Fortunately, many people prosper with structure or order. Leading operations companies also have figured out how to motivate people by appealing to their eagerness to provide distinctive value.

The attention to and improvement of process management that was born with total quality and grew up with reengineering is a natural fit for operations companies. Orderly, efficient, and documented processes are their heart and soul. This kind of workforce must be centered on following and delivering established, regulated, and uniform processes.

With *efficiency, order,* and *process* as its foundation, the general workforce strategy for operations companies looks like this.

The Operations Workforce Strategy

- Compete and win by building teams to deliver high-value, low-cost processes
- Place heavy emphasis on creating motivation and esprit de corps
- Make sure everyone knows the rules and plays by them
- Measure everything you can, and reward what you measure
- Build a continuous improvement mindset and environment

These strategies are how outstanding operations companies manage talent. First and foremost they build teams, because teams deliver processes; individuals can't—processes are too complex. These may be different kinds of teams: permanent teams, like the distribution center teams at Grainger; project teams, like the teams that came together to help reengineer Wisconsin Electric; or temporary teams that keep reforming, like the flight crews at Southwest Airlines. Whatever the type, they deliver their basic products and services in teams.

Team Spirit

As a result these companies spend considerable time building team spirit to compete and win against the competition, as well as to beat their own previous accomplishments. This keeps motivation high.

In *Built To Last,* James Collins and Jerry Porras wrote that it is not necessary to be a charismatic CEO to build a visionary, successful company. They cite examples of 3M, Hewlett-Packard, Procter & Gamble, and Merck, among others. They appear to be correct for the products companies they discuss. There, the emphasis on technical excellence and the required freedom to produce it would make charisma, zeal, and exhortation seem phony, or at least out of place in many cases.

What I see is the great operations companies most often have been built or renewed by charismatic or strong-willed CEOs. These are people who can rally the troops and align them to the vision or challenge at hand. Sam Walton of Wal Mart, Herb Kelleher of Southwest Airlines, Fred Smith of Federal Express, and Michael Dell of

Dell Computer are contemporary examples of charismatic or visionary founders. Bob Crandall of American Airlines, David Johnson of
Campbell Soup, Dave Whitwam of
Whirlpool, and Phil Carroll of Shell are
leaders of vision and spirit who reshaped
and revitalized their companies. If you
are striving to become an outstanding operations company, you will need to find
a source of inspirational motivation
somewhere.

> **Many of the great operations companies have been built or renewed by charismatic or strong-willed CEOs.**

These companies also thrive on procedures and measurement. Many are
regulated businesses, or businesses
where safety is an issue, like airlines,
trucking, and utilities, so procedures are
critical. Others are commodity businesses
and/or low-margin operations, like food and materials processing,
everyday product manufacturers, financial transactions processors,
or distribution operations. Standardization is critical to efficiency.
With these high levels of process and procedure, it's possible to measure not only end results, but most of the steps in the process too.

This makes operations companies "measurement fanatics,"
putting some kind of metric to everything they do. This reinforces
staying on process or procedure, since the behavior likely is being
counted. One issue with the annual incentive plan at Whirlpool is
not how to measure results, but which of the many good results
measures it has to use in the plan. If Whirlpool used all of the solid
measures it has, no one would be able to understand the plan. The
dilemma is solved by selecting the biggest outcome measures for
reward purposes and using the other results and process measures
to help get to the outcomes.

Distinctive Value

In many of these companies, what's being created and measured is
distinctive value. This is where operations companies distinguish
themselves from other operations companies competition. Since it is
harder to distinguish product or service features among these companies, and a high value-to-cost relationship is a given, then it becomes imperative to have a distinctive value for customers.

At Whirlpool, the distinctive value is reliability. Washers and dryers don't differ that much in price and features, but consumers have to feel they are getting appliances that will last a long time when they buy Whirlpool or Kenmore washers and dryers. In fact the quality and durability of Whirlpool's laundry products are legend. This is a main reason why Japanese and Korean manufacturers have not yet tried to compete in this country with major appliances.

Whirlpool measures quality and reliability in several different ways, including its service incident rate, customer satisfaction, the number of service calls "off warranty," the age of the product being serviced, and others. One aspect of continuous improvement at Whirlpool is to build more reliability into its products every year.

Most people think credit cards are pretty much alike in cost, convenience, billing procedures, and other features. At MBNA, the Delaware-based credit card company, the distinctive value that sets it apart is service speed. MBNA markets to affinity group members, producing premium customers with larger balances. What these affluent people want is faster service, a quicker resolution to their problems.

MBNA measures 15 standards around customer service, most pertaining to speed, and posts the results every day. Team incentives are based on meeting or beating these standards. Quality measures ensure speed and quality go together and are tied to individual rewards. These standards provide targets for continuous improvement so MBNA can offer better service every year.

Southwest Airlines' distinctive value is fun. When the airline started, it changed the economics of the industry. It showed how to make money by flying short hauls between cities, avoiding hub-and-spoke systems of other major airlines, and usually bypassing larger, busier airports. As others adjusted their prices, costs, and route structures to meet Southwest, sometimes launching direct shuttle-type competitors, Southwest retained its distinctive value that flying should be an enjoyable experience. This was a lesson lost a long time ago by many big carriers.

Southwest gets top rankings from the U.S. Department of Transportation and from passengers by getting people to their destinations with their luggage, safely, and on time. Passengers like the cheap fares, but also the employees who ensure they relax and enjoy some laughs along with their peanuts. To do this, Southwest hires to an employee profile for people who can follow procedures but also love to laugh and enjoy themselves.

From a talent management perspective these distinctive values give employees something to aspire to besides just providing a low-cost/high-value offering. Offering a great deal is important, but usually it's not enough to inspire people. An energizing workforce strategy for an operations company needs to include something to give employees the added boost they need.

A Utility Workforce Strategy

A workforce strategy for a utility company I consulted to embodied the principles of efficiency and reliability and the distinctive value of community service. The company arrived at this to fuel the needs of people who had joined a highly regulated, public utility to provide a critical basic service. It also needed to upgrade its abilities to compete as the industry began to deregulate and open to competition.

The strategy focused on the character of the company, what it needed from its employees, and what they could expect from the company. Then tactics and initiatives were begun to realize the strategy. Here is a sample from the strategy.

First, the utility company suggested these characteristics as the basis for a new workforce strategy:

- A company with shared mission and common goals
- A work environment that maximizes high performance
- A company that meets the changes facing the industry
- A company that acts as a good neighbor, responsible citizen, and steward of the natural environment

With this backdrop, the workforce strategy summarized company and employee needs as shown in Table 5-1.

This strategy led to new initiatives in selection, training, labor relations, workforce upgrade, and compensation, along with new financial, operating, and employee measures of performance. These measures were communicated frequently so employees could develop a better business understanding.

TABLE 5-1

Utility Company Workforce Strategy

What the Company Needs from Employees	What Employees Can Expect
People who understand the whole business, not just their jobs or functions, and can make good business decisions	Increased training and education for greater business knowledge and continuous skill development
More cost-consciousness, while increasing safety performance	New efforts to rebuild personal trust and security through better communication about business performance and organizational issues that affect employees' lives
Greater technical and interpersonal skills for improved performance and teamwork	Stronger benefits and more ways to share cash rewards for company financial success
More measurable, bottom-line results from people who are held to greater levels of accountability	Opportunities to take reasonable risks without punishment for failure

From its business and workforce strategies, the utility was able to achieve significant cost reductions and safety improvements, while maintaining high levels of customer satisfaction. This enabled it to secure its financial future, the first step it required to play a bigger role in the rapidly consolidating industry.

PRODUCTS COMPANIES

In the great products companies, like 3M, Motorola, and Hewlett-Packard, the workforce must focus on invention. The creative process has to come first. Many talent management practices, like supervision, evaluation, and rewards have to take a back seat. The workforce strategy must emphasize *freedom*—the freedom to pursue your own creation without obstacles, bureaucracy, or fear getting in the way.

Products companies usually have the freest cultures of all the strategic styles, especially around operational issues. Business units and functions enjoy extraordinary autonomy in how and what they create, and, to a lesser extent, how they go to market. A free culture can be a very strong culture when it is held together by strong values and norms. In some of the biggest companies, like Hewlett-Packard and Motorola, there is a powerful coalescing around company values and administrative procedures. Business units have lots of room to explore and invent, try out new things, and run their businesses their own way.

The other key tenet of a workforce strategy in products companies is *support*. Companies provide a great deal of support to employees for their abilities to create, but also in managing their careers and work lives. Asking product employees to do many administrative things for themselves, like putting considerable time into thinking about their own training, benefits decision-making, or career development just gets in the way of focusing on product development and invention.

When you combine freedom and support with the drive for technical creation, you get an *inside-out* management strategy. These companies drive invention from the minds of their people out to their customers. This is the "if you build it, they will come" mentality that characterizes these companies.

Products companies don't ignore their customers. They just are more likely than other styles to lead their customers with their products or services, rather than wait for customers to express specific needs before they create. The now famous stories of Chrysler's invention of the minivan and Sony's creation of the Walkman are great examples. Nobody was asking for either product, but each revolutionized their industries and people's lives.

Still, many products companies today, like 3M and Chrysler, are doing more than before to bring customers into creation and design processes. Perhaps bringing customers into these processes may become a key organizational capability in this style. For now, products companies seem to do an amazing job of creating needs that people never knew they had.

A products company's main workforce strategy must be to create a positive, comfortable, and resource-rich environment where people feel free to create. Fortunately premium product offerings and the margins they generate enable them to afford it. The general workforce strategy looks like this:

The Products Workforce Strategy

- Provide a positive, comfortable, resource-rich environment that allows people to create
- Take care of basic needs at a very high level; provide outstanding training, compensation, and benefits, and make them very easy to access and use
- Don't distract people with too much information, things to do themselves, or worries about policies, organization, or management
- Constantly work to remove organizational barriers to creativity
- Don't create a reward system that differentiates too much among individuals—you'll wind up punishing failure or creating the fear of it

Products companies are famous for managing this way. 3M is known for its stable workforce and environment, generous benefits delivered with terrific employee service, freedom to work on individual ideas, rewards and recognition for innovations and patents, and an organizational chart that is so fluid it's hard to describe. One 3M executive pictured the organization as a "centipede table, upside down," with at least 33 technology platforms and 500 to 1000 businesses growing out of them. Holding these together are company values, financial goals, and human resource principles, rather than a tight organizational structure.

Just as importantly, 3M scientists and technologists are urged not to take no for an answer when it comes to getting money to finance their inventions. If the immediate supervisor says no, the scientist is encouraged to go to other business units who might see value in the idea. If that doesn't work, there are opportunities for other kinds of grants and funding sources. With a goal of getting 30 percent of revenues from products less than four years old, individuals have to be encouraged to keep pushing ideas and asking for support, without letting any bureaucracy stop them.

W.L. Gore, the maker of Gore-Tex, also breeds an environment for invention. According to Gore, "our environment is its own reward," and it's rich in teamwork, celebration, and freedom. Gore carefully selects people who want to work in teams and then provides an organization where team leaders emerge from their accomplishments and because other associates want that person to lead. Leadership roles can be lost when teammates lose confidence or no longer approve of a leader's actions.

Gore's reward systems heavily reinforce team and organizational success, much more than individual contribution. There is a lot of celebration, a whole plant will celebrate a team's success. "Golden Eggs" are given for patent acceptance. Safety programs, idea awards, service anniversaries, and profit-sharing results all are heralded with great fanfare, food, parties, T-shirts, and anything else Gore people can conceive.

At Gore, freedom comes partially because supervisors have been replaced with "sponsors." Sponsors are chosen by the associates who want them and primarily focus on feedback and development. Sponsors can be peers or leaders from other areas, and associates can change their sponsors frequently. People volunteer to be sponsors, but they have to show appropriate characteristics to perform the role.

Everyone at Gore takes communication skills training, because Gore believes "being valued is being listened to." Those who are good at listening and feedback can become sponsors.

Other companies with this style plan and manage their workforces in similar ways. Chrysler and Merck have broken down functional barriers to speed new product creation and design. Chrysler engineers work with sales and marketing people, dealers, and even outside suppliers to create new cars and trucks. Merck uses "worldwide business strategy teams," cross-functional teams of executives, to tackle diseases on a coordinated, global basis. These teams have broken down the compartmentalized, functional approaches to development, marketing, and selling that used to exist.

A Pharmaceutical Workforce Strategy

Here is a sampling from the workforce strategy of a pharmaceutical company. It is expressed primarily as a "strategic intent," a broad direction that forms the basis for new initiatives, tactics, and programs. This company's strategic intent around people is to:

- Hire and develop people who can discover great products
- Enable people to execute as high-performing, global teams
- Break down barriers to create faster, more effective decisions
- Provide an environment that kindles and maintains employees' creative spark

With this strategic intent, the company is able to complete its workforce strategy and tactics in a number of specific ways. It put in place efforts to:

- Identify the competencies and behaviors employees should demonstrate to deliver on its business plans
- Revise its selection, training and development, and promotional criteria and programs to use those competencies
- Reorganize, as appropriate, into global teams to work on discovery and development of new compounds
- Measure and improve the speed of decision-making, especially around new drugs (This required removing obstacles to effective, timely decisions. Most of these

obstacles turned out to be organization structure and policies.)

- Provide a variety of opportunities and recognition for stimulating and sharing new ideas and information, including information networks, recognition awards for discovery, team celebrations, and so forth

These efforts turned into a comprehensive action plan for deploying talent to maintain its market advantage.

CUSTOMERS COMPANIES

If operations companies manage top-down and products companies manage inside-out, then customers companies manage *outside-in*. Front-line employees are the key to knowing and serving customers with individualized help. Keeping these employees satisfied and motivated is essential to customer success. Outside-in can feel like *bottom-up* in these companies.

This perspective applies to more than just retail operations. Anderson Windows with its made-to-order windows, Johnson Controls automotive seating division, and Pitney Bowes outsourcing mailroom operations are customer-focused manufacturing or service organizations. The recent turnaround at IBM, engineered by Louis Gerstner, has been attributed to IBM returning to its customer roots. The key is that these companies and their people create customized, total solutions to produce distinctive results for their customers.

A workforce strategy for this style of company must be directed at *responsiveness* to employee issues and concerns, but in a different way than in products companies. In products companies, the strategy is to take care of employees so they can be left alone to invent. In customers companies the strategy is to respond to employees to make their lives easier to serve customers.

Notice I said "lives," not jobs. In these companies, "doing whatever it takes" to serve customers often means going above and beyond the job. Personal time and work time blend into each other, so the boundary disappears. Nordstrom and Home Depot love to tell stories about how their employees take their own personal time to deliver purchases to customers or help them fix things.

This "doing whatever it takes" requires a devotion to service that is another critical part of the workforce strategy. Getting people to show this devotion requires *selection and socialization* of the right people. Individuals who can become service masters seem to be born, more than made. Selecting the right people becomes key. A person who is more comfortable with machines or data is not going to be world-class at serving other people.

Once the right people are on board, there needs to be constant reinforcement and expansion of the customer service values. In fact, service values often are discussed in these companies in a spiritual sort of way, so that delivering fantastic service is a higher-order calling, one with great moral authority and reward. A colleague once told me training on client service at Hewitt is more like cultural indoctrination than skills training. He meant it as a compliment.

A final piece of this workforce strategy is *autonomy* at the customer interface. Employees have to feel free to problem-solve, go around policies, and generally "move mountains" to get customer results. If they have to stop and ask or check with a higher authority, it may be too late. The customer's need or problem has to be the single-most important and immediate thing on the employee's mind.

With *responsiveness, selection and socialization,* and *autonomy* at its core, the workforce strategy is:

The Customers Workforce Strategy

- Keep people satisfied so that they will satisfy customers
- Pick people who have a customer service mindset
- Promote service as the highest-order activity
- Rely on values messages to shape a service culture
- Give people plenty of independence to meet customer needs.

The customers workforce strategy, more so than the others, begins with a strong, but adaptive, corporate culture. Other types of companies may have this type of culture, but the customers company must have it.

Values, Values, Values

An operations company can run hard on numbers, at least for a while, and pay less attention to values and norms. The right people and processes will still produce the numbers for a time. Some products companies start with an invention, long before a company really grows up around it. With the right technology and enough personal freedom to create, a products company can manage as a loose confederation at least for a while, without a lot of attention to values and norms. But a customers company has to start with and build from a set of values that center on both the employee and the customer to produce results for the customer.

In retrospect, Thomas A. Watson's founding credo for IBM forms the basis for any customers culture. Watson's three points: 1) respect the individual employee, 2) make the customer very happy, and 3) put in the extra effort to create superior results, would be just as appropriate at Nordstrom, Home Depot, or any other customers company. In fact, if you looked at the mission statements or ideologies of these companies, you will see very similar words.

A culture that listens to customer and labor markets keeps adapting. When a company is willing to be led by its customers and employees, rather than its products or processes, it will keep changing by design. This adaptability is a built-in advantage in a customers company, as long as the company keeps listening and responding.

Paradoxically, the strong and the adaptive parts of a customers culture often fight with each other. Strong cultures tend to be insular, shutting out the outside world. This is the opposite of adaptation. The only way to avoid this hardening of the cultural arteries is to put the customer at the top of the organizational chart and respond accordingly. The most important people in a customers company aren't the executives, they're the customers who pay the bills. Similarly, keeping employees satisfied is also at the heart of this style, but it is done to serve customers, not for the sake of employees.

> **The most important people in a customers company aren't the executives, they're the customers who pay the bills.**

Responsiveness begins by setting out to treat both employees and customers well and then listening carefully to improve on that baseline. Customers companies usually offer some types of compensation, benefits, or working condition advantages to their employees as part of their way of doing business. Nordstrom employees average about $29,000 annually, more than other retail employees. IBM employees have a long tradition of enjoying some of the richest compensation, benefits, and training opportunities in any industry.

Generally these companies can afford to provide more because superior service typically commands a premium price, though usually not as much as technical superiority. These companies keep these practices current and build on to them by listening to employees' changing needs and modifying plans accordingly. It may be less important to offer the richest pay or benefits than it is to communicate to employees that changes were made to meet their specific needs or requests. As a result, employee satisfaction stays high to support customer satisfaction.

Another distinctive part of the customers culture is it's seen by both insiders and outsiders as very special and different from other companies. Many people have described the tight, almost "cult-like" cultures of IBM and Nordstrom. Like other customers companies, there are high hurdles to entry, reasonably well-defined ways to behave, and cultural "heroes" who exemplify the right behaviors.

I've said selection is particularly important for customers companies. Most have very rigorous selection procedures—lots of testing, interviews, and other devices—to find the right people for customer service, and because these companies believe you have to be a very special person to join them. This is one of the self-perpetuating beliefs that keep the culture going—if you have a special organization, you wouldn't want just anyone to join. This can be insulating, but it's not dysfunctional if people are listening carefully to the customer. Careful selection helps build the company's beliefs around fantastic service.

Indoctrination to the culture, or socialization (as I called it earlier), actually begins in the interview process before a person gets hired. People doing the interviewing in these types of companies often spend a lot of interview time talking about and probing for the behaviors valued by the organization. They'll spend much of their time looking for and discussing fit, rather than evaluating technical or problem-solving skills.

Once in the company, there is a lot of pressure to conform and behave in prescribed ways. Employees at Hewitt and IBM often are described as "clones" by their competitors because of the consistent ways they behave. However, many customers appreciate the consistently excellent treatment they get, regardless of the particular employee providing the service. When you shop at Nordstrom you expect to receive enthusiastic and attentive service. Rarely are you disappointed, no matter who waits on you.

Pressure to conform in these companies comes in lots of different ways, and most aren't that subtle. IBM and Nordstrom have pretty explicit rules of conduct, though most tend to be passed down verbally, not in writing. Home Depot is famous for its management training which still is delivered by its founding executives, not management trainers. The training focuses on six things: "Serve the customer, serve the customer, serve the customer, serve the customer, serve the customer. And No. 6, kick ass."

A standing joke at another customers company is the "culture police," the imaginary enforcers who come around when an employee isn't showing the right behaviors. This is a verbal invention that enables employees to use peer pressure to get others to conform. It's a third-party fiction that enables people applying the pressure to appeal to a higher order.

Despite this heavy socialization, freedom reigns in customers companies at the customer interface. There the exact opposite attitude is expected—don't worry too much about rules. Do whatever it takes to make the customer happy. At Nordstrom this attitude is stated clearly, "Don't listen to the boss, listen to the customer."

Actually, this is no contradiction. The heavy values socialization is designed to produce people who will do the right thing for the customer without having to check a policy manual or ask a boss. When a front-line employee needs to make a quick decision to please a customer, he or she has to rely on his or her values to help guide the decision. If the organization's values have been inoculated into the person, the person should make the right decision.

This freedom also pertains to employee relations. Many customers companies take the same individualized, everybody-is-important approach to making policy decisions about employees that they do with customers. This obliterates the need for a policy manual, but makes it more difficult to ensure consistent decisions about people. Nordstrom is famous for its one-page policy manual, which basically says the only rule is to use your best judgment in all situations.

At Hewitt we have a similar framework: Do what's fair for the client and the firm. When we have a concern with a person or need to make a transition, we consult each other and spend a lot of time discussing what's right for the client, the person, and our firm rather than consult a set of policies. Obviously, McDonald's or American Airlines cannot run this way.

This goes back to the strong belief in the individual that Tom Watson proclaimed many years ago and is the bedrock of a customers company. This is how a customers workforce strategy must differ from an operations workforce strategy in which teams are primary because they deliver process; or products companies where invention may be done individually, in pairs, in small teams, or even sequential groups.

Only individuals form relationships. They can be supported by teams, but buying and selling takes place person-to-person. These strong cultures celebrate organizational values to appeal to personal motivation and affiliation, but the heart of value creation is the individual employee dealing with the individual customer.

A Professional Services Firm Strategy

A professional services firm was experiencing extraordinary growth, like many similar firms. It became concerned with two issues. The first was finding enough people to support its growth. The second was to make sure these people understood the desired relationship between firm and individual.

To solve the hiring issue, it grew its internal recruiting staff and dedicated them to specific practice areas. It also expanded its external search and resourcing capabilities. It changed its internal processes to move candidates through its extensive screening procedures and make decisions about candidates much more quickly, rather than risk losing them to competitors looking for the same people. Finally, it resigned itself to slightly more turnover than it experienced historically as the price of loosening up its selection screens.

To build understanding about the employee-firm relationship, it committed to paper what the relationship should be and conducted a communication process that reached all employees. The relationship was based on the long-stated goals of the firm, including client satisfaction, individual respect, teamwork, and financial growth. The relationship was described as "shared responsibilities," and these were detailed in five areas:

- Contribution and rewards
- Workplace flexibility

- Personal development
- Financial security
- Health and well-being

To emphasize its seriousness, the firm launched new initiatives to either communicate existing practices or create new and improved ones in each of the five areas.

You can see the three types of companies, their cultures, management styles, and workforce strategies in Table 5-2.

TABLE 5-2

Workforce Strategy Summary

Strategic Style	Culture	Management Style	Workforce Strategy
Operations	A hard, bottom-line culture, focused on efficiency, order, and process	Top-down management, with more need for charismatic leadership	Compete and win by building teams to deliver high-value, low-cost processes and continuous improvement
Products	A free culture that emphasizes operational autonomy and employee independence, with great support for invention	Inside-out management, generally more low-key	Provide a comfortable, resource-rich environment without management or organizational distractions so people can create
Customers	A strong but adaptive culture that stresses responsiveness to customer and employee, selection and socialization, and autonomy with customers	Outside-in and bottom-up management, with emphasis on shared values	Keep people satisfied so they will satisfy customers

A workforce strategy that supports your business strategy and style is required to make alignment work. Strategies come alive through tactics, and that is the next step; looking at the management practices you need to use. Before going there, try answering these questions about your workforce strategy.

CREATING THE TALENT SOLUTION

1. Do you anticipate being able to hire and retain the people you think you'll need to grow your business over the next several years?

2. Have you tried to create and write down your workforce strategy? How well does it align with your business strategy and strategic style?

3. Regardless of whether you have a written strategy, take a good look at your workforce from a strategic viewpoint. What do you think you are emphasizing? Efficiency, order, and process? Freedom and support? Responsiveness, selection and socialization, and autonomy? Is this what you think you should be emphasizing?

4. How would you describe your culture and management style? Does this seem right for your business?

Use the Lead Practices that Fit Your Style

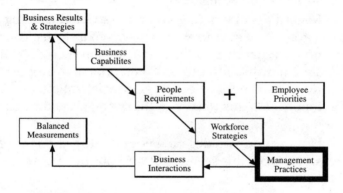

Your workforce strategy is implemented through your talent management practices. This chapter tells you:

- What talent management practices are, and what criteria you can use to judge them
- How practices keep changing, but beware of "best practices"
- How each strategic style has a particular lead practice
- Why learning must be a lead practice for every style

ALIGNING TALENT MANAGEMENT PRACTICES

What would your company or business unit be like if you used one set of very consistent practices to hire, train, manage, reward, promote, and fire people? What if those practices were so closely linked to your value offering and business strategy that they communicated, encouraged, and reinforced precisely the kinds of interactions and results you wanted? What if you could change these practices easily when customer and labor market situations changed? What if every manager used them effectively and every employee understood them fully?

If your company did this, it would be very, very unusual. No organization I know is completely like that. Many smart companies do some of these talent management practices very well, closely in line with their business strategies. These smart companies review what they do on a frequent basis so they keep getting better, slowly inching closer to this form of management utopia.

Workforce strategies come alive through your management practices. This is how you operationalize your talent solution. If your practices are aligned with your strategies, then deploying them will ensure your leaders and managers make decisions that put your strategies into operation so your employees do what you need them to do.

When your management practices are properly designed, aligned, and implemented, you should see these things happen:

- People will be carrying out your business strategies as you want them to do. This is the definition of alignment.
- You will be building and implementing the kind of business strategy, organization, culture, and employment relationship you want for long-term success.
- You will be acquiring the kind of talent you need, and getting your people trained and utilized properly.
- You will be shaping the kinds of interactions you want people to have with your customers, vendors, suppliers, and each other. This will get you the business results you want.
- You will be giving your employees what they need to understand the big picture of your business, what you are doing about it, how they can help, how they will find satisfaction, and how they will be paid and promoted for

doing it. This will help create a meaningful work experience for them. It will make it easier for you to hire and retain talent.

The talent management practices I am talking about are how you staff, organize, help people learn, manage performance, and reward people. Most writers refer to these as *human resource systems*, but I don't like that term. When you call them human resource systems, it sounds like they are owned and operated by the human resources department. That's dangerous because experience shows that your managers won't use them as effectively as they must.

My Hewitt colleague, Dave Jones, identified this problem in his work with the Lincoln Electric Company. Lincoln recently has gone from being privately held to public ownership and has brought on new executive leadership. The company is in a fairly straightforward and unglamorous business, manufacturing and distributing arc welding machines and materials. It recognized a long time ago that its competitive advantage lies in motivating its workforce to be more productive than the competition. Lincoln has been extraordinarily successful over the years. It is famous for, and rich in, unique traditions, culture, and management practices that keep motivation extraordinarily high, especially its Incentive Management System.

Dave was leading a team consulting with Lincoln to update many of its people practices, and the company did not want to lose the competitive edge these practices have inspired. Though it also strengthened its HR department while Dave was leading the project, Lincoln realized if it called these human resource systems, there would be a much greater likelihood these practices would become the property of that department. Then managers would decrease their high levels of ownership and use of them.

To the contrary, Lincoln's President Tony Massaro and HR Vice President Ray Vogt felt strongly that managers need to own and use these practices to make the business work, just like reviewing budgets every month keeps managers on track about money and production. Budgeting is a management practice, and so are talent-related practices.

Wayne Anderson, Senior Vice President of Amoco, likens them to building a house. According to Wayne, "If you were building a house, you'd go out and hire an architect, contractor, carpenter, plumber, electrician, and the others that you'd need. Then you'd have them develop the plan, understand it, coordinate their activities, and build to it, each according to their specialties. You'd pay them for their work, talk with them while they were building about what you like and didn't like, and have them make the changes you want. This wouldn't be a separate function from building the house—this is how the house gets built. People management practices are not separate functions from running a business, this is the process of running a business and producing results."

CRITERIA FOR EXCELLENT PRACTICES

There are three major criteria you can use to determine how well your management practices are working. Excellence demands that you meet all three: alignment, integration, and execution.

Alignment

Your management practices are aligned with your strategy when they spell out what people should do—how they should behave or take action to make your strategy work. This means being very clear about the specific behaviors and results you need from people—the how and the what they should do to serve customers, make products, deal with suppliers, show leadership, work in teams, and engage in other activities.

Many companies now are using competencies to describe the knowledge, behaviors, and processes that are important to their strategies. These are used along with the objectives or goals they set for results. If the competencies support and extend your strategic style, business capabilities, culture, and management style, and the objectives link closely to the business results you want, you start to get alignment.

Integration

Your practices must connect to and reinforce each other to produce the business outcomes you want. You cannot be doing one thing in one practice that produces a counterresult in another.

One company I know did all its hiring through its decentralized business units. The units hired people as cheaply as they could because of the costs to their bottom lines. While this got them the people they needed, it had the unfortunate side effect of hiring people who didn't have the abilities and potential to run the bigger, global corporation, no matter how much experience they received. The company eventually solved this problem by hiring high-potential entry-level employees through its corporate center, sending these people out to the business units, transferring them across units, and maintaining them on the corporate budget for a number of years to minimize the effects on the business units. This solved the problem, but it also created some unnecessary budget games and not very helpful distinctions among people.

General Gordon Sullivan, Retired Army Chief of Staff, provided what I think is the most powerful description of integration. General Sullivan said, "High-performing systems talk to each other." These practices have to communicate and deliver results for each other. Hiring people who are promotable may seem like a "no-brainer," but there's an amazing number of companies that don't and end up with too many expensive, outside hires in key management positions. Or companies may invest heavily in training, only to find out that the training topics are no longer related to the kinds of work that need to be done.

Consistency is a part of integration. Practices need to send a consistent message to employees about what's expected and valued, and what's rewarded. Employees look for clear signals about what to do. Inconsistencies among practices cause confusion and skepticism. An old French proverb says "Skepticism quickly hardens into cynicism," and cynicism can destroy a workforce.

For example, if a company touts itself to be a learning organization, it had better make sure it offers meaningful training and development opportunities. Cutting training first when budgets tighten, or offering training opportunities primarily to managers and salaried professionals instead of the whole workforce soon will have people treating your pronouncements about valuing learning the way many Americans treated the 55 mile-per-hour speed limit. A split between what you say is valued and what you offer and reward damages credibility and puts your claims for integrity at risk.

Execution

Management practices don't mean much if people don't use them or don't use them well. One chemical company spent several months and tens of thousands of dollars designing and training managers on a new performance management process. However, the senior managers objected to being told they had to use it. They didn't want to mandate it to supervisors either. Senior management figured if it was such a good idea supervisors would gravitate to it naturally, so their reviews did not include whether they had used the new process with their people. The senior managers didn't realize people want feedback, but giving it is basically an unnatural act.

The result? Two years later less than 20 percent of employees had reviews, and there was no noticeable improvement in productivity, knowledge of performance expectations, or communication in the company. I don't argue for mandating these kinds of policy changes. Still, if a company thinks these practices need to be done, there has to be accountability.

ACCOUNTABILITY AND CONSEQUENCES

As part of decentralizing its organization, Amoco decentralized many of its management practices. It allowed its business units to abandon the corporate performance management process as long as: 1) people had objectives tied to business strategy, 2) they received regular and timely performance feedback about results and competencies, and 3) the units met their business objectives for productivity. Some of the units maintained the existing process, and many revised it or created new processes to better fit their specific situations. Amoco did the right thing by holding units accountable for the outcomes, but not mandating the process. Subsequently, Amoco decentralized its Variable Incentive Plan to give business units more autonomy about pay.

The only way you can ensure your practices are used is to hold people accountable for making them work. This demands demonstrating positive and negative outcomes in line with meeting or not meeting these accountabilities. Installing practices without creating consequences is a waste of time and effort. Worse, like inconsistency, it will cause your credibility to erode and place your integrity in peril.

> The only way you can ensure your practices are used is to hold people accountable.

When Tony Massaro took over at Lincoln Electric, he was appalled that meetings didn't start on time. Massaro is a nuclear engineer by training. Probably no education and discipline values precision more dearly. What did Massaro do? He locked the doors at scheduled starting times. People changed behavior quickly because of the consequence. No one wanted to endure the embarrassment of having to knock on the door to be allowed in after the meeting had started.

When Larry Fuller, Amoco's CEO, began the renewal process, he publicly raised the bar on Amoco's financial and operating performance and demanded his leadership group meet it. Then he formulated leadership competencies to tell his executives how he wanted them to perform. Since 1990, Amoco has replaced over 100 of their top 350 executives who didn't fit or meet the new demands. These are very strong consequences for performance, and Amoco's performance keeps getting better.

Consequences should be positive whenever possible. These are the strongest reinforcers. Continental's on-time bonuses are big positives. So are W.L. Gore's recognition plans for patents, sales, and financial success. Herman Miller always has stressed the importance of family and community to its employees. It provides a rocking chair to employees when they have their first child. When Amoco and Whirlpool each said employee learning was a key to their futures, they both created outstanding new learning centers and enhanced their educational programs.

An extremely powerful signal and reinforcer is who gets promoted and developed. Several companies have declared that managing people is an essential basis for competitive advantage and have altered their promotion practices to ensure good people managers, not just good technical performers or operators, get promoted. Avon, Cargill, and Shell are examples of this.

As Shell Oil has gone through its highly successful business transformation, it began to formulate a new approach to leadership, organization, and business results. It formed a corporate leadership council of approximately 200 of its top people, created leadership competencies that were tied to business results, and began a much more intensive education process. This included new approaches to learning and 360° feedback for this leadership group, with the intent of pushing these practices further through the company.

Following the criteria of alignment, integration, and execution, and then holding people accountable and providing appropriate consequences will help you get your talent management practices right. No company is perfect, or even highly effective, at all of these. It's a matter of making constant progress toward getting good and then getting better.

CONSTANT EVOLUTION

Let's get more specific about these five management practices—staffing, organizing, learning, performing, and rewarding—and how you can use them to manage talent and implement strategy. Each of these five are made of several specific components. I can list the components, but the listing doesn't imply that everyone does all of these things, or even should do all of these things. There also are companies who do even more than what's on the list.

- **Staffing**—All of the activities that put people into their assignments, including recruiting, selecting, hiring, promoting, succession planning, management and workforce planning, diversity, downsizing, layoffs, and firing.
- **Organizing**—The ways work is structured into tasks, jobs, assignments, processes, or teams; how these are formed into organizational units; and how these units interrelate, including organization structure, restructuring, teaming, job design, and communications.
- **Learning**—Activities that enhance the knowledge, skills and abilities of the workforce, including individual development planning, career development, on-the-job training, off-site training, management and executive development, self-directed learning, workplace education, specialty certification, rotational programs, and educational reimbursement.
- **Performing**—The business and individual performance management processes of the company, including forming organization goals and the assignment of goals to functions, units, teams, or individuals; and the individual or team-level practices and activities involved in performing, including job and/or role descriptions, performance expectations (behaviors and results), performance measures, coaching and feedback, performance evaluation, suggestion systems, special projects and assignments, presentations, and supervision.
- **Rewarding**—The total compensation and recognition the company offers, including base pay or wages, pay or wage increases, incentives and bonuses, recognition awards, savings plans, pensions, stock purchase plans, ownership, and options; psychological recognition, health benefits, wellness benefits, lifestyle/lifecycle benefits, vacations and paid time off, a pleasant workplace, celebrations, and mementos.

Since these practices need to come from your workforce strategy and be aligned and integrated, I often portray them as the connected points on a star (see Figure 6-1).

FIGURE 6-1

Talent Management Practices

These practices are changing constantly, but there's not much revolutionary about most of them. Even ideas that are trumpeted as new and different usually have been tried by someone else already. For example, beginning in the late 1980s and continuing today, there has been considerable attention paid to companies providing more child-care support to employees. That is actually an old idea in America and other parts of the world. In the 1910s and 1920s, R.J. Reynolds Tobacco provided day-care for the children of women workers.

Another recent development is the movement to broad-banded salary structures among large companies, a response to the need to be more flexible in pay administration. This actually imitates the way smaller companies and many professional service firms have managed their compensation plans for years.

Changes and improvements to talent management practices are a continuing evolution, as companies keep deploying and upgrading them. Generally, companies try something, get good at it, and then they try to do more. Phillip Morris USA started out to create an assessment center to evaluate prospective supervisors. That one center has grown over the years into a full-scale competency management and development approach using assessment centers for directors, competency-based executive development, a new performance management process, and other related activities.

There often is a lot of debate in management journals and business magazines about how to use some of these practices and whether to continue them. It's quite clear the immutable, long-term trend among larger- and mid-sized employers is to continue using more of these techniques and keep getting better at them.

A quick scan of developments in process from the mid-1990s until the start of the next century would include increasing or improved use of:

- Competency-based selection techniques
- Succession management and planning
- Management and executive development in broader, more action-oriented settings
- Mentoring programs
- Computer-based learning
- Work teams and team-based performance systems
- Workforce planning, including broader approaches to diversity
- Elimination of summary performance ratings on appraisals
- 360° feedback
- Broad-banded salary structures
- Broad-based incentives and bonuses
- Stock ownership and options for larger numbers of employees
- Greater spending on capital accumulation and financial security programs
- Broader choices among lifestyle benefits for things like fitness, child and elder care, and college savings accounts
- Alternative work schedules and other approaches to creating more flexible work/time arrangements

This is only a partial list, but don't rush out and implement them. These practices are useful only in the context of what you need to do as a business and what your employees need. The term "best practices" can be misleading.

Practices are "best" only if they align to your strategic style. Trying to copy what someone else is doing makes no sense out of context. Broad pronouncements that appear regularly in the management and business press, like "skill-based pay is the wave of the future," or "no one should use pay for performance," are irrelevant and could be counterproductive to your company's success.

Unfortunately, the first question many companies ask when they are considering changing their management practices is, "What are other companies doing?" The second question is, "What is our competition doing?"

Practices are "best" only if they align to your strategic style.

I say forget about other companies and the competition. Above all, your management practices should be directed at getting people to do what you want them to do. For example, if you want to encourage risk-taking, you should:

- Hire people who are risk-takers—there are tests and other indicators you can use to tell who these people are.
- Keep your organization relatively flat—too many organization levels means too many bosses checking too many decisions and squashing risk.
- Help people learn what you mean by *risk-taking*—define it, explain it, give enough tangible examples of it and when and how should you do it.
- Set expectations for risk-taking performance, measure it, evaluate it, and give feedback about it.
- Reward and recognize risk-taking when it meets your expectations.

This should result in a highly effective approach to risk-taking regardless of what your competition is doing.

USE THE RIGHT LEAD PRACTICES

At Lincoln Electric an operations strategic style that focuses on cost and productivity, combined with a work design that is individually based, aligns directly to a fabulously successful individual incentive plan on the production floor. Lincoln employees are famous for being more productive and making a lot more money than others doing comparable work. Cash compensation of 30 to 50 percent above competitive levels is the norm. Lincoln employees like what they do, how they do it, and how they are rewarded. Lincoln enjoys long-tenured employees, high morale on the production floor, very low turnover, and long lines of applicants when there are openings.

This compensation system is not the only good thing Lincoln does in its management practices, but it is the *lead practice* it depends on most heavily in talent management. In my benchmarking, consulting, and speaking I have had the chance to visit, observe, or talk to hundreds of companies. A key conclusion I have drawn is most smart companies are like Lincoln Electric. They have one lead set of talent management practices they do very well. These lead practices are what they get known for, and they come to depend on them. They rely on them over time to carry the biggest messages to their workforces about strategies, cultures, and desired behaviors.

These lead practices are what these smart companies fall back on to help create change and manage through tough times. A study team I worked with at Shell concluded that without an identifiable lead talent management practice, a company has a very difficult time managing change. The lead practice is a familiar source of knowledge, a credible message carrier to management and employees, and often comes to define how the company manages people.

Some examples of these lead practices are management planning at PepsiCo, the Incentive Management System at Lincoln Electric, the performance and reward system at Whirlpool, Motorola University, performance management and the ESOP at Cargill, stock-based compensation at General Mills, diversity at Xerox, and the Scanlon Plan at Herman Miller. These all are key to aligning the workforce to strategy to create lasting value. When you don't have a lead practice, or it's not well-aligned to your strategy, you may not have the focus you want, or you may be sending the wrong messages.

Table 6-1 illustrates a few of these practices and the messages they send.

Other talent management practices still are important to these companies. All five—staffing, organizing, learning, performing, and rewarding—will help you gain alignment. You need to be at least competitive in these other areas to manage talent effectively.

Still, talent management is just like other strategic management. It's very hard, if not impossible, to focus on doing many things very well. It's highly unlikely you will find a company that is really world-class in more than one of these five areas of management practices.

Not surprisingly, these lead practices carry a halo effect. When people hear about them, they assume the company does a great job overall in its management practices. I invite you to look at the other talent management practices in companies that have an identifiable and well-known lead practice. You will see some good ones, but they

TABLE 6-1

Examples of Lead Practices

Company	Lead Practice	Messages
Cargill	Performance management and ESOP	Here are the results and behaviors we need to succeed; when we execute, the value of your ESOP will increase
General Mills	Stock-based compensation	Our mission is growth; as we grow you benefit from the growth in your stock holdings
Herman Miller	Scanlon Plan	We all participate in our success—financially and with your involvement
Lincoln Electric	Incentive management system	Productivity is crucial and individual production workers are empowered to get it
Motorola	Motorola University	Learning and staying on the leading edge is how we will shape our culture, technical expertise, and management skills
PepsiCo	Management planning	Constant, planned attention on who will be ready for the next, larger assignment
Whirlpool	Performance and reward system	Tangible results are key and that's how you will be rewarded; amended in 1997 to put more emphasis on behaviors
Xerox	Diversity	A diverse and flexible workforce is required to meet the changing and varied needs of customers

won't be as powerful or play as crucial a role in company success as these.

For instance, if a company has a world-class compensation system where it focuses its time and resources, it's very likely its staffing practices will vary somewhere between poor and good. In fact, the compensation system may do some of the work of the selection system, encouraging the hiring of some people and discouraging or eliminating others.

Also, like any message givers, these practices send unintended messages that are not always positive. Aggressive management planning at PepsiCo tells people they have to stay on the fast track, keep getting promoted, or they run serious risks to their careers. Not surprisingly, PepsiCo has a well-known history of high turnover among salaried and management staff. Whirlpool's performance and reward system was so heavily focused on bottom-line results that many people would do only the objectives listed on their performance plans. The company felt the need to put more emphasis on behaviors in 1997 as a way of balancing and enhancing its culture. The Scanlon Plan at Herman Miller is a great group reward plan, now updated to include an Economic Value Added (EVA) measure. However, the company has struggled for years to try to increase individual accountability.

A LEAD PRACTICE FOR EACH STYLE

This brings up a key question. Is there a lead talent management practice best suited to each strategic style? I say there is. Market-leading companies with the same strategic styles are very similar in their lead practices. These practices, in turn, are different from the lead practices in companies with different styles. You should focus on building the lead talent management practice that fits your strategic style.

These patterns didn't arise because companies were focusing deliberately on creating these specific practices. Instead, I think these particular practices made the most sense to these companies at the times they were considering them—they fit best in helping to deliver customer value. They became part of the way these leading companies sustained their abilities to outperform their competition. It makes sense that different management practices help create or reinforce different types of customer value. It also follows that if you are delivering the similar types of value, you will rely on similar types of practices.

This approach can help you understand how to align your management practices to your business strategies. It also can tell you which practice you should try to concentrate on as your lead practice—the one you ought to build into a real, enduring strength. This will increase your abilities to manage talent to meet or exceed your customers' expectations. It also will enable you to manage change more effectively—the lead practice can become your stalwart change agent if you use it properly.

Conversely, this framework also suggests which practices aren't as important to your strategic style. I doubt it's possible to do every practice terrifically. It's also not necessary. This approach tells you where to concentrate so you can get the most out of your investment in talent.

The lead practices for each strategic style are:

Strategic Style	Lead Talent Management Practice
Products	Fluid organization
Operations	Performance-based compensation
Customers	Selection for fit

In the next chapter you will see several examples of these. You also will see examples of another key point—each strategic style also suggests how you should operate in the five management practice areas. You should conduct each of these differently depending on your strategic style.

Before going there, let's discuss an exception to this framework.

THE SPECIAL CASE OF LEARNING

When I first identified and developed the idea of lead talent management practices, I was unable to include learning as a lead practice for any of the strategic styles. Somehow learning didn't seem to fit this framework very well. Then it became clear to me why.

Learning is always a lead practice.

Learning and education are absolutely crucial to success in all of them. Learning is always a lead practice.

Unless cheap labor is the key to your success, your company, like companies all over the world, has critical needs to keep increasing "smart work," the knowledge-added components of your products and services. This requires you to continually raise the bar on employee learning. To drop it for even a minute puts your company at risk.

Earlier I said avoid blanket statements about best practices. I still mean it because even with learning, different kinds of companies will use it in different ways, consistent with their strategic style and initiatives. For example, Amoco created its Amoco Management Learning Center (AMLC) early in its renewal to create a place where managers could learn about its new strategies. About 3,500 people a year attend the AMLC to share perspectives on how to accelerate success.

Shell Oil is using its new Shell Learning Center to train leaders on the business transformation at Shell. This includes focusing on the new Shell business framework, organization model, alignment processes, workforce strategies, and key management practices like diversity, rewards, and recognition. Shell is using learning as a transformational tool, in addition to its usual technical and management training.

Chaparral Steel uses learning to be the fastest steel producer in the U.S. To a greater extent than other steel mills, Chaparral's operating model promotes employee learning as the way to build competitive advantage. Chaparral emphasizes cross-training, education, and outside learning so employees will apply their minds to making steel. Employees can learn all of the jobs in their departments and cross-train into other departments. They get paid higher rates for being able to do more jobs, as well as for going to company-sponsored training programs. Education reimbursement for high school and college degrees also is a management practice.

FedEx similarly stresses learning to improve process management. Its training programs for employees primarily focus on customer service. Employees must complete several weeks of training before ever delivering a package or answering a phone call. Then they are tested on job knowledge every six months. If they pass, they are eligible for pay increases, but if they fail, they must go back to training. To ensure they stay sharp, employees are required to attend at least 40 hours of training per year.

This is not just a U.S. phenomenon. Other countries have grasped the need to upgrade the skills of workers on a continual basis. For example, the Chinese government has based the reform of its state-owned enterprises away from public ministries and towards privately owned businesses, heavily on the concept of training. Every state-owned enterprise lists training as its first priority for management practices.

CITIC

The outstanding example is CITIC, the China International Trust and Investment Corporation. CITIC was the first state-owned enterprise to go through the reform process and has been at it the longest, since 1979. It is among the world's larger banks, with more than $20 billion in assets and over 58,000 employees, and is China's investment arm and financial window to the world.

CITIC's training philosophy and practices are as sophisticated as any I have seen anywhere around the world. CITIC's training philosophy is linked directly to its organizational mission and role—to be China's economic window to the outside world and to act as a laboratory for its economic and social reform. According to CITIC, this requires its people to be "versatile." The training of versatile staff is its most strategic talent management task.

It defines a *versatile* employee as:

- Suited to both the market economy and the planned economy
- One who can develop in two directions—professional accomplishments and relevant business disciplines
- Proficient in both technology and management
- Having a field of vision that covers both domestic and international markets
- Possessing an open mode of thinking
- Having understanding of both Oriental and Western cultures
- Showing mastery of more than two languages

The knowledge, skills, and experience to become versatile are offered in a variety of ways. CITIC structures jobs so lower-level employees focus on technology, mid-level employees get a mix of technology and business experiences, and senior-level employees have comprehensive knowledge across business lines. The enterprise offers technical training to employees and management training that includes corporate finance, global finance, international trade, principles of investment, and the principles and practice of management and law. In addition, all employees are offered training in computer applications and foreign languages. To supplement this classroom training, CITIC offers rotational assignments, university-based education, studying abroad, and various self-development opportunities. A career-path system was under development in 1997.

Finally, CITIC goes one step further than many other organizations in the world by measuring specifically how it's doing in cultivating versatile employees. These measures include:

- Standards and tests for each position prior to employment
- Performance on professional tests sponsored by China
- Promotion on the basis of identified job criteria, testing, and competence, as assessed by interviews, psychological assessments, and observations
- Financial assistance to those who go to training during their spare time

According to Jinping Wen, Director General of CITIC's personnel department, "Our strategic focus on training versatile employees helped us to establish and maintain CITIC's position and role in China's economic reform, as well as strengthened our foresight and adaptability in the changing marketplace."

CREATING THE TALENT SOLUTION

1. Think about your talent management practices. Would you say they are aligned with strategy? Integrated with each other? Well-executed?

2. How well do you hold people accountable for using your talent management practices? Are there appropriate positive and negative consequences?

3. What's your lead talent management practice? How well does it fit your strategic style?

4. Do you treat learning as a lead talent management practice for your entire population? What would it take for you to be world-class at learning?

CHAPTER 7

How Different Styles Manage Talent

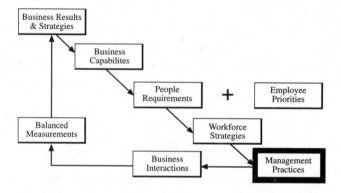

You've just read that each strategic style has a different lead talent management practice and each style manages all the practices differently from the other styles. This chapter will take you through the differences in detail and with many examples.

PRODUCTS COMPANIES

Products companies attain alignment by hiring and training for intellect and technical skills, maintaining a loose and easily changeable organizational style, and offering above-average pay and benefits. They do not do much in the way of highly leveraged individual pay-for-performance. This last point is crucial.

Heavy emphasis on performance evaluation and pay differentiation usually is detrimental to encouraging the creative process. Creative discovery depends on trial and error, experimentation, risk-taking, and serendipity. To practice a great deal of highly leveraged individual or team pay-for-performance may reward success, but it surely will punish failure and thwart creativity.

Smart products companies stay away from this outside their sales functions, despite the exhortations of many compensation professionals and the "conventional wisdom" in human resources over the last 15–20 years. This is where the "don't distract people with management policies and practices" workforce strategy really can be seen.

Strategic Use of Pay

This last point came home to me a few years ago in a conversation with the compensation and benefits director of Ford Motor Company. Ford is one of the few companies that has been able to successfully migrate from one style to another. Ford started as the original operations company—after all, Henry Ford invented the modern assembly line. For many years later, all the way into the late 1970s, Ford was run by financial types who stressed efficiency, including Robert McNamara who went on to be Secretary of Defense under Presidents Kennedy and Johnson.

However, by the early 1980s Ford was in a financial crisis. With such a strong emphasis on cost control, quality and design had slipped so consumers didn't want its cars, and the company was losing billions of dollars. Chairman Donald Peterson led the company through a transformation that focused on products, including the launch of the Taurus, the car that saved Ford. Current Chairman Alex Trotman talks about Ford people as needing to have a "passion for the product," and Ford's products are usually somewhat more expensive and have more features than comparable General Motors vehicles.

In my conversation with the compensation and benefits director, I asked him what Ford's compensation philosophy was. He said it was to be "fair and competitive, and provide above-average rewards when business was good." As I probed more, I realized there was no real interest or attempt to align pay any more closely to business goals. To do so might distract from the "passion for the product." Pay and benefit levels are competitive with other Big Three automakers and leading industrials. When the company does well, there is profit-sharing at all levels. Profit-sharing is distributed equally by dollars or percents among hourly, salaried, and management employees. Ford's performance management process, which Peterson revived and used as a transformational tool, stresses performance improvement and development, not rigorous or rigid evaluation.

When I compared what Ford does with the policies at 3M, Hewlett-Packard, Motorola, and the pharmaceutical companies I have consulted to over the years, I saw much the same thing. They offer competitive or better pay levels, bonuses or incentives tied to company or business unit success, and little or no real individual performance differentiation in bonuses and pay increases. Many of these companies talk about paying for performance, and some, like Hewlett-Packard and Motorola, occasionally used forced distributions of performance appraisal ratings, which often are an unfortunate part of pay-for-performance schemes.

Still, they don't really do it the way operations companies do, with individual and/or business unit incentive award opportunities that could account for a big part of pay, and a tough focus on performance measurement and evaluation to determine awards. More typical is 3M, who, as recently as 1994, commissioned an academic review of the literature on pay-for-performance to see if it works. This was long after other companies were using extensive, highly leveraged incentive plans. These companies often talk about it or study it, but they appear to know that considerable individual pay differentiation doesn't make good sense in a products company.

That's when it occurred to me—this is a strategic use of pay. Plans like Ford's, or Motorola's long-time RONA (return on net assets) bonus, which rewards employees when Motorola and its business sectors hit their financial goals but doesn't differentiate by individuals, enable products companies to do what they need to do. They let people focus on product development rather than trying to make their bonuses, allow the companies to move people around organizational units fairly easily because they are not tracking unit bonuses, and reward success without punishing failure. This is alignment and integration for a products company.

W.L. Gore

W.L. Gore does much the same thing. Though it ranks people on performance, it doesn't create much of a spread according to the rankings. Instead, rankings are used to determine how fast to move people up to their appropriate market pay levels and to insure internal fairness. Gore stresses paying the person rather than the job. To do so, it looks at overall contribution, which it defines as a combination of factors including impact; effectiveness; past, present, and future accomplishments; expectations of worth; notable achievements; special skills and talents; time and effort on the job; leadership; and teamwork. As you can imagine, with a select population to start with, all those factors to consider, an emphasis on internal fairness, and a cap essentially at the external market average, how much individual differentiation can there be?

Far more important at Gore are the two group incentives. Gore profit-sharing is tied to worldwide EVA. EVA goals are set, communicated to everyone on a constant basis, and when they are hit, whenever that occurs throughout the year, they are paid with great fanfare and communication. Usually there's a party or some type of celebration. Everyone gets the same percentage payout, usually about one week's pay. There is no penalty for plants or business units that aren't profitable; everyone shares. This is rewarding success but not punishing failure.

The other big group reward at Gore is the ASOP, the Associate Stock Ownership Plan. This is a phantom stock plan that is the cornerstone of retirement for Gore employees. The ASOP is a 15 percent of annual salary contribution, the maximum allowed by law. There is no 401(k) or other savings plan at Gore. The plan vests in five years, it's portable if an associate leaves, and people can withdraw 50 percent at age 55 with 15 years of service.

Gore associates are very aware of the ASOP. There is a great deal of communication, it's highly lucrative, and it is at risk if the value of the company does not continue to rise. The ASOP is valued and communicated quarterly at financial updates that associates attend. There the associates discuss how to increase its value.

NIKE

NIKE also emphasizes team rewards for performance, more than individual rewards. They have performance-sharing, gainsharing, profit-sharing, and 401(k) plans as part of their "LifeTrek" total compensation plan, though the performance-sharing plan does include a 50 percent individual component.

LifeTrek is particularly notable for its comprehensive approach to benefits, which attempts to consider employees' "whole life experience" and goes well beyond traditional benefit plans. This is in line with products companies offering rich benefit packages to their employees to take care of a number of their needs so employees can concentrate on product development.

LifeTrek was designed using the same market research approaches with employees that NIKE uses with customers to design new shoes. NIKE asks consumers about their lifestyles to formulate new shoe ideas. The company asked employees about their aspirations, needs, and fears in work and life to create LifeTrek. LifeTrek includes eight different categories of total compensation shown in Table 7-1.

TABLE 7-1

LifeTrek at NIKE

Keeping Healthy

Health excellence program
- Earn up to $150 in credits for not smoking, taking a health risk assessment, and wearing a seat belt

Medical coverage (also available to domestic partners of employees)
- Point-of-service plan, health maintenance organization, preferred provider organization, two indemnity options, and "no coverage" option

Vision coverage
- One option and "no coverage" option

Employee assistance program

Health-care spending account

Taking Care of Your Family

Dependent care spending account with NIKE match for incomes under $60,000

Child education savings account

NIKE scholarship fund

Making Life Easier

Direct deposit

Fleet car buying service

Product discounts

On-site fitness centers

Taking Time Off

Paid time off bank

Sabbaticals with NIKE match of additional paid time off

Protecting People

Short-term disability

Long-term disability

Life insurance (employee/spouse/child)

Universal life

Accidental death and dismemberment

Managing Your Money

Profit-sharing

401(k)

Retirement accounts (for after-tax dollars)

WorkTrek

Coaching for excellence

Learning at NIKE (training and tuition assistance)

Pay, Performance, and Teamwork

Pay for performance

V.A.L.U.E.S. (broad-banding)

Performance-sharing and gainsharing

Another aspect of LifeTrek is a broad-banded salary structure to provide more flexibility to manage pay without worrying about jobs and hierarchy. It enables NIKE employees the opportunity to focus on developing their skills as a way of increasing their contributions to the company. This more flexible approach supports a more fluid and flat organization, one of the characteristics of many products companies.

Fluid Organization Structures and Practices

These approaches to compensation distinguish products companies from other types of companies, but compensation is not the lead practice at products companies. The key to products companies' workforce strategies is that their organizations are more fluid. Products companies have to build this kind of organization so their smart people can feel the freedom they need to pursue the most challenging opportunities for creative fulfillment and commercial success.

Fluid is not the same as flat. Products companies will vary in how flat a structure they use, though it's true most companies are moving toward flatter structures. Fluidity comes from creating, disbanding, and re-creating product development efforts and teams quickly to pursue the most promising leads. The quick deployment of smart people across organization boundaries makes everything else work. Increasingly, this deployment is into cross-functional teams including discovery, design, development, marketing, sales, and even vendors, like the development teams at Chrysler and Merck.

What's distinctive about organization at many products companies is what I call "operational autonomy." I've already described aspects of the 3M organization style, with its "centipedal" structure—many different business units springing out of common technology platforms and bound together by common financial and workforce practices. The structure may not be as insect-like at other products companies, though the Microsoft structure has been described as "like a spider web." The overall approach is typical of this strategic style.

Business units or sectors have great freedom in how they conduct their businesses—what to create, what markets to pursue, how to go to market, and so forth. This is not the same as true decentralization, because these companies are often administratively quite centralized. They will use one set of financial, information, and people systems and practices to bind the business units together. Gore's "lattice organization" fits this description, as do the structures at Motorola and Hewlett-Packard.

This makes strategic sense because it enables people to combine and recombine in different teams across different organization units without worrying about whether administrative procedures are following them or reforming to align with the organization. The administrative management of the company is more permanent than, and somewhat separate from, the organization structure, which must flex to meet the demands of product discovery and development.

Usually this means keeping hiring, pay, training, and other practices constant while people are forming and reforming into teams to support different processes involved in bringing products to market. It also means giving these teams lots of decision-making power and at the same time, leaving room for individuals to create and make decisions as necessary. At 3M, though you can be on one team one day and on another team in a different business the next, you can be confident that your employment status, pay, or training arrangements usually won't be affected.

Products companies do a lot of merging and acquiring, and many of them are quite good at it. It often is the easiest and fastest way to get new brains and products, as opposed to building them. Additionally, products companies often merge or buy other businesses easily because they are the most likely type of company to leave the target company alone for quite a while. Trying to integrate the target means combining administrative systems. With a strong value on organizational freedom, it often makes sense just to leave the targeted company intact as long as it is producing.

The need for a fluid organization proved to be a decisive factor in one of my consulting assignments. I was working with a large research lab where discovery had slowed down, and people were feeling stifled by the organization's bureaucracy. We administered a Hewitt organizational diagnosis tool called CultureFit™ to assess six dimensions of culture and organization.

Then we compared the responses of different populations. In this lab, executives felt they were creating an organization where people had great flexibility and control over their activities. Employees felt the lab was very hierarchical and experienced tremendous management and systems control over their activities. They saw this as the biggest block to creation. Our intervention consisted of reducing some layers of the organization and moving to a more flexible, team-based structure where people could make many more decisions. It took a long time for the company to implement this large change, but the result was a much improved environment for innovation.

Staffing and Learning

Staffing and learning for products companies center on hiring very smart, technically-minded people and helping them stay cutting-edge. Microsoft has become a role model for this, working hard to find and hire the smartest people in the software world. Bill Gates, Microsoft's chairman, has been quoted to the effect that intelligence and creativity are mostly innate and can't be taught. He looks for the brightest and most creative programmers and developers who also can grasp new knowledge fast, are intellectually aggressive and challenging, are pragmatic, verbally facile, respond when challenged, and are obsessive problem-solvers when it comes to understanding and developing code.

Microsoft believes its people's brains are its competitive advantage. Even now that he is one of the richest men in the world, Gates continues to spend a great deal of his time recruiting, and the company is hyperselective about whom it hires. The company's director of recruiting has said, "The best thing we can do for our competitors is hire poorly. If I hire a bunch of bozos, it will hurt us because it takes time to get rid of them... then they start hiring people of lower quality... we are always looking to hire people who are better than we are."

Getting smart, technical people in the door is the staffing challenge for products companies. Keeping them up to speed technically and helping technical people become good strategic, process, and workforce managers are the learning challenges. Much of keeping people sharp technically comes from offering bigger and more difficult problems to attack and providing the necessary resources. These type of people love the technical aspects of their work and take great joy and meaning in staying on top of their fields. Look at how many Microsoft millionaires keep working.

Products companies also do other things to spur learning. Opportunities to work on independent research, support and awards for patent discoveries, in-house and external technical training and symposia, encouragement to write articles, and investment in research and development tools all are techniques used frequently.

A pharmaceutical client of mine developed formal relationships with the leading universities in its area. This enabled it to do a variety of things, including sponsor faculty research into related areas, obtain greater access to new compounds from the faculty, and invite faculty members to participate in discovery projects inside the company. One plan rotated company researchers and faculty members into each others' jobs for limited periods of time to provide fresh perspectives and new learning opportunities.

Turning technical people into great managers is a constant challenge facing products companies. There are no easy solutions to this. Dual career ladders help by separating out those who want to manage from those who prefer to remain in technical jobs. Ladders equalize rewards for both types of people.

Part of the impetus for establishing Motorola University was to provide leadership training for technical people who needed to broaden their skills. At Motorola U. one action learning approach used to help develop executives is to put them on learning teams to work together for three years with big goals, milestones, and quarterly updates. The charter for these teams is to address a real business problem that requires cultural change, enables them to learn to manage change, and helps them learn to learn. Teams have to develop, implement, and own their solutions.

OPERATIONS COMPANIES

Operations companies run their businesses by using teams and highly variable, performance-based compensation. They hire and develop people who like this way of working and who want to deliver tangible results and great deals to their customers. These results will be washing machines, hamburgers, airplane rides, or other concrete products or experiences.

Teamwork and Staffing

Teams abound in operations companies, and you can see them. They are the flight crews at Continental, Southwest, and American Airlines, the counter and kitchen crew at your local McDonald's at mealtime, and the salespeople at Wal Mart. They are machinists and assemblers on the washer and dryer production lines at Whirlpool who are there to build what you will use for years. They are the fossil fuel teams at the Wisconsin Electric coal burning plants and the exploration teams at Shell.

Teams deliver processes. Individuals really can't. Operations companies are about teams involved in process management and delivery. Lincoln Electric's focus on individual production is one of the few notable exceptions, but its production methods haven't changed much since the 1930s.

This has big implications for staffing. One of the first criteria operations companies have to look for in hiring is people who like working closely together on a regular basis. This is beyond cooperation and collaboration. It's "in-your-face" everyday interaction on all sorts of issues, little and big.

From a teamwork standpoint, it's more like a basketball team, a constant movement of people together. When one player goes to a place on the court to do something, the positions and duties of everyone else are affected instantly. A flight crew or an assembly line is like that. Not everyone is able or willing to work together this closely so teamwork behaviors become the crucial staffing criteria.

There's also the issue of permanence in staffing. Many operations companies, like Cargill, Lincoln Electric, and Whirlpool, are long-term employers. They value the advantages experience brings in operating their work processes. Others are long-term by nature of the collective bargaining agreements they have, like airlines and utilities.

Yet for many operations companies, more so than for other types, long-term employment is not the issue, especially on the front lines. Many retail businesses, like McDonald's, Wal Mart, Disney amusement parks, and most branch banks, see considerable turnover. For them it's the product or service experience that's permanent. The processes are so strong that people can come and go. As long as people can be trained quickly in the operating processes, they will deliver the needed quality levels.

Even many nonretail operations companies behave this way. PepsiCo has always experienced higher-than-average turnover in its beverage and snack food businesses, especially among salaried employees. In recent years the company has expressed a growing concern about this. It has taken a few runs at improving this situation, but has not realigned practices to create a solution yet.

General Electric has experienced much higher voluntary and involuntary turnover in recent years, as it keeps raising the bar on its performance. GE also has experimented with several unique approaches to staffing. Its Medical Systems' Customer Support Center partnered with Manpower Inc. to create a workforce comprised of 50 percent GE employees and 50 percent Manpower Inc. employees. This was a permanent situation, not a temporary cushion for peak workloads, made possible by strong process management, technology, and operational improvements. GE also has gone to outsourcing large amounts of its staffing activities through an independent company, something a customers company more concerned with fit would be reluctant to do. For operations companies, picking the right people is important, but fitting the people into the process is more important.

Organization

This emphasis on process management and delivery mean structure and policy are more important when it comes to organization. Operations companies have to preserve and improve their processes and the teams that deliver them. To do this there will be more structure, and it will be more rigid, than at other types of companies. Most operations companies are founded on the concept of delivering large, consistent volumes of product or service—airline miles, electricity, grain, light bulbs, small motors, beverages, washing machines—and this cannot be done without tight and efficient organization.

This doesn't necessarily mean more hierarchy, but I usually see it in these clients. Sometimes safety demands it. For example, airlines, other transportation companies, and utilities all are dealing in potentially life-threatening situations and have to exercise careful control. Many of these types of companies are the last vestiges of command and control, military-type organizations. In other operations companies, the demands of on-time delivery, cost control, or continuous production or processing require greater attention to fixed formulas, policies, and management control.

Fortunately the kind of highly structured person who likes things, methods, and efficiency also is better suited to enjoy a more structured organization. There's an order to the universe and a logic that may not exist in products companies and customers companies. To the extent that employees are empowered in these companies, and many are, it's within limits dictated by processes that other types of people might find stifling.

This approach to organization often affects mergers and acquisitions. When operations companies merge or acquire, they aren't the kind of company to leave the target alone. Processes and policies are integrated or imposed to achieve efficiencies and economies of scale. Sometimes this goes so far as to redo everything at the merged or acquired target to make it unrecognizable from the acquirer.

We recently conducted some research into operations companies' structures and found these types of characteristics:

- The focus on gaining substantial economies of scale tends to result in functional, rather than business unit, organizations, or limited (not full-featured) business units organized inside very large functions, sectors or regions.
- Lean or efficient manufacturing and/or materials processing still use relatively long product runs, though not as long as 10 years ago.
- New product development and manufacturing is done outside existing structures; thus not disrupting efficiencies of existing products.
- All customer-related positions—administration, sales representatives, and technicians—tend to be grouped in one functional organization that services multiple product lines.
- Administrative functions tend to be grouped in "shared services" or other types of centralized operations to maximize efficiency and also take advantage of economies of scale.
- Outsourcing decisions tend to be made more on cost than other criteria.

According to my Hewitt colleague, Mark Hoyal, who conducted this research, "Operations companies may appear somewhat more traditional in structure than other types of companies, but they tend to use more leading-edge quality teams and information technology to build business capability, integrate across functions, and deliver value."

Performance and Rewards

Where operations companies really need to distinguish themselves in talent management practices is in performance-based compensation. This combines two management practices areas, performing and rewarding. Performance compensation can be the strongest opportunity for operations companies to tell employees what's important. Operations companies that don't have strong performance and reward systems are missing this opportunity, and their practices are misaligned.

Though teams are key to operations companies, whether they reward individuals or teams depends on how they organize work and the emphasis they place on individual performance. Their reward systems keep score for these companies and communicate the workforce strategy of "compete and win." A few, like Lincoln Electric, focus more on individual winners, though even Lincoln evaluates individuals on their teamwork behaviors. Whirlpool is more typical and tries to balance individual and team performance. W.W. Grainger prefers to reward teams because this supports its business strategies and work design. Still others are limited to rewarding organizational or team performance by collective bargaining, like Southwest and Continental. Regardless of whom they reward, these performance and reward systems have real variability and tell employees what tangible results are important.

> The more focus a company puts on measuring individual performance and tying pay to it, the more risk it can share with employees.

The more focus a company puts on measuring individual performance and tying pay to it, the more risk it can share with employees. By *risk* I mean offering lower-than-average base pay levels, with opportunities to earn well above average total cash compensation based on performance. By necessity this means much larger-than-average bonuses. Not many companies have tried this outside of their sales forces. Lincoln and Whirlpool are two who have done it. The Shell pay plan has some elements of this too.

Instead, most companies do what I call "reward sharing." They offer something additional on top of competitive base salaries. This is what a lot of short-term executive and salaried compensation plans look like in the U.S. The base pay levels don't change relative to the competition. They always stay at competitive levels. So where's the risk? It only occurs when there is true variability in the bonus or incentive. Some smart companies really allow the bonus or incentive to vary greatly, but many companies shy away from that too.

The Lincoln Electric Company

The Lincoln Electric incentive management system has been written about frequently, but it takes on a whole new perspective when you can see it up close. Production employees work extraordinarily hard for their merit rating, which is a point system based on productivity, quality, level of supervision required (how independently you work), and cooperation and ideas, a measure of teamwork and contribution to the Lincoln suggestion system. Employees compete with each other for points, except on the quality measure. The number of points translates directly to how large a bonus someone can earn.

Since the bonus runs 50 to 100 percent of pay and pushes compensation well above competitive levels, the work level is fierce. Employees are given considerable freedom within the system to run their own businesses, and they behave as if they do. The cooperation and quality points ensure that people don't engage in counterproductive internal competition.

What's fascinating is how the values and environment created by this system permeate all of Lincoln Electric, including office workers, salaried employees, and executives. This is by design and creates tremendous alignment. Everyone is mindful of building up the bonus pool that gets allocated to all levels of the organization and any spending that can detract from it. The production workforce scrutinizes this as closely as management in this open book company, but then this is a company where "managers work and workers manage." Whenever there is spending that ultimately will detract from the bonus, including business investments, there is considerable dialogue and questioning about it through the advisory board that enables production workers to comment on what management's doing. Also, since production workers are expected to put in long hours to meet their production goals, everyone else is expected to work long hours too.

Whirlpool Corporation

The Whirlpool performance and reward system has created tremendous alignment. When designed in 1988, the system had the following characteristics:

- A compensation philosophy of base pay levels at 90 percent of the competitive market average, and annual incentive opportunities that paid at 110 percent of market when business and individual objectives were met.

- Incentive opportunities based on corporate return on equity (ROE), business unit (RONA or product earnings), and individual performance according to measurable stretch goals. These goals are set to produce high levels of earnings and breakthrough performances by people.

- Tough-minded performance evaluation of people against the results they created, calculated using weighted objectives and rating points to produce a performance score.

- A managed distribution of performance scores to determine both base pay increases and incentive awards, with strong differentiation among individuals.

Some companies talk about these kinds of things. Whirlpool did it. They used this system to build record-breaking corporate performance for six years. In addition to this system, which applied to all salaried exempt employees from entry-level to executive, gainsharing plans were put into Whirlpool's manufacturing plants. Just in case people still did not get the performance message, Whirlpool tied its contributions to its 401(k) plan to the same measure of corporate financial performance—return on equity—that it used to fund the short-term incentive.

An inequality in the system was that salaried nonexempt employees did not participate in these incentive rewards, other than the 401(k). One reason for this was this smaller group of employees already was paid above market when this plan was put into place. A second reason was that the company could not find meaningful measures of nonexempt performance that could be linked to financial performance.

As the company went from being North American-based to global, and the culture became so heavily focused on financial results that people became concerned about company values, the system was redesigned in 1996 for 1997 implementation. The changes included:

- Modifying the 90 percent base pay philosophy to acknowledge that local markets around the world need more flexibility in pay rates. Some will be higher and some will be lower. Tightening of talent markets around the world may require that some star performers should be paid at or above market—but no across-the-board market adjustments.
- Greater emphasis on behaviors in the performance evaluation system to focus on building a winning corporate culture around the world, including learning, teamwork, integrity, and leadership.
- Broadening corporate and business unit objectives to focus on a balanced scorecard with customer service and employee objectives, in addition to financial objectives.
- Inclusion of nonexempt employees in the incentive plan.

All of these changes were made to help build a global, high-performance culture that could carry the company for the next several years. According to Chairman Dave Whitwam, "To create the advantage that a truly global company can deliver, we must develop a global culture—a culture that is aligned around the world. We are working to align our key business systems and processes to support our behaviors and values... how we measure performance... how we reward ourselves... how we train... how well we communicate... and how we report on business measures. Think about the power this culture will create!"

Cargill

Not all operations companies structure their incentives to focus on the short-term or the individual. It depends on what's important to the company in delivering customer value. Cargill has a worldwide performance management process designed to communicate one set of behavioral competencies around the world. The process sets expectations and measures individual performance for these competencies and the key results areas that cascade down from business unit planning.

Employees at various levels throughout Cargill's different businesses may be eligible for annual incentives, mostly based on unit financial results and individual performance evaluation, if the business unit wants to offer them. The company puts greater emphasis on its long-term incentive for everyone—an employee stock ownership plan that ties employees' long-term financial security to increases in the company's book value. Cargill sees itself as one worldwide team, despite being one of the most diversified large companies in the world.

Shell Oil Company

Shell Oil Company instituted a variable pay plan at the beginning of its transformation to a more focused, low-cost, high-productivity competitor. Prior to that, it operated more like a products company, a characteristic shared by many of the giant petrochemical companies. At first, Shell was contemplating a less aggressive, less leveraged variable pay plan, more like what some of the other oil companies were using. Instead, the team that studied the issue saw how aggressive operations companies manage incentive pay and decided to go for it. The result was the most dynamic pay plan among the big oils. Shell:

- Froze base pay for three years to move its competitive position from high-average among the seven major oils to average among a larger group of 14 oils, thus lowering its average pay levels.
- Provided market-based incentive opportunities based on net income results, relative to its competitors, and return on capital employed (ROCE).
- Awarded most of the incentives based on corporate and business unit performance, with some individual adjustments when necessary, left to the business units to determine.

The message from Shell to employees: "Financial results and lowered costs are absolutely crucial, and if we perform well on these, you will be rewarded for being part of the team that produced them." This is the essence of successful talent management practices in operations companies—produce results and enjoy the rewards.

CUSTOMERS COMPANIES

Staffing

Every smart company ensures its hiring practices get the absolute best talent it needs. What's different about the lead practice for customers companies is that staffing and selection must focus on personal fit, the extremely close match of values and behavior between the employee and the company. According to a vice president in the private bank at U.S. Bancorp, the customers companies part of the bank, "We have to get deep inside peoples' heads."

A good match also is important to other types of companies, but not as important as in customers companies. The environment of freedom that characterizes products companies can accommodate a wider range of personalities, as long as people are smart enough to contribute to building world-class products. In operations companies the relative weight of processes over people and the short-term nature of employment in some of them,

> In customers companies personal fit is everything.

mean that fit is not as big an issue. People have to be well-matched to the processes and team-oriented, but processes, policies, and the drive for results will govern their behaviors. In customers companies personal fit is everything.

Hewitt Associates LLC

At Hewitt, selection for fit is our lead practice, and it affects all of our staffing decisions. We involve as many people as we can in staffing processes, including hiring, promotions, transfers, relocations, and firing. Considerable conversations resulting in careful consensus and correct decisions are what we seek.

Our CEO always has been involved in all key hires, and we define that broader than most companies do. If the CEO is not involved, then a large number of experienced managers are. Our objectives in hiring are not only to assess critical competencies, but to really get to know people and to let them get to know us. This takes time. The downside of being this thorough is that we occasionally miss out on a good candidate who is in a hurry. We don't find this particularly bothersome. If a person is not willing to go through a careful selection process for his or her own reasons as well as ours, then we're not sure he or she would be a good fit.

In addition to the critical consulting competencies we look for, we have a long-time model of fit that everyone who does hiring at Hewitt can recite. The acronym is SWAN, someone who:

- Is **S**mart
- **W**orks hard
- **A**chieves—creates results
- Is **N**ice—fits our collaborative culture

The purpose of all this selectivity is to keep a high barrier to entry, but to practice the "benefit of the doubt" once someone joins us. One Hewitt colleague, Rob Weinberg, commented, "It took forever to get hired, but I was accepted instantly." Another way to understand this is we select then hire. "Up or out" companies hire, then select.

This enables us to begin cultural socialization right away. Since our culture stresses teamwork and cooperation, sharing of information and assistance to clients, open communication, and a "one-firm" mindset, it makes sense to get people into it as positively and as quickly as possible.

Another business purpose of this selectivity is we want people to select us because they want to join a company with our values. This is a more important factor than money to people who place a high premium on shared values. Obviously we need to be competitive in making financial offers to new hires, but we don't buy them. People turn down more lucrative offers to join us if they want the values-oriented environment we work hard to nurture and sustain.

Other customers companies operate in similar fashion. Leo Burnett, Nordstrom, Rosenbluth Travel, and USAA all hire for very close fit to their values. These companies recognize they have to be highly selective if they are going to carry out their strategies. They also know if they can find someone who fits their values, they can, in many cases, find them a job that will fit their skills. So often hiring isn't for a specific job, but more to join the organization. If the person proves to be a good fit and does quality work, the company will work with the person to find the right role, even if this means trying several things out over a number of years.

This emphasis on fit can cause some customers companies to have problems with diversity, particularly in accepting and selecting people with different backgrounds or points of view. Here a good lesson can be learned from a small business, Gold Medal Cleaners. Like a number of small employers with a workforce paid less than at many big companies, Gold Medal has learned to live with and celebrate diversity faster and to a much greater extent than most large companies.

Gold Medal serves an upper income, mostly white clientele in an affluent Chicago suburb. It provides premium dry cleaning with outstanding service at premium prices. Over the years the workforce at Gold Medal has gone from being mostly white to mostly African American to mostly Hispanic. How has Gold Medal managed to maintain its terrific service with a changing workforce?

According to owner Stuart Friedman, the key is hiring for attitude. Stuart says that in interviews, "I look for attitude, eagerness, enthusiasm, and pride. That has nothing to do with a person's background. The major reason you lose customers in any retail business is a bad attitude at the counter." After Stuart hired and trained his first Hispanic employee, he turned to her for help in recruiting and screening others. Now she and her cousin do most of the word-of-mouth recruiting, screening, and hiring when new employees are needed. The more senior people act as group leaders and exert peer pressure over others to maintain Gold Medal's standards and reputation for customer service and cleanliness. In turn Gold Medal provides a good place to work.

Learning

Selective hiring means a long-term employment relationship for people who fit, and you also can see this in the learning practices of these companies. Learning focuses more on socialization to values and long-term knowledge building than on technical skills or process behaviors. Learning in customers companies has been likened to "brainwashing" by several people who have observed it.

This brainwashing isn't dangerous or designed to produce mindless automatons. On the contrary, it's intended to create employees who will make good decisions for the customer and the company in real time during the customer-employee interaction, usually without being able to consult anyone else or a procedures manual. Since these interactions typically are more complex and expensive than shopping elsewhere, the decisions have to be right.

What does this "brainwashing" look like? A lot of it is mythology, featuring the values and service orientation of the founder or mythic leader of the company. This is meant to inspire people to higher levels of service to the customer. At Leo Burnett and IBM, people still talk about Burnett and the Tom Watsons, Sr. and Jr., even people who never met them. When people who did know them start to talk about something these founders said or did, reverent silence engulfs the crowd.

Another part of the learning at customers companies is motivational, designed to keep enthusiasm up for meeting sales goals and the day-to-day demands of customers. Nordstrom and Home Depot are famous for this. In fact, one of the succession issues facing Home Depot is that as one of the founders looks toward retirement, the other founder who will remain to run the company is a quieter, much less inspirational personality. In nonretail environments it may not be quite as necessary to have this "rah-rah" form of inspiration, but there must be a good deal of sentiment and sincerity to communicating company values.

A third part to learning at many of these companies is centered on continuous career learning for employees, designed to make them smarter, more well-rounded people. Learning may or may not be directly job related. It is based on the idea that customer-centered work takes bright, broad-based people who can bring many resources to bear on customer problems. It also reinforces the need for people to stay for the long-term to keep building relationships and to grow wiser to encourage and manage more complex relationships. Educational reimbursement and external education work well here. USAA's career development program, including extensive reimbursement and even offering college courses on-site, is a good example.

At the same time, product knowledge is stressed. It's crucial, because employees have to be able to discover and coordinate solutions and resources for their customers. This could be understanding what's sold in other departments at Nordstrom or how to move across client server and desktop solutions at IBM. While much of this is offered in training programs, more of it is learned through on-the-job experience.

Long-term learning signals a strong promote-from-within mindset in these companies. The heads of these companies are almost all people who have worked their way up from the bottom. This is, of course, how you keep the powerful culture going. From an organization standpoint, customers companies with these kinds of cultures aren't very good at, and don't attempt, many mergers and acquisitions. It's just too hard to transfer the culture. Burnett and Hewitt each have done one small acquisition in their respective histories. Home Depot may take over stores from other companies but it remakes them over completely in its image. IBM has tried various ventures over the years with very mixed success.

Organization

It's hard to generalize much about customers companies' organizations. Usually they are quite flat, though IBM, as large as it is, is something of an exception. At Hewitt there are never more than three or four levels from entry to our Chief Executive. Our competitors often have many gradations of consultants—we have associates and principals. It's vital to have as few layers as possible so decision-making stays close to the customer.

Organization structures vary between team- and individual-focused, depending on what it takes to build relationships and deliver to the customer. Though it takes a team to deliver on a process, ultimately it takes an individual to build a close relationship. There may be teams backing up the individual relationship-builder in many situations, particularly when it's necessary to integrate across different areas to build complex solutions. Whether the customer knows about the team or sees team members will vary depending on the situation.

Performance and Rewards

Performance and pay systems are quite diverse in customers companies and can be somewhat problematic. They range from Nordstrom, which was the first department store to feature an all-commission system, to companies that offer subjective bonuses, like Hewitt, or no bonuses or incentives at all. Hewitt and IBM both were

relatively late among their competitors in offering bonuses or variable pay to broader groups of employees. Again, the key to understanding performance and pay is what it takes to serve the customer.

When the interaction between customer and employee is a short-
cycle sale, like clothing or hardware, or a phone transaction, like a
travel reservation or insurance question, it makes more sense to use
a commission or incentive system. In these cases, the relationship
being built is really between the store or agency and the customer,
more than between the individual employee and the customer. Customers actually may deal with many different employees, so the store
wants consistent, energetic, and personal service. A formula-driven
commission or incentive can be a good way to get that.

When the relationship is a more complex, longer-cycle sell and
service situation, and more likely to lead to a relationship between
the customer and the individual employee, it becomes more difficult to structure the performance and pay package. Performance
expectations can be aggravatingly hard to specify. An employee is
supposed to do whatever it takes to serve the customer. How do you
boil that down to a limited number of objectives or behaviors? There
also may be conflicts between the short-term results the company
wants and the long-term relationships it also wants.

Typically it's possible to assess the quantity and most important outcomes of the targeted relationships in these companies. This
can include growth in revenues or profitability, as well as things like
market or client share. Yet it can be extremely difficult, if not impossible, to stipulate and evaluate all of the important steps or milestones needed to produce the outcomes. Additionally, the behaviors
needed to produce these relationships are critical for success. These
should be identified, assessed, and evaluated. Finally, for the sake of
the relationship, it may be vital to sacrifice something in the short-
term for the long-term, and that's quite difficult to measure or assess.

When it comes to the pay side of the equation, it becomes crucial not to reward short-term success at the expense of the long-term.
This can happen if current incentives become too powerful. Or, if
results are the only things that are rewarded, employees may not
pay attention to the behaviors needed to create positive, long-term
relationships.

Another bewildering issue is how long or often do you pay for one-time success. If a person takes an account from $5 million to $8 million in a given year, how long should he or she be rewarded for that? What happens in year two if the account stays at $8 million? Is the person paid for managing $8 million, or does he or she see a reduction because there was no growth in the account that year?

The complexity of these issues leads many of these customers companies to more subjective or collegial bonus schemes. This may be the only way they can take a total, balanced view of performance. Bonuses are different from incentives in that bonuses are not tied to strict formulas. The award opportunities and performance targets are not communicated as clearly in advance so it is difficult, if not impossible, to know what someone will earn as the year progresses. The decision around how much a person earns often is subjective, decided by a group of people who may be making a holistic judgment of performance.

The customers companies workforce strategy of "keeping people satisfied so they can satisfy the customer" is shown clearly in the benefits plans of these companies. They tend to be rich, like products companies, and usually offer a good deal of choice. The idea is to be responsive to employees, the same way that they are responsive to customers. Usually a lot of time is spent listening to employees to modify benefit offerings to meet current needs.

Since customers companies want to give their customers tailored products and services, they often carry this into employee benefits, with flexibility offered to individuals, not just groups, and an "early adopter" mentality when new benefit ideas surface. Today this includes things like alternative work arrangements, new child- or elder-care services, wellness and lifestyle enhancements, and employee convenience services, like on-site dry cleaning or car repair. Employees have considerable abilities to modify their benefits to meet their own particular needs, just as their customers receive tailored solutions.

BRINGING IT ALL TOGETHER

You have now covered a lot of ground about the talent management practices of each strategic style. I summarize how these align in Table 7-2. Lead practices are highlighted in bold.

TABLE 7-2

Alignment of Talent Management Practices and Strategic Style

	Products	**Operations**	**Customers**
Staffing	Staff for intelligence and long-term employment	Staff for tangible results and teamwork, tenures will vary	**Staff for tight fit with values, and the ability to build long-term relation-ships**
Organizing	**Fluid, changing frequently, mostly teams but leave room for indi-vidual contribu-tors, "operational autonomy"**	More structured, some rigidity or hierarchy is OK, heavily focused on teams to deliver processes, business units	As flat as possible, mostly determined by individual relationships, team-based if it suits the customer, integrated
Learning	**Keep technical people at the leading-edge**	**Teach process management and improvement**	**Educate on values and service**
Performing	Behaviors that contribute to discovery and development, behaviors are more important than results for individu-als	Measure and evaluate on tangible results, behaviors support results—especially team behaviors	Balance behaviors and results that produce growing relationships
Rewarding	Above-average levels, long-term focus, little individual differen-tiation or much variability, broad-based cash profit-sharing	**As variable and differentiated as possible, based on measurable performance, team or individual depends on work design, formula-driven incentives**	Variability and differentiation varies depending on customer situations, great diversity from immediate and individual commissions to holistic and subjective bonuses

Sometimes when characterizing companies and their practices, it can be easy to get carried away and see things as "pure types." This exaggerates things and makes it seem that if a company fits a particular strategic style, then it must have one set of practices and cannot do anything else. This isn't the case. There aren't many "pure types" out there.

Instead, I see smart companies aligned predominantly in one direction, following their strategic styles, but with exceptions in some of their practices. For instance, Microsoft, a products company, offers somewhat below-average base pay but makes up for it with large stock option grants. Often companies are in some stage of realigning to get a better fit with practices that are misaligned or could be improved.

Other not-so-smart companies appear to have talent management practices that vary all over the place and don't seem to align to any particular model. Either they haven't put much thought, energy, and resources into creating strong practices, or they have tried to copy best practices out of context, opting for what works for others rather than what fits best with their business strategies and strategic styles.

Aligning talent management practices in the ways I have described will help you and your employees clearly see the link of practices to business strategy and the integration of practices with each other. It will also help you create an environment that parallels your customer experience. The messages delivered by your practices will be consistent with how you want to deliver value to your customers and treat your employees. This will help you create success for your business and make your employees feel like they are successful too.

CREATING THE TALENT SOLUTION

1. How well-aligned are your talent management practices to your strategic style? What's in alignment? What's most out of alignment?
2. What would it take to fix your most glaring misalignments? How would you benefit if you did?

CHAPTER **8**

Align Leadership and Other Interactions

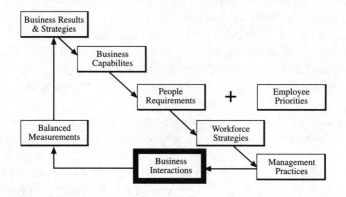

Your talent management practices will shape interactions among employees and leadership, customers, and other employees. If you have aligned your practices to your strategic style, you will get the interactions that produce success. In this chapter you'll see:

- What people want from leaders
- How leadership is defined by competence and empathy
- How each strategic style requires a different kind of leadership and personal style
- That employee-customer interactions are very different in operations, products, and customers companies
- A process for changing employee-employee interactions

All business results come from interactions—leaders with employees, employees with employees, and employees with customers. These interactions are changing, and some are becoming much more electronic. Sometimes the "employee" now is an ATM machine, a voice-mail box, home page, or voice response circuit.

Still most really important business still is done person-to-person. When you use the alignment model and structure your talent management practices to implement your business strategies and strategic style, you create the kind of successful human interactions you want.

Let's review each kind of interaction, starting with leaders and employees.

LEADERSHIP INTERACTIONS

Leadership should occur everywhere in your company, not only in interactions between employees and management. Nonmanagement employees show leadership frequently, though usually this gets described as initiative. I don't subscribe to the idea that says an organization needs some people to lead and others to follow.

In my ideal, everyone should show leadership all the time. They should do it in complementary ways and for interdependent and varied responsibilities. They also collaborate, another form of leadership. All of this should be done to satisfy your customer, and the outcome should be a high-initiative, high-energy, and high-results company.

> A company without money can always borrow it, but a company without leadership is bankrupt.

Still, you should be able to see leadership most readily in employee-management interactions. If it isn't there in your company as an example for others, it's going to be hard to find it elsewhere. As someone once said, "A company without money can always borrow it, but a company without leadership is bankrupt."

I worked with a team of managers from Shell on the issue of leadership interactions some years ago. After studying how to increase and improve leadership, the team issued the following recommendation for their vision for Shell. It said, "The role of leadership

is well-defined and balanced between business results, people management, and transformational leadership. Employees have a much
higher quantity and quality of interactions with their leaders. A continually abundant pool of diverse leadership resources is being
primed and readied."

Though this recommendation was written by Shell people specifically for their company, it touches on a number of issues about
leadership I see in other organizations. These are:

- Often, what leaders are supposed to do seems vague or ill-
  defined to others. Employees want a lot of communication
  from leadership.
- Leaders are so focused on getting bottom-line results they
  don't invest much time or attention in people, except on an
  exception or problem basis. Employees want their companies to be successful, but even when they are, people will
  complain about leadership if employees feel their issues
  and concerns aren't being heard.
- Today, leaders have to be change managers. The most
  important role of leaders going forward may be guiding
  their organizations through an unending stream of change.
- Executives constantly are concerned about "bench
  strength," the availability and development of the next set
  of leaders.
- Leadership, in American business at least, is still dominated by white males.

Most of these problems cut across many levels in companies,
regardless of their success, strategic style, or situation. They certainly
get in the way of managing talent to get the most out of it. Is it possible to use the strategic styles and alignment model to address some
of these issues? I think so. I'll begin by suggesting what companies
and employees want from leadership, how this might fit into my
approach, and how it can help you.

WHAT DO PEOPLE WANT FROM LEADERS?

Since both companies and their people want to be successful, I think
there actually is pretty good agreement among top management and
employees about what leadership should do and be like. Gary Wills,

the author, professor, and social historian, describes a *leader* as someone who "mobilizes others toward a goal shared by leader and followers." Dave Whitwam, Whirlpool's CEO, interprets this for his job from his "stretch goal" mindset. He says, "The CEO's role is to get groups of people to accomplish what they didn't think was possible."

There may be more written on how leaders should do this than on any other topic in business, but I prefer to keep it simple and use just two terms: *competence* and *empathy*.

Competence

A brief definition of leader *competence* comes down to:

- Setting a direction
- Communicating it
- Getting it done

Setting a direction involves lots of things, including looking at your target markets and business capabilities realistically, pinpointing your customer value proposition, determining how you can position yourself competitively, ensuring and enhancing your particular advantages, and making a decision about which way to go and going there. These can be tough decisions, especially when others don't have the whole picture or see things realistically. Nancy Siska, a Cargill vice president and a relatively new member of senior management, said this last item has been a real learning experience for her. According to Nancy, "Now I know why senior managers get paid more. They make decisions other people don't want to."

Gaurdie Banister, President of Shell Continental Companies, reinforces this. "You have to take a stand and take it with conviction. It has to be heartfelt and meaningful to you, so you can appeal to others."

Leader competence also involves the courage to stick to your direction when things are going bad. Yet there seems to be another kind of courage too, the courage to get feedback and change direction when necessary. Ed Dunn, Whirlpool senior vice president, says, "Leaders who are successful in the long run recognize mistakes early and have the courage to do so, say so, and do something different. This prevents them from elevating a commitment to a failed course of action."

This type of courage seems founded on a bedrock of listening, a skill people almost universally cite as an attribute of effective leadership. It's unlikely you could set a useful direction if you didn't listen well. When Arthur Martinez started the turnaround at Sears, he began by identifying and listening to Sears' target customer, the middle-income mother. He was shocked to learn that many Sears executives didn't even know who the target customer was.

Earlier I noted operations companies seem to have more charismatic leadership types, products companies could do well with more of a quiet style of leadership, and customers companies need to be led by strong appeals to values. These are not mutually exclusive styles and a variety of communication styles can work well for leaders. What all leaders have in common is they communicate a lot, and the communication is authentic. A quick look at championship coaches in sports suggests lots of different styles can win. The common element is their players say winning coaches treat them honestly and let them know where they stand.

> ## What all leaders have in common is they communicate a lot, and the communication is authentic.

This leads to another key area of leader competence—ethics. There clearly are different ethical standards around the world, but in Western cultures ethics are defined in terms of honesty, truth telling, integrity, quality, and following the rule and spirit of the law. We admire leaders who show strong ethics. Sooner or later, hopefully sooner, a lack of ethics catches up with weak leaders and knocks them out of their positions.

Competence and Performance

There's an old psychological distinction between competence, the ability to do something, and performance, getting it done. In the arena of leadership, competence is nothing without performance. Part of leader competence is results. A significant issue is how long can a leader survive without competent performance. In this country there is no clear set of criteria for dismissing poorly performing leaders.

Accountability for corporate leadership performance rests with boards of directors, but they seem to have widely varying standards. When I spend time in China, the leaders of the state-owned enterprises are fascinated by our concepts of boards and their accountabilities. This is new territory to them since they are used to political control of their organizations. They ask about it constantly, but unfortunately I find it hard to talk about boards' management of performance in anything other than generalities because of the wide variation.

In recent years, the Quaker Oats board seemed to have a large supply of patience with William Smithburg, putting up with a long period of low performance because of the Snapple purchase before Quaker finally sold it and Smithburg was forced to step down. However, at another Chicago company, Waste Management, a board led by outside investor George Soros dumped CEO Phil Rooney for lackluster performance after less than a year on the job. Likewise, the AT&T board acted quickly to dump John Walters after it decided he was not a good fit to succeed Robert Allen, though Allen was allowed to stay on through years of poor financial performance. A board dominated by insiders and close friends let the price-fixing scandals at Archer Daniel Midlands go on for years until long-time leader Dwayne Andreas stepped aside as CEO. Even then, his nephew took the job, and Andreas retained the chairman's title. Certainly it takes strong outside leadership on a board and active investors to ensure accountability for performance, but some boards seem to have it and many don't.

Empathy

The other part of leadership is empathy. Interestingly, empathy shares something very important with competence—listening. Listening is the basis for all human relationships. Leadership is nothing if not a relationship.

I find a lot of business writing ignores this. The myth of the lone, tough, heroic leader is still alive and well, especially in several American business publications. Many years ago, Dwight Eisenhower said, "You do not lead by hitting people over the head—that's assault, not leadership." Yet read company profiles, and they seem mostly to be about the "tough as nails" CEO. The best CEOs I know are far more empathetic people than that.

Empathy generally is defined as identifying with another person, either intellectually, emotionally, or socially. Yet I see leadership empathy as something slightly different. An empathetic leader identifies with other people enough so that people can identify with him or her. In other words, the leader shows enough of a human side so people know he or she has feelings and can understand theirs. Gaurdie Banister says, "You have to be willing to expose your emotions to people and just live with it." Given a choice about leaders, people will choose the one who can show some empathy by displaying appropriate emotion.

Empathy in leaders also helps set a direction. It's positive, uplifting, and points to opportunities, not limitations. This doesn't mean it's Pollyanna, or based on false optimism, but in the face of insurmountable obstacles, leaders see paths to glory. They see abundance where others see scarcity. They see the greater good when others can only imagine personal threats or gains.

The last few U.S. presidential elections show this. Ronald Reagan was a master communicator of emotion and defeated two people who weren't—Jimmy Carter and Walter Mondale. George Bush was widely perceived as a very competent man, but not very good at communicating empathy or emotion. He defeated someone else who couldn't convey much emotion, Michael Dukakis, but lost to a master of empathetic communication, Bill Clinton. Even some people who thought Bush was more competent—the cornerstone of his campaign in 1992—voted for Clinton because they thought he was more in touch with people and the times.

If anyone ever doubted elections are about personalities and not programs, then 1996 should have given them their final answer. Bob Dole ran on a traditionally popular issue, tax cuts, that was brought up again immediately after he lost. Clinton had strong disapproval ratings, but his ability to communicate emotion far outdistanced Dole, who was seen as a competent career politician but out of touch with people and their feelings. This may be an oversimplification of current politics, but never bet against the more empathetic candidate.

In business, employees don't have much choice about who their leader is, so what does empathy have to do with it? Simply this, people need to identify with a leader personally before they can identify with the mission, strategy, or change effort of the company or unit. Both Sears and Shell call this "personalizing the transformation." Cargill refers to it as "personalizing the vision." The key point is getting your people to feel in their hearts, not just understand, the direction you want your company to go. Understanding comes from competence; feeling comes from empathy.

This is crucial because you cannot change a direction or sustain the change without empathy. Evidence suggests in a crisis competency may be enough for a while. It's better if you're like Gordon Bethune at Continental and have both, but you can do without empathy for a short period if you can convince people the ship is sinking fast, and you have to take drastic actions just to stay afloat. Also, if you are just managing for the short-term, then competency alone should work to correct the financial situation. Particularly if you favor Al Dunlap-like solutions, it may be better not to have any empathy.

However, in a steadier or long-term situation when change may be more incremental, or where a large-scale change effort may take years and be just one event in the term of a leader, you have to have empathy or you won't have any followers.

Empathy and Toughness

Please don't confuse empathy with weakness or being soft emotionally. Larry Fuller at Amoco, Ernie Micek at Cargill, Bob Ingram at Glaxo Wellcome, Mike Volkema at Herman Miller, and Dave Whitwam at Whirlpool, are very tough CEOs who have accomplished record earnings at their companies and continue to demand better performance every year. What makes them empathetic leaders also are their abilities to identify sincerely with the emotional concerns of their employees and enable their employees to identify with them. This creates the sense of belonging and connection people need to go out and perform over the long run.

A story to illustrate what I mean: I was walking through LaGuardia Airport in New York on a Friday a few years ago, more than ready to catch the 4:00 flight home to Chicago. Just ahead of me was Bob Crandall, Chairman and CEO of American Airlines, the very definition of a tough CEO and no stranger to hotly contested marketplaces or labor negotiations. Many years ago, American was headquartered in New York, and the people at the ticket counters, mostly women, were a very senior group. Many of these women saw Crandall walking by to catch the 4:00 to Dallas, they probably were expecting him, and ran out to greet him. It was a scene more befitting a movie star, with smiles, hugs, kisses, and even a few friendly shrieks of "Bobby, Bobby!" I can't think of a more visible demonstration of identification or connection, especially from a unionized group.

It may be easier to show empathy if you have grown up in a company because people know who you are and you have worked in the same types of jobs they have. The people I cited in the paragraph above are all long-time company men. Also, it may be easier to be an empathetic leader if you are a long-time company person because you are more like your employees. Long-time exposure to cultural values, work environment, and management practices affect leaders and make them more like others in the company. Employees have to be aware of this on some level and connect easier to an insider. The language and points of reference are the same, in addition to knowing the leader and sharing values.

Can too much empathy become a weakness? Clearly empathy turns to sympathy in some situations and gets in the way of tough decisions. That's where competence has to balance empathy. Several CEOs have been fired in recent years because boards have seen them wait too long to make realistic business decisions. GM, IBM, and Kodak come to mind quickly as examples. In these cases boards seem more likely to turn to outsiders who are unencumbered by years of personal history, socialization, and friendships.

LEARNING LEADERSHIP

If competence and empathy define the effective leader, can a person be taught these things? Can leadership be learned? The myth of the heroic leader tends to describe leadership as innate characteristics present at birth.

On the other side of the argument is someone who often was described as a heroic leader, the late Vince Lombardi, Hall of Fame coach of the Green Bay Packers. Lombardi said, "Contrary to the opinions of many people, leaders are not born. Leaders are made, and they are made by effort and hard work."

Ed Dunn from Whirlpool takes the most practical approach to this issue. Dunn sees a big part of his job as creating generations of global leaders for his company. According to Dunn, "Leadership can be taught and learned, but some people have more inclination to it than others. We have to be sure we teach it to the right people—people with the right raw material. Companies waste a lot of time in leadership development on people who will never be leaders."

Earlier, I said in an ideal company everyone leads, yet I also agree with Dunn. Everyone can and should lead in their areas of responsibility, but not everyone is able to get to the top, or even close to it. You need to spend your best leadership development resources on the people most likely to provide a return on your investment.

> Spend your best leadership development resources on the people most likely to provide a return on your investment.

The need to increase the pool of leadership is causing many companies to create lists of leadership competencies and devise new and varied ways to teach them. The ways of teaching leadership are limited only by the imagination of those creating the methods, but only a handful seem to work. Research into behavior change is fairly clear that the opportunity for deep, objective, and realistic self-assessment of one's leadership character—competence and empathy as I define it—coupled with strong personal motivation to change is the most powerful way to develop leadership. Any development approach that doesn't insist on this is probably a waste of your time and money.

When done right, leadership competencies should reflect the views of today's and tomorrow's leaders about what it takes to be successful, now and in the future. These competencies will include a mix of values, knowledge, skills, abilities, experiences, and attitudes. They need to be linked closely to your company's business strategy, core values, and strategic style.

To develop its list of leadership competencies, Cargill gathered opinions from its Chairman's Leadership Forum, the top 200 officers and up-and-coming executives. Shell gathered these data from a similar group, the Chairman's Leadership Council. Shell's leadership competencies are divided into three categories, and the labels look like this:

1. Maximize what we have
   a. Priority-setting
   b. Continuous performance improvement
   c. Quality decisions
   d. Problem-solving

2. Leverage our people resources
    a. Effective conversations
    b. Effective team development
    c. Values diversity
    d. Personal responsibility for development
3. Create a future from uncertainty
    a. Dealing with ambiguity
    b. Relentless learning
    c. Business perspective
    d. Perseverance

These 12 competencies match quite well with both a current and future perspective for a company that is quickly and sharply increasing its operations focus. They also match well with the five values Shell chose to guide it through its transition. These include belief in people, trustworthiness, excellence, innovation, and sense of urgency. You can see the emphasis on both leader competence and empathy.

The specific definitions of the competencies derive from the business strategy, values, and descriptions of what it will take for successful performance that Shell gathered from its present and future leaders. Shell is engaged in action learning, mentoring, and other techniques to try to help leaders learn how to lead using these competencies. However, as Gaurdie Banister said, "The most important use of these is to hold them up as a mirror to your own behavior and figure out what you need to do to change, and then do it."

LEADERSHIP ALIGNMENT

Assuming leaders have or can develop competence and empathy, is there an optimal way for leadership to be expressed in a company? Is there a type of leader who aligns better to a company depending on the company's strategy and style? Should the personal style of the leader match the strategic style of the company? Some leaders are successful in some situations but not in others. I think this indicates that alignment of company and personal styles must be important. Without alignment, either the leader or the company is going to have to be extremely adaptable.

From the alignment perspective, companies will be better off over the long-term if a person who likes things runs an operations company, even a service business; an idea person runs a products company; and a people person runs a customers company. This is depicted in Figure 8-1.

In operations companies you want a leader who likes to make things happen fast. The drive for speed, quality and efficiency in those companies comes from the need to make things faster, better, and cheaper. The satisfaction comes from achieving and seeing the concrete results.

The products leader is a thinker, someone who takes the time to pursue the big picture and encourages others to do it too, through freedom of expression and the support to pursue their thoughts. The intellectual side of the work appeals to him or her. The reward is the big idea, the breakthrough product that changes the world.

FIGURE 8-1

Leadership Alignment

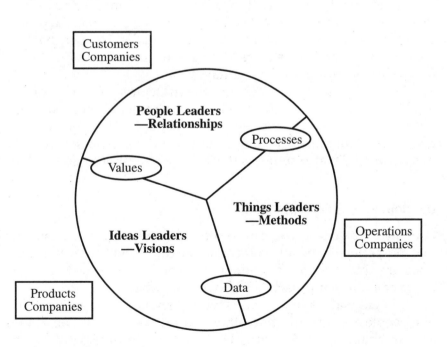

Leadership alignment probably starts all the way back at hiring, with good selection processes. As people get weeded out, or take themselves out of an organization, this type of alignment grows. By the time a person reaches the top, the alignment presumably is almost complete.

The customers leader is concerned with how people feel and wants them to enjoy their jobs, careers, organizations, and, ultimately, lives. These leaders deal with the whole person, so the person can serve the customer totally. The quality of work is judged on the quality of relationships with customers or clients.

This approach to leadership alignment suggests the potential rewards and dangers of high-level outside hires. If a leader's personal style matches the strategic style of the company and has a fresh outside perspective, I predict success for the outsider. George Fisher is an idea-oriented person who went to Kodak from Motorola, both products companies. His idea style is a good fit for Kodak. Lou Gerstner started at McKinsey, a customers company. His relationship orientation made him a great fit later for IBM. Is it just coincidental the turnaround he has led at IBM started with getting IBM back to its customers-focused roots? Arthur Martinez led Sears back to its operations focus to bring it back. Martinez is a financial professional by background, not a merchant or retailer. His penchant for measurement and his vision of serving Sears' target customer fit perfectly with Sears' operations heritage.

If personal style doesn't match the strategic style, the new high-level hire won't be in alignment. If close alignment is needed, either the person or the company will have to adapt. Since people adapt faster than companies, the onus will be on the person. Fortunately, this circle model also suggests what the person should do to adapt.

Overlap, Versatility and Change

Looking at the circle, you can see how the styles meet and overlap. The most effective people and companies are good "at the borders." They are able to move far enough into contingent areas to bring in complementary approaches without losing focus.

In personal behavior, this is widely known as *versatility*. Effective people are versatile, but retain a strong core orientation so they are not chameleons. Versatile leaders bring in diverse ideas and people while retaining core style, values, and direction.

Things and ideas have data in common, and that's where operations and products companies speak the same language. Ideas and people meet in values. Both products and customers companies tend to be held together by values. People and things come together in processes. Processes can help people understand how to work together to satisfy customers, solve problems, participate in teams, and make things.

For instance, if an idea person is hired to run a customers company, she or he should focus first on values because that will be comfortable for both person and company. As time goes on, the leader will have to get more accustomed to the people, rather than to the intellectual, implications of the values.

However, a company may hire someone with a different orientation to change the company. My circle would indicate if an operations company needs to improve its products, it should hire an idea person. If it wants to improve customer relations, it should hire a people person. These outsiders should try to move the company using data or processes as the bridges to change.

Your company probably needs all three types of people in leadership positions to be successful. You can align people to company functions according to their personal style. This puts the things people primarily into manufacturing, distribution, finance, and some sales jobs; the people people primarily into human resources and some marketing and sales jobs; and the idea people into R&D, product development, systems development, and some aspects of marketing. This diversity of styles will make for a better executive team.

Still, the person who succeeds at the very top usually has the personal style that fits with the company's strategic style, the way Dave Whitwam's things orientation fits Whirlpool, even though Whitwam came from sales and not manufacturing. Similarly, Gordon Bethune's things style helped him lead Continental back. What makes these and other leaders most effective is they have enough of the other styles to be versatile.

When the CEO is versatile and can meld people of diverse styles and backgrounds, there will be a much greater understanding of the marketplace, the customer, and what it takes to win. Just for fun I can demonstrate this by reviewing the personal leadership styles of the most successful organization around, the Chicago Bulls (see Figure 8-2). Michael Jordan leads by doing, Scottie Pippen makes the people around him better, and Phil Jackson is a versatile leader who uses Native American, Zen, and Red Holzman ideas and philoso-phies to blend individual talents and personalities together.

EMPLOYEES WITH CUSTOMERS

Ultimately what pays the bills are employee-customer interactions. By aligning to strategic style, U.S. Bancorp gets its tellers, sales, and service people to respond to customers quickly and resolve their needs fast. Learning and performance measurement practices en-able tellers to understand that "moving the line along" contributes to successful branch banking. On the other hand, a different set of management practices helps private bankers probe their high-worth customers' needs in depth and solve their unique problems. Private bankers take as much time as they need so their customers get the level of personal attention they expect.

This is alignment in action. U.S. Bancorp lines up its retail bank to operations and its relationship bank to customers. You probably experience this all the time in your various interactions with differ-ent service providers. You don't see the practices that direct them, but these are their natural outcomes. Real-life examples abound, and some of the more interesting ones come from the retail world.

FIGURE 8-2

Leadership on the Chicago Bulls

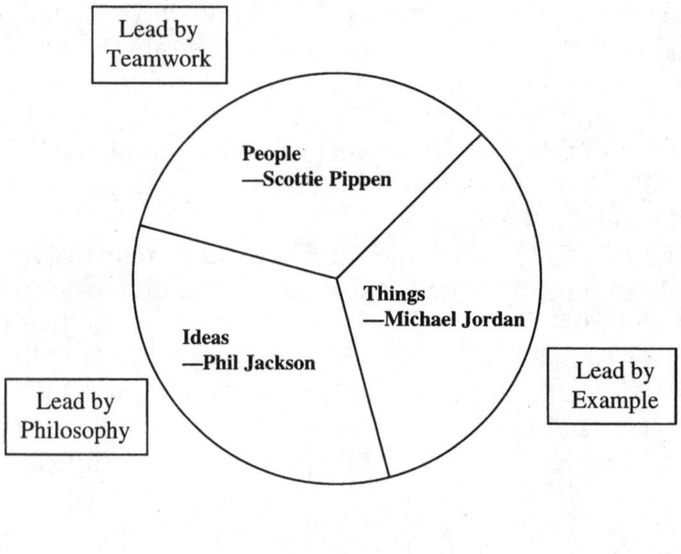

Dayton Hudson Corporation

For many years, Marshall Field's was *the* department store in Chicago, and Dayton's occupied the same premier place in Minneapolis–St. Paul. These were the signature department stores in each market, where people went for a great, hometown shopping experience based on selection and service. Each was tremendously successful in its own right and came to symbolize shopping in their respective cities. Going to Field's or Dayton's for holiday or special occasion shopping became part of family tradition in both places. In the 1980s, Dayton Hudson Corporation bought Marshall Field's and folded it into its department store division, which also included Hudson's of Detroit. Dayton Hudson also operates a midpriced division consisting of Mervyn's stores and its discount powerhouse, Target Stores.

Dayton's bought Field's in response to the ferocious retail competition that started reaching new levels through the 1980s . The rise of new types of competitors, stores like category killers, fashion outlets, and giant discounters, along with the proliferation of high-end boutiques, squeezed department stores that traditionally served the broad middle market. Department stores started suffering, and all of them eventually changed or refined their strategies to survive. Penney's went through a radical transformation, to be joined much later by Sears. Others, like Nordstrom and Bloomingdale's, refocused on their basic value offerings and made themselves better.

Dayton's and Field's went through a transformation of a different sort. The real star in the Dayton Hudson Corporation is Target. Target is a great example of an operations company with a distinctive value. It is a high-end discounter, offering merchandise at prices and quality slightly higher than Wal Mart and with a brighter, more pleasant shopping experience. The stores are lighter, the aisles are wider, the brands are somewhat better known, and there are additional services, like wedding and baby gift registration. Target also takes Dayton's, Hudson's, and Field's credit cards. Target is wildly successful, with wonderful growth and profitability, and fiercely loyal shoppers. It is the discount store of choice for many upper-middle income shoppers.

Since Target is the star of the company, its people ascended at Dayton Hudson, taking over the department store division. The new executives promptly did what executives do all the time—they set out to repeat what worked for them previously. They "Targetized" the department stores.

Since they are very talented people, they brought operations focus to the department stores where it hadn't existed, and they did it very well. They focused on the supply and delivery chains to cut costs and improve the speed and volume of transactions. Target people even invoked the same "boundaryless" term to reengineer their department stores, that was introduced by operations-oriented General Electric.

Being boundaryless enabled Target to move its systems, including talent management practices, into Dayton's, Field's, and Hudson's. Among many other actions, the new leaders centralized department store buying functions in Minneapolis, reduced the number of merchandisers, started buying more of the same merchandise for all three chains of stores, moved many parts of the merchandise to lower price points, and even centralized alterations in Minneapolis. The most notable difference to the customer, and a huge cost savings, was store personnel were cut. In most departments the sales help acted more like they did at Target. There were people to ring up sales at the register, but far fewer to really help the customer on the sales floor.

What happened is just what you would predict using the alignment framework. Employees focused on speed and efficiency instead of individualized responsiveness and problem-solving. They followed rules closely about how to handle sales and became tougher on exceptions. They became more like the bank tellers at U.S. Bancorp, friendly, but eager to move people along quickly according to procedures. This became the definition of good service.

This isn't bad, if it meets the expectations of the customer. There are many operations retailers who deliver great service within a limited framework and at low prices. Wal Mart, for example, is ranked second to the much more customers-focused Nordstrom on the well-regarded American Consumer Satisfaction Index.

Still, this change in style hasn't worked well for Dayton Hudson, whose customers were accustomed to a more service-oriented shopping experience. The department store division has lagged its competition in earnings for many years and has missed participating in the revival some department stores have enjoyed in the last few years. Dayton's, Hudson's, and Field's are frequent targets of takeover or spin-off rumors because they continue to be a drag on corporate profitability.

Recently the department store division has put more people back on the sales floor and added more upscale merchandise. Unfortunately for Dayton's, unless either customer expectations change or it realigns its management practices back to a customers company, more salespeople and more expensive clothes will not translate into higher customer satisfaction.

Sears

There is a different story going on at Sears, where its turnaround is resulting in record earnings. Sears began its transformation in 1993, about the time the famous *Fortune* magazine cover story appeared, featuring the dinosaur figures of Sears, GM, and IBM. Not many people saw much hope for the company, but, led by Arthur Martinez, Sears is restoring itself to vitality.

At Sears the transformation means refocusing on its operations history. The operations style is where Sears always has been or should have been, and it is making great strides in logistics, teamwork, merchandising, store remodeling, and measurement, among other activities. Its target shopper is a female co-head of household, married with two children, and household income between $25,000 and $55,000 annually. This is why its emphasis is on the "softer side of Sears." Increasingly, harder goods, like appliances and hardware, will be offered outside of the department store framework and in free-standing specialty stores.

Sears' research shows customers expect the right merchandise at the right prices with friendly sales help and easy returns. It can improve against these expectations by recommitting itself to operations because this strategic style fits customer expectations. To get there, Sears is using the types of workforce strategies and management practices that are part of this style. Above all, it's measuring things, tying pay to them, and treating the stores as teams.

Through extensive measurement, Sears has determined that increasing employee satisfaction leads to increasing customer satisfaction, which in turn, leads to increasing revenue growth. It has found that every five-point improvement in employee satisfaction leads to a two-point improvement in customer satisfaction the next quarter, which results in a 1.6 percent growth in revenue. With this focus, Sears measures employee satisfaction every quarter using a ten-question survey, and customer satisfaction continually, using a two-question, 60-second survey. It tracks and publicizes this data to improve financial performance.

These metrics are tied to pay. The incentive plans of the top 200 officers are based 50 percent on financial performance, 25 percent on employee satisfaction, and 25 percent on customer satisfaction. These survey metrics also give Sears leaders a way to study and improve performance on a constant basis. According to one Sears executive, these measures, and their impact on business performance and compensation, have made top managers "survey experts." They know when they move the numbers up on employee and customer satisfaction, the financial numbers and incentive awards go up too. Metrics and incentive plans are being pushed lower in the organization in a continuing fashion.

Sears also is doing a lot of training to improve associates' understanding of the retail business, their abilities in customer service, and teamwork. Learning maps and town hall meetings at the store level are designed to help associates learn about cash flow, customer expectations and satisfaction, competitors, and retail economics. They also are used to build teamwork and solicit ideas to improve the stores and customer service.

Teamwork is one of five factors influencing Sears associates' attitudes about their jobs which affects their behaviors toward customers. Sears' goal is to be as good at customer service within an operations style as Nordstrom is within its different style. Sears knows it has a very long way to go to reach that goal, but imagine how it could raise the competitive bar on customer service for Nordstrom.

The results so far are encouraging. Sears estimates it's about halfway towards its destination. Financial results are very encouraging. Total shareholder return since 1992 is over 300 percent. Employee satisfaction is good and getting better. Customer satisfaction is still the middle of the pack but is showing strong gains. Sears is intent on pushing it higher so shareholder returns become even stronger. The company is on the right track to alignment with its strong pursuit of measurement, teamwork, incentives, and process improvement.

In customers companies employee-customer interaction is proactive, probing, and personal. Walk into a Nordstrom or similar environment and a friendly, personable individual approaches you, asks how he or she can help, and works with you to help you buy something or get your needs fulfilled. In operations style stores the service tends to be fast, efficient, and helpful when it's done right. Once you link up with the Sears associate, he or she takes care of you in a quick, friendly manner. In the big-ticket commission departments, like appliances, associates will spend more time and attention on you, but they are not yet ready to help you redesign your kitchen, which might be the case if Nordstrom sold white goods.

What is the employee-customer interaction like in a products company? To find out, I asked several regular customers of Bloomingdale's and Crate and Barrel. This was an unscientific survey, but these regular shoppers were quite uniform in their reactions. They all said they could spend a long time wandering through these stores, happily looking at the terrific and exciting merchandise without being approached by a salesperson. Since there is so much to see, customers didn't necessarily want to be approached by a sales person right away. When they did need sales help, they asked for it and got it, usually well informed, and as much or as little help as they needed. Returns were no problem. Again, this is what you would expect given the organization, culture, and management practices of a products company.

EMPLOYEE TO EMPLOYEE

I will cover employee-employee interactions only in a very general way, though they are essential to delivering value to customers and bottom-line results. There is a complexity and variety to them that would require a whole separate book. These kinds of interactions do seem to be governed primarily by two things—culture and organization structure. Since culture and organization differ so much depending on the strategic style of the company, you can see alignment in operation.

Culture and Hierarchy

Culture may be the biggest influence on informal interactions, while culture and organization together guide formal ones. This suggests culture has the biggest overall impact on employee-employee interactions. Whether you are thinking about culture as the internal brand experience or high-performance culture characteristics, like achieving excellence, doing whatever it takes for the customer, and treating each other with respect, cultural issues shape employee interactions significantly.

It has been observed many times that employees who live in a "hard" or internally competitive culture interact with each other in more direct and confronting ways than people who live in softer cultures. This isn't bad or good. It just is. The opposite also is true. Employees who work in a softer culture usually have trouble confronting each other in a direct way. They aren't very good at it and have trouble handling it.

It's also clear that getting people to act differently inside a company is a much tougher and slower change than treating customers differently. Changing to meet customer needs differently has a much stronger appeal to people and is perceived to be more directly related to business success than employee-employee interactions. Also, internally there's all that culture and personal history to undo.

This internal aspect points back to organization because hierarchy is the great inhibitor to honesty in employee-employee interactions. Look at all of the effort in the last ten years to move to process management and its accompanying emphasis on teamwork. So much of that came about because functional or business unit hierarchies have people looking up to their bosses instead of out to the customer. This can preclude a realistic look at the marketplace.

Similarly, fact-based decision-making, a concept that came with Total Quality, was designed to help make more accurate decisions. I think it also came about to help move away from hierarchical decision-making, where the people on top get to call all the shots. You can see clearly when you focus on the customer, many top executives won't have all the answers because they are not as close to customers as front-line employees.

Changing Employee-Employee Interactions

If you want to change employee-employee interactions to improve business results, you need to focus on two characteristics of culture and organization: accountability and sociability. Accountability is the results dimension, and sociability is the relationship dimension. Addressing these will help you change closely related issues around values, participation, and structure.

To decide how to change things, you'll need to begin by asking:

- How much accountability should different people have at different organizational levels? For what issues? How much shared versus separate accountability should there be?
- What level of involvement in business processes is appropriate? How does this differ by process or business unit?
- Will a team structure work best, or will an individual focus? Possibly some combination?
- How should people get along with each other in the organization? Strictly business? A broader range of personal and business issues?
- Is organizational level a strong factor in interactions today? Should it be downplayed? Do you have to make a separate effort in training or restructuring to downplay it?

There are more questions to ask, but these will get you going. You can tell by reading through them that your alignment to your strategic style will have a big effect on how you answer them. In fact, you will get to three different kinds of answers based on style. These answers will tell you how to form your workforce strategy and your talent management practices to make the changes you want.

Whatever answers you come to—greater accountability at lower levels, a more relaxed hierarchy, more team spirit, more involvement in key business processes—there is a straightforward way to implement them. I see this change process, or a close variation of it, whenever I participate in attempts to change interactions on a large scale. It looks like this:

- Leaders define clearly how they want people to interact with each other (or the customer) and in what situations.
- Leaders insist the interactions have certain qualities; for instance, openness, timeliness, fact-based, participation levels, equalitarian, and so forth, and write these down into some sort of code of behavior.
- Leaders communicate this code clearly throughout the company.
- Leaders review the management practices that shape these particular interactions and change the relevant ones—staffing, organizing, learning, performing, and/or rewarding.

- Leaders insist all affected or participating employees go through some learning experiences about the change—the more action-oriented, experiential, and personal, the better.
- Leaders start the new interaction behaviors by doing them themselves—they are the role models for the new patterns.
- Leaders hold each successive level of leadership accountable for pushing the new practices through their areas until it covers everyone who is supposed to be involved.
- Leaders recognize and reward people who demonstrate the new interactions. Others who cannot or will not are counseled to change or leave.

You probably recognize this process. These steps are a big part of the transformation Gordon Bethune is leading at Continental Airlines, Arthur Martinez at Sears, and Phil Carroll at Shell. At the same time, it is possible to change interactions on a smaller scale with more limited efforts, like trying to introduce more team-based management in a specific work unit. Usually you can do this with communication, training, and rewards or recognition. These efforts may spread out past the unit as far as there are champions to push them. They won't become company-wide until leadership takes them on and follows the path I described.

CREATING THE TALENT SOLUTION

1. How would you rate yourself and other leaders on competence and empathy?
2. Does your personal style match your company's strategic style? Where are you strongest "at the borders" between styles?
3. Do your talent management practices produce the employee-customer interactions you want? How could you improve them?
4. Are your culture and organization well-suited to create the employee-employee interactions that you want?

PART TWO

ENGAGE

CHAPTER 9

Your People Are More Valuable than Ever

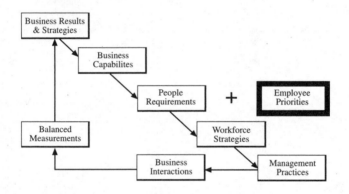

The next three chapters cover employee priorities and their importance in creating a workforce strategy, employment relationship, and talent management practices in depth. These chapters focus on the changing nature of the employment relationship as a context for engaging employees, what engagement is and how you can increase it, and the psychology of engagement and change. In this chapter you will learn about:

- Contradictions in today's employment relationship
- Why people are more valuable than ever
- The changing nature of the employment relationship
- What each side—company and employee—wants from each other
- What the immediate future holds for these relationships

TODAY'S EMPLOYMENT RELATIONSHIPS

A lot has been written on the current state of employment relation-ships and how they are very different from the old "deal" of loyalty for long-time employment that people used to have with their com-panies. When I look at what's going on, I see a mass of contradic-tions and confusions. Things can appear so bewildering, it's not possible to arrive at a firm set of conclusions.

As evidence:

- Employment is growing, but layoffs continue at a strong pace. U.S. unemployment in early 1997 hit its lowest point in the last 20 years. The U.S. economy continues to create jobs at about the rate of 200,000 a month, and by most reports, these are good jobs—well-paid, highly skilled, good working conditions. Still, layoffs in 1996 were about 8 percent higher than in 1995, almost equivalent to the recession of the early 1990s. Job elimination continues at a slightly slower rate in 1997. American Management Asso-ciation data show the same thing—job creation and job elimination coexist at the same firms, at the same time.

- Employees say they are quite satisfied with their jobs today, but they're also full of insecurity about them and concerned they will lose them. Suzanne Kenney, Hewitt's practice leader for employee communications, reports our data show 82 percent of people are satisfied with the work they do, and 84 percent are satisfied with their coworkers. Meanwhile, a recent *New York Times'* survey suggests about half of American workers are concerned about being laid off.

- People are working longer hours than ever, but they don't seem to mind. Employees now work about 163 hours—4 working weeks—more than in 1969, according to Depart-ment of Labor statistics; and 42 percent say they feel "used up" by the end of the workday, according to a study by the Families and Work Institute. However, a new study by sociologist Arlie Hochschild shows that people like the hours they work and prefer the work environment to the greater chaos of being at home. Hewitt's LifePlan Re-sources database projects to responses of more than 1 million employees nationwide and shows the item "more

time for family" is a distant tenth on a list of employees'
top ten needs, fears, and goals. Only 11 percent of employees are asking for it, compared to 42 percent who are
concerned with job security, or 38 percent concerned with
saving for retirement.

- Or are they working longer hours? Time-use experts John
  Robinson and Geoffrey Godbey contend in a new book that
  Americans have more leisure than ever. They use different
  data than the Department of Labor to claim that Americans
  are working less. The problem they see is not the amount
  of work but the pace has increased so dramatically that
  people feel rushed and out of control. Nobody disputes
  this last point, but their findings about hours worked are
  subject to much questioning and debate.

- Productivity is up, but overall wages aren't growing very
  quickly despite dropping unemployment. The increase in
  worker productivity in the U.S. in 1996 was the best in five
  years, 0.7 percent. That's hardly robust, but it's twice the
  increase in 1995. Still, the employment cost index went up
  only 2.9 percent in 1996, the same as in 1995. Some sectors
  of the economy—technology and professional services, to
  name two—and many "hot" jobs are experiencing very fast
  wage inflation. Yet, overall wage growth is slow and
  steady, just like the U.S. economy.

- Despite a growing distrust of management, people aren't
  quitting in huge numbers to start their own businesses.
  Hewitt data are similar to data from other sources and
  suggest only about one-half of employees know what to
  expect from their employers, about one-third think senior
  management knows what's on their minds, and only about
  40 percent feel that senior managers care about them.
  Similarly, a little more than half feel they are paid fairly for
  what they do, and a little less than half think promotions
  are fair at their companies. Still, the contingent workforce
  is growing as a result of changes companies are making,
  not people opting out of full-time work. New business
  formation is about the same as it always has been, mostly
  influenced by the economic cycle.

These paradoxes and confusion arise because employment relationships are in transition in many companies and in the country as a whole. There probably never was just one contract or understanding in industrial America, but the predominant one started right after the Great Depression and lasted about 50 years, until the economic restructuring of the mid-1980s. We are in the first decade of the new era, and things haven't settled yet. I suspect whatever patterns we see now are transitional and will look very different in another ten years.

This cloudy picture makes it hard to tell what's really happening with company-employee relationships today. Yet these issues have huge bearing on your abilities to create results for customers and shareholders. Your relationships with your employees shape the relationships you have with your customers and those determine what you can bring to your bottom line.

PEOPLE KEEP BECOMING MORE VALUABLE THAN EVER

There's one thing that is clear about today's employment relationships. Simply put, people are more valuable than ever to your company. How can I make such a claim? Easy—companies continue to eliminate or keep from adding jobs as much as they possibly can these days. Some of this is shrinkage to cut costs. Other reductions are due to increasing abilities to substitute technology for people.

This leads to the most important paradox in business today. If you can do much more with fewer people, then the people who are left are much more valuable to you. They are more productive and more highly skilled. They carry a lot more responsibility for the success or failure of your company on their shoulders. That's why effective talent management is so crucial to you.

> If you can do much more with fewer people, then the people who are left are much more valuable to you.

Data comparing the business results of the *Fortune 100* from 1983 to 1993 confirm this incredible increase in the value of people (see Table 9-1). This ten-year period was an era of rapid corporate shrinking. It included some very good years for the U.S. economy and some recessionary years. After 1994, *Fortune* added service companies to its list, so this represents one of the last times this comparison can be made.

Looking over the data from this ten-year period, you can see sales increased from $1.2 trillion to $1.7 trillion, about 42 percent. Inflation, measured by the Consumer Price Index, increased about 41 percent during the same period, meaning most of this increase could be accounted for by rising prices. However, the number of employees at these companies decreased by 12 percent, about 1 million. The effect of this is a tremendous increase in sales per employee, a gross measure of labor productivity. Sales per employee went from $144,578 in 1983 to $232,877, an astronomical increase of 62 percent, or 20 percent in real terms after inflation.

This was a strong period of investment in physical plants and equipment, technology, global expansion, and other working assets. Assets and assets per employee also showed tremendous growth, meaning the financial and physical resources deployed by companies for each employee went up markedly. Equity in these companies did not go up much over the period. Perhaps investors were waiting for the payoffs from these investments that appear to be occurring now.

These data clearly show your employees now carry far more responsibility for the sales, assets, and ultimately, the productivity and value of your company. Every decision you make about your employees has far greater impact on your competitive abilities than it did when you employed more people. Decisions that enable employees to serve customers better or use resources more wisely are likely to have far greater impacts than previously. Conversely, decisions that erect barriers that keep people from doing their jobs or that disrupt their relationships with you and your customers will be much more destructive to your business results.

TABLE 9-1

Productivity Increases Among Fortune 100 Companies

	1983	1993	% Change
Sales	$1.2 trillion	$1.7 trillion	+42%
Assets	$914 billion	$2 trillion	+119%
Equity	$422 billion	$494 billion	+17%
Employees	8.3 million	7.3 million	-12%
Sales/Employee	$144,578	$232,877	+62%
Assets/Employee	$110,120	$273,972	+149%
Equity/Employee	$50,843	$67,671	+33%

Since I first did this analysis three years ago, business has been able to keep pushing productivity higher by continuing to substitute technology for people. This is a primary reason for the continuing business expansion in the U.S. throughout this decade. No one knows the limits that can be achieved here, and I would be foolish to try to predict it. The more you push, and the more you are able to eliminate jobs as a result, the more valuable people become. This leads to the inescapable conclusion that companies doing the best job in building effective employment relationships and managing talent will be the biggest long-term winners.

FOUR CHARACTERISTICS OF RELATIONSHIPS

With the transitions occurring in employment relationships and the increased value of people, what can be concluded about today's employment relationships? Employment relationships in North America now are marked by four characteristics. They are:

- Market-based
- Personal, rather than job-centered
- Complex
- Changing

Let's look at each of these in turn.

Market-Based on Both Sides

Market-based employment relationships occur because external marketplaces, both customer and labor, have much greater impact than they used to have. While layoffs and downsizing, job hopping, and getting raises based on outside offers always have existed, there was more shelter from the outside world for many companies and their employees before the massive corporate restructurings of the 1980s and 1990s.

The contract really was more relational, to use Denise Rousseau's word. Companies were more likely to shield people from downturns, and employees had much longer tenure on the job, showing much more loyalty to employers that treated them well. Most reward systems—pay and benefits—were set up to provide big payoffs to people who stayed most of their careers with one company.

This appeared to be what both sides, company and employee, wanted.

This type of deal clearly is gone from many places today, though there are some exceptions. Now companies say as long as we perform and you perform, and we stay in your line of business in your location, there likely will be a place for you. If business stalls, if we exit the business line or category, if we move, or any other of a long set of contingencies, then who knows what will happen to you and your job.

For the first several years of this new market-based deal, the prevailing opinion was how terrible this is for employees. This still seems to be the predominant view in the mass media. I think things are changing, though.

To me, this market-based contract is fairer to both sides, as long as it's out in the open. Especially now, as we enter a period of an almost worldwide talent shortage, your skilled employees can do quite well if they pay more attention to the labor market and know what their skills are worth.

For example, Harvard University economist James Medoff has been advising younger workers to seek as much pay as they think they can get, and it's employers who have caused this. According to Medoff, "Employers are no longer honoring the arrangement that you are underpaid when you are young, and overpaid when you are old." Since nothing seems permanent anymore, and the pendulum is swinging heavily toward rewarding talent, skilled employees can prosper, particularly with the growing portability of benefits. Employees who are aware of this market-based contract and are willing to risk some uncertainty will do better than ever.

It's no wonder many companies are beginning to talk about regaining lost employee loyalty. They now are seeing what it costs them to lose and replace people, not only in direct personnel costs, but also in accomplishing business plans, customer retention, and quality. When there is an abundance of good labor, companies gain from the market-based contract, but when skilled labor is in short supply, it is very expensive.

If employees become as aware of this as companies seem to be, and benefits continue to become more portable, there will be a new, much fairer equilibrium established in employment relationships. In fact, Suzanne Kenney thinks this already is happening. The employees she surveys are, "much more savvy and realistic. For years, companies have been trying to get people to take more personal responsibility and show prudent risk-taking. Now people are applying those traits to their careers, and it's better for them but more costly to their employers."

The Person, Not the Job

Relationships today also are more personal and less job-focused. The emphasis in industrial America used to be on defining jobs and filling them. It may always have been true to some extent that "you made the job, and the job made you." Now, in the information economy, it's much more true that you make the job. Every hire becomes more personal and more strategic. Talent and potential are more critical than the current job you are trying to fill.

Technology has made the information available to everyone so rich and the tools so powerful that people are able to do as much or as little as they want in their work. Employees can apply as much discretionary effort toward greater results as they can give and you can elicit from them. They are no longer constrained by job descriptions unless they want to be. Instead of fixed jobs, work increasingly gets done by individuals assigned to special projects, teams, or task forces that form to accomplish a goal and then disband. "Whatever it takes" is the new reality.

Additionally, old ways of selecting and rewarding people are changing to fit this personal focus. Companies now are selecting for broader competencies and potential to grow, rather than specific job skills. This enables people to be brought in, get done whatever needs to be done in the current assignment, and then move on to other, bigger tasks.

Reward systems have become more focused on total contribution, rather than just job performance. *Contribution* means current role and behavioral performance, impact on the company, growth in responsibilities, and business results achieved. The external market plays a much larger factor than before because talent is in short supply, so there's more market pressure. The price of replacing a broader contribution costs more than just replacing a job holder.

Complexity Reigns

Employment relationships also have become more complex. There are likely to be more and different categories of relationships within a company than there used to be. Companies have gotten sharper about who is a core employee and who is more peripheral to the core business.

Shell is an example. It placed most of its internal support staff into a services company to provide many sorts of facilities, information processing, financial transactions, payroll, engineering support, and other services to its upstream, downstream, and chemical businesses. Increasingly the services company is being asked to compete with outside professional services firms to provide assistance to Shell on a cost and quality basis. Many other companies have moved to some form of this "shared services" model.

If you are a supporting employee whose main job is not finding oil in an oil company, discovering or marketing drugs in a pharmaceutical firm, or making and manufacturing semiconductors in a semiconductor company, you always have been a cost rather than a profit-maker. Still, it was more likely ten years ago that you were part of a business unit or a highly valued corporate staff. Now your staff group has been cut, or you have been moved into a centralized shared services organization where your work is being compared to outside vendors. Moreover, some or much of what you or your co-workers used to do is being outsourced. If it isn't currently done outside, it is constantly being studied to see if it can be reduced, eliminated, automated, or outsourced.

That's what being peripheral is these days. You have management constantly looking at whether what you do is valuable and should be done at all, and you have outside vendors continually figuring out how to replace you. This is not a comfortable place to be, especially if you have spent your career outside the main line organizations in your company and your money-making skills aren't in great shape. The only consolation for employees is that if they are peripheral to their companies, they can be a core employee to the outside vendor.

Core/peripheral is just one distinction in contemporary employment relationships. Companies also will include greater numbers of temporary, part-time, contract, and joint venture employees today. Is there one main type of relationship you want to have with all of these different types of employees, or are there several? How do you communicate this so people understand what you expect, and what they can expect in return?

Jack Bruner, Hewitt's practice leader for employee benefits, cautions against trying to communicate several different categories of employment relationships. Bruner notes most companies aren't too good at communicating the main one, so they shouldn't try to communicate several. Instead, he counsels companies to communicate the kind of work environment they want, create an identification with the customer, and help employees figure out their roles in the environment and the outcomes they will get when they are successful.

According to Bruner, "People want to make a meaningful contribution, but they realize it's mostly transitory. They want to see growth, meaning, money, and security while they're there. Communicate the desired environment, not a particular relationship, because that's more meaningful to people and more flexible for the employer." Bruner points to NIKE's LifeTrek as one of the most successful examples of this.

Constant Change

The last characteristic that describes employment relationships is they keep changing. What appears to be a peripheral business today may be core tomorrow and vice versa. Work that was done inside today may be done by outsiders next week. Pitney Bowes and General Electric are two companies basing more and more of their businesses on service instead of manufacturing and sales. Pitney Bowes now has become a major outsourcer of mailroom services, beyond selling postal machines. GE people have become consulting engineers, cost cutters and logistics experts, selling time and services to several of its customers in different lines of businesses, ranging from medical supplies to aircraft engines.

Every week more companies announce they are turning their information technology, accounting, benefits administration, and other functions over to outsiders. The list of functions seems to expand all the time. For example, W.W. Grainger is changing its integrated supply activities from a small, sideline business into a major business unit and direction. It is gaining long-term contracts to replace parts of client purchasing departments and handle huge portions of their supply needs. This has gone from being peripheral to core for Grainger, but it has gone from peripheral to nonexistent for its clients.

When companies change their relative emphasis on lines of business or functions, they cast huge uncertainty onto their employees, who now are valued like pieces of the business, not enduring assets. Many companies compound this by not communicating, re-training, or redeploying. This costs you a tremendous opportunity, because it misses how valuable talented people are today and the increased loyalty and engagement you get from someone you re-tain.

Some of this is caused by lack of company awareness, and some of it comes about because so many organizations are so weak at internal redeployment. They end up casting people aside and sending the message to employees: Don't get too comfortable in whatever you're doing. I have noted how expensive this can be, but it will take an even greater scarcity of skilled employees for this situation to change. In the meantime, companies run the risk of losing employees who might be strong contributors to new business ventures as things keep changing.

WHAT EMPLOYERS WANT, WHAT EMPLOYEES NEED

The content of employment relationships depends on what companies expect from their employees and what employees expect from them. These will be unique to every company, since expectations reflect company values. Still, I can summarize from experience with several organizations what the mutual expectations of companies and employees seem to be today (see Table 9-2).

TABLE 9-2

Mutual Responsibilities

What Companies Need from Their Employees
- A sense of urgency
- Results
- Learning
- Collaboration

What Employees Need from Their Companies
- Freedom from worry
- Freedom to focus
- Freedom to learn
- Freedom to try new things, take risks, and make mistakes

Company Wants

Businesses expect basic values from their employees—honesty, integrity, ethical behavior, and compliance with law. Beyond those, companies have at least four performance expectations they need from their employees in much greater quantities than before: a sense of urgency, results, learning, and collaboration.

A Sense of Urgency

Your company probably expects a much greater sense of urgency from your employees now. Employees have to work as if their jobs depended on it—in most cases they do. Action has to be taken immediately because your customers won't wait. Performance delayed is performance failed. If there are fewer people to do the work, there is less margin for error and less tolerance for nonperformance.

> People who put their heads in the sand and wait for the change to pass are likely to be run over.

A further aspect of this is the need for quicker acceptance of change. Organizations are demanding their employees adapt to new situations and processes fast, without lots of hand-holding, stalling, fretting, sabotage, or complaint. People who put their heads in the sand and wait for the change to pass are likely to be run over, if not by the current change, then by the next one. Simultaneous, complex changes are the norm now, and your people have to get used to them.

Results

When you think about the three types of customer value, remember customer expectations are not stagnant. They keep going up all the time. This means your employees need to take accountability for producing levels of results far beyond what they are used to doing, and these levels keep rising. The quality movement and its emphasis on customer satisfaction has helped make most of us grumpy consumers. We expect high performance from our purchases all the time, and we are quick to scream when we don't get it. A friend says she "fires" a store if she doesn't get fabulous service. With competitive suppliers appearing worldwide, there's almost always somebody else ready to provide goods or services better and/or cheaper to someone looking for more value. The only sure thing is that demands for better results will continue to grow.

Learning

The only way to produce these kinds of increasing results is to continuously learn new skills and ways to do things. You have to keep learning to keep adding "smart value" to products and services. If your employees stand still in learning, they will stand still in results and fall behind.

I can remember discussing performance issues with clients years ago and often hearing from them that it was okay to have some people just do their basic jobs from 9:00 to 5:00, while the stars and fast trackers pushed the company ahead. Clients don't say that anymore. Today everyone has to be a go-getter when it comes to learning. If people aren't learning, they are jeopardizing their performance and your company's competitiveness.

Collaboration

Your employees need to collaborate in new ways, one-to-one, on permanent and temporary teams, within, across, and outside your company. Even if your basic organizational unit is the individual and not the team, you still have to generate and share information faster than ever to remain competitive. Electronic databases and networks are useless unless people populate them with knowledge. In many professional service firms, employees are evaluated on how much they contribute to knowledge networks.

The best way to share knowledge and create new results is through collaboration. Hoarding knowledge to protect turf is counterproductive at best, and highly destructive in the worst cases. It's also impossible when boundaries between functions are disappearing and your total supply chains start at your vendors, run through your company, and end with your customers.

No doubt you have other, more specific things you expect from your employees, but every list I have seen in the last several years includes a sense of urgency, results, learning, and collaboration.

Employee Needs

What's the other side of the equation? What do your employees expect from you? Your situation will be unique, but I can generalize from observing many organizations. I equate these employee expectations with the four freedoms that President Franklin D. Roosevelt expressed on the eve of World War II. Employees want four freedoms from their employers today: freedom from worry, freedom to focus, freedom to learn, and freedom to take risks.

These employee expectations match up closely with company expectations. Again, what your company needs to have from your employees to be successful is similar to what your employees need from you so they can be successful. Done right, there should be mutual interdependence and simultaneous success.

Freedom from Worry

Your employees can't be worried about their social, psychological, or physical safety and be expected to perform at the high levels you need. You have to free your workplaces from obstacles to doing a good job, like safety risks, environmental hazards, inadequate tools, mental or sexual harassment or abuse, discrimination, and above all, bad management. Of all of these obstacles, companies have done the least to remove bad management. Hewitt data suggest North American employees think their supervisors lack the skills, training, motivation, and rewards to provide effective people management.

Freedom to Focus

If freedom from worry takes care of basic needs, then freedom to focus removes concerns about current life situations, pay, and benefits. This kind of focus means being on the job psychologically as well as physically. Earlier I said employees seem to have become more realistic about the impermanence of their jobs. People are concerned about losing their jobs, but they no longer are afraid. Good economic times and seeing others go through transitions successfully seem to have "toughened" people.

One employee need that has remained constant is fair treatment. Your employees will list fair treatment in performance evaluation, pay, and promotion as top on their list of concerns about how you treat them. Fairness sets up the basis for respect and the other workplaces values that will make you an attractive employer. However, as I noted earlier, fairness does not have to mean slavish adherence to consistency. Different business strategies may mean reasonable differences in what constitutes fair employee treatment.

This is another reason to decentralize if your company is pursuing different business strategies through different strategic styles.

Since so many people are working longer hours and returning more economic value, many companies are providing more support for taking care of home/life concerns. Competitive and reasonable levels of pay, health-care benefits, and long-term compensation for retirement now are just a starting point, even if many of these today are more variable and tied to performance. The best employers are listening to their employees and stepping forward to offer some form of assistance with child-care, elder-care, health and fitness, time management and alternative work schedules, mortgage and education savings, investment education, and many day-to-day conveniences like access to car repair, dry cleaning, messenger services, even already-cooked meals to take home. Many of these are low-cost efforts that are more than paid for by higher focus and productivity.

Freedom to Learn

Your employees have gotten the message about learning. Many understand that it now has to be at least a career-long process. Employees need help in finding and funding learning opportunities, as well as being free to take advantage of them. Some companies have become famous for providing learning opportunities—Chaparral Steel, Levi Strauss, USAA, just to name a few. In-house training, educational reimbursement, and easy access to community education are some of the more effective things employers do.

Freedom to Take Risks

Learning, collaborating, and pushing hard and fast to achieve stretch results require people to take calculated risks. Taking risks means your people will make more mistakes and fail more often. Your employees will do this when they know they won't be punished if prudent and appropriate risks don't work out well. People have to feel they can go outside existing procedures and policies to delight customers, innovate, and solve problems without being punished for the occasional failure. Earlier I noted that this kind of freedom is more likely in products and customers companies, but all types of organizations have to provide this freedom or it will not occur.

RESOLVING CONTRADICTIONS

Having reviewed the current state of employment relationships, can the contradictions I cited at the beginning of this chapter be resolved? Can resolving them lead to better understanding of what's going on between companies and employees? Can you use that knowledge to improve your employment relationships and business results? The answer to all of these questions is "yes." Here's where things are today and where they may go tomorrow.

Obviously, companies are leaner today than they were 10–15 years ago. They are more efficient and productive, and use technology to do more with less. Fierce competition has them more focused on doing what they do well and trying harder to avoid overextending their reach. The feedback from even minor missteps is immediate and painful.

Being lean has huge payoffs in cycle time, decision-making, and economic value creation, so it's clear that smart companies will continue to try to operate that way. They will not add jobs unless they have to, will use layoffs more surgically and strategically, and won't use a shotgun approach. They will continue to eliminate jobs as technology enables them to, or as they exit businesses and locations. Most of this elimination will be on a much smaller scale than the massive cost cutting of the past. Business results have shown that massive cost cutting of people and operations is born of desperation and only marginally successful.

> Really smart companies will try to redeploy people as much as practical.

Since globalization and new technologies are bringing a new era of growth to those who are capable of taking advantage of it, namely the focused, lean, and nimble, job elimination and growth will continue side-by-side. Growth will create new jobs in different lines of business and locations. Really smart companies will try to redeploy people as much as practical because they understand experience and loyalty bring a lot to the bottom line, even though redeployment often seems more challenging than hiring.

This means the talent left in companies not only has more challenging work to do but is more valuable, and will demand to be treated better. Lean companies with great technologies offer huge personal growth opportunities for people. Employees can stretch themselves as far as they want, and achievement-oriented people love to stretch themselves. This feeds their sense of mastery—the desire to be the best—which is an almost universal motivation.

More challenging work provides more psychological rewards to people, but people are working more, and they're tired. They complain about it, but this seems like it's more to relieve stress because high performers aren't cutting back much or even voluntarily leaving big companies in large numbers. Some are doing this, but more people appear to be concerned about securing their futures. Given a choice between increased work and pay, versus increased time off, more people still pick the work and pay. The exceptions to this are people with awful jobs, and the dwindling number of people in unions who still are asking for both more pay and more time off.

Additionally, there's some evidence that working conditions are getting better. Thanks to TQM and reengineering, along with workplace regulations and the growing psychological awareness of the educated population, job tasks are more complex and interesting. There's not nearly as much mindless, "rivethead" work anymore—more people are in teams or doing broader, enriched jobs.

Also some of the worst management behavior is gone. There are still plenty of insensitive people in supervisory and management jobs, but considerable time and money have been spent on supervisory training. Talented people are quicker to complain or sue about abuse and harassment, so that there may be less really bad management than there used to be. Skilled employees can and do change jobs because of bad management in a growing economy. Finally, there's less management than there used to be since companies have flattened their structures. This has to be a positive development.

Pay and Benefits Are Increasing

Along with working conditions, pay and benefits keep getting better all the time. Through the first half of 1997, pay and benefit inflation has been kept in check, though real income is starting to grow for the first time in years. Additionally, this low inflation masks the fact that educated and skilled individuals are making a lot more money. Not everyone is sharing this bounty, but enough are that the overall economy continues its long expansion fueled by consumer spending.

Leading employers also are doing some extraordinary things with work/family and convenience benefits, and these innovations are trickling out to other companies. Who would have thought 20 years ago that you could pick up a hot meal at your company cafeteria and take it home for dinner at a fraction of what you would pay in a restaurant? Or that an employee could call a toll-free number to get help with elder-care in another part of the country? Or business casual would replace business suits as the mode of dress for salaried and professional workers? Yet these things are not unusual anymore, and all of them make the workplace better for employees. Every day you can read about another employer who is trying something new to meet a broader range of employee needs.

Certainly there are some real problems and resentments, and I am not hopelessly optimistic. A huge number of workers have fears about job security, even those who are skilled, have "toughened up," and know that things are impermanent. There is resentment about the otherworldly amounts being paid to executives. This has put a distance between employees and executives and contributed to employee feelings of mistrust and not being valued. Many employees think they would be quickly sacrificed for more stock options if some executives were given the choice. Some people can't get the full-time, secure work they want. Finally, there is the problem of what to do with people who aren't as highly skilled, because they will be left behind. Almost one-third of the U.S. workforce is stuck in low-paying jobs.

Realistic Relationships

Still, work life will keep getting better for talented employees, and I think it's because of the market-based employment relationship. This forces employers and employees into an adult relationship based on realism, performance, and market worth. Unrealistic expectations, inappropriate demands, and immature dependencies are disappearing on both sides. To meet all of the hurdles that competition poses, and to achieve the high levels of psychological and financial rewards that are available, both sides have to deal with each other in more effective and positive ways. Adversarial relationships cost too much.

This also points the way to everyone who wants to do better. Get an education and work hard. The more skills and talents you can develop, and the more you contribute, the more you'll get paid and the better you will be treated. There is a way up through this workforce that begins with low-paying work and steadily, usually slowly, progresses up to increasingly better jobs based on skills and performance.

This is a U.S., and maybe U.K., perspective, derived from the massive economic restructurings that both countries have experienced. Other mature European economies have not yet restructured the way we have, and some resist doing it or feel it's the wrong economic model. Japan is just beginning to realize that it must go through some deregulation to compete more effectively on a global basis. China and other Asian/Pacific nations who are less developed economically have very different cultural feelings about work and the relationships between people, their employers, and other social institutions. So this view is unique to these places, and I think, to this point in time.

Indeed, my hazy crystal ball says the pendulum is swinging dramatically in favor of skilled, educated people in the very near future. We should be just beginning a very positive era in employment relationships from these employees' points of view. I foresee a time in the next few years when smart employees will be able to greatly increase their expectations and demands on their employers, and employers will have to deliver on them or fall very short of talent.

My prediction comes because information and knowledge keep playing a bigger part in value and wealth creation in advanced economies. Information and knowledge arise from human talent. There's really no other source. There are more markets than producers in the world so accelerating global competition will put even more pressure on talented people to produce, just as talent becomes more scarce in the next several years. This will produce the rather ironic and wonderful result that the same information technology that makes job elimination an everyday occurrence also will yield an era of great abundance for talented employees who can deliver knowledge-rich goods and services.

How can you use this information to become a more attractive employer to get the people you need and build the employment relationship you want? Follow these steps:

- Identify the kind of employment relationships you need to have with your various groups of employees.
- Communicate the type of work environment you are trying to build.
- Provide the most competitive compensation, benefits, and working conditions you can afford.

- Create challenging work and outstanding training, along with the best work tools you can, so people are able to achieve excellence.
- Most importantly, treat people like adults, with respect, dignity, and mutual expectations of support and success.

CREATING THE TALENT SOLUTION

1. Describe the types of employment relationships you have now with your people. How well do they match up with what you need from them to create extraordinary business results?

2. What do you need from your employees? What do they need from you? How open and explicit have you been about this with them?

3. Have you made it easy for people to stay focused and contribute as much as possible? What more could you afford to do?

Engage Your Employees to Energize Results

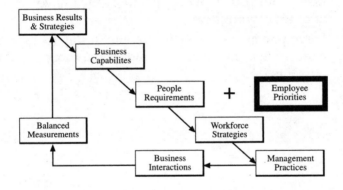

Your employment relationship forms the environment for how you respond to and engage employees. Now you need to go beyond that and determine how to engage your employees to create results. In this chapter, you'll learn:

- A definition of engagement and why it's important
- Some simple and direct ideas about how to engage employees
- A clear picture of how alignment and engagement fit together
- An understanding of employees' search for meaning and what you can do to create a more meaningful work experience

RESPONDING TO EMPLOYEES

A quick story: Some years ago, I was flying with a group of Chevron managers on a benchmarking trip. We boarded our flight and encountered a three-hour ground delay on a hot, steamy tarmac. The airline had just acquired a competitor, and the flight attendants were from the acquired airline.

The acquiring airline had decided to fold its new employees into it, so the flight attendants had to buy new uniforms, learn new procedures, and so forth. However, the airline refused to pay the new flight attendants according to its much higher pay schedules. This situation created a two-class system. Attendants flew side-by-side, dressed the same, and followed the same policies, but one group was paid much more than the others.

As the hours wore on, the inside of the plane grew hotter. People were sweating, and tempers grew shorter. To add to our misery, there had been no drink service the whole time. Finally, in the nicest voice I could muster, I asked a nearby attendant why there hadn't been any beverage service while we sat roasting on the ground. Her quick and sharp reply: "This airline doesn't give a _____ about me, and it doesn't give a ____ about you, either." That was the end of our conversation. The seven people I was flying with all vowed not to use that airline again. I kept my promise for three years, and I had been a frequent flyer on that airline.

You can see the effect of a lousy employment relationship on service behavior. It's direct! Aligning to business strategy and delivering value to your customers clearly requires you to consider employee needs and wants.

It's one thing to say what you want to do with your workforce. It's quite another to make it happen. To get, keep, and move talented people in the direction you want to go, you have to respond to their priorities and motivations, or somebody else will. Bill Gates has been quoted as saying, "Take our 20 best people away, and I tell you that Microsoft would become an unimportant company." That applies to every company, not just one of the most successful in the world for the last 20 years.

You may think this only matters in a service or knowledge business, but it's not true. A recent study showed that while seven of ten service workers have direct contact with customers, four of ten manufacturing workers do too. You cannot create and implement an effective business strategy without a supporting workforce strategy and a responsive employment relationship, regardless of your industry.

ENGAGEMENT AND WHY IT MATTERS

Smart companies go beyond just responding to their employees. I use the term *engagement* to tell you what you should do to go beyond just responding so you can enlist your employees to achieve extraordinary results. Then you'll become an attractive employer and get the talent you need to succeed.

A brief definition of *engagement* is putting "above and beyond" energy and dedication into what you do. This energy shows up in many ways; most of all, creating outstanding value for the customer and the enterprise. I recently heard a General Motors executive say their business turnaround now depends on having "excited" employees. That's another "E" word, like enthusiastic, engaged, and energized. They all describe what I mean.

Engagement may strike you as a strange term for discussing how to relate to your workforce. You may equate it with a more intimate set of activities, like the step between courtship and marriage. That's why I picked it. You really have to engage employees in an emotional sense if you want them to deliver big.

> If you want employees to deliver big, engage them in an emotional sense.

Think about it. "Being engaged" for most people is a pretty wonderful time. Engaged people are excited and enthusiastic. They devote a lot of time and energy to their relationship. They eagerly anticipate the joy and security of making a commitment and entering into a long-term relationship. Even when the marriage doesn't work, most people look back on their engagement with fondness, a pleasurable and memorable experience. They often remember it as a period filled with growth, as they learned new ways to relate to another person.

Now look at the last paragraph again. Pick out the words and phrases that describe engagement—excited, enthusiastic, devote a lot of time and energy, eagerly anticipate, fondness, pleasurable, memorable, filled with growth, learn new ways to relate. Is that how you would like your workforce to feel about their jobs and company? Would those feelings produce great discretionary effort and productivity? Wouldn't an engaged workplace make it easier to attract talented people? Do you think engaging employees is a big reason why Southwest and Continental ground and flight crews deliver on-time flights and customer satisfaction? Could Whirlpool build reliability into their washers and dryers without engaged employees? Could NIKE designers create new trends in athletic fashions without them?

The opposite of engagement is alienation, just like the flight attendant in my earlier story. I have a very hard time thinking of a great business built on alienation. On the other hand, I can think of several that have sunk when employees became alienated.

ALIGNMENT AND ENGAGEMENT

Alignment and engagement are not two separate topics. They are complementary parts of the same process. You probably can achieve some alignment for a while without really engaging your workforce, but it wouldn't last. Nor do I think you would get very high levels of performance for very long. A high-performance culture requires an aligned and engaged workforce.

One reason for this was explained very powerfully by my Hewitt colleague John Bausch, a communications consultant. John notes that alignment from the company perspective looks like Figure 10-1.

FIGURE 10-1

Alignment from the Company's Perspective

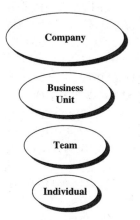

In this view the company is the big player, pushing its message down through successively smaller levels. Each level is responsible for lining up the next level to implement the desired direction or change.

However, to the employee alignment looks like Figure 10-2.

From the employees' view, they're the center of the universe. What and how, or at least how well, they do things is up to them. Your business unit and company are distant influences on their behaviors.

The importance of these two drawings is the relationship of alignment to engagement. Employees see things from their vantage points, the world immediately around them. To get them aligned to your corporate, business unit, or team direction, you have to engage them, help them see their roles in delivering business results and why it's important to them—what's in it for them—so they can put the perspectives together. This enables them to equate your company's direction with their own needs. This is what true alignment and engagement look like as illustrated in Figure 10-3.

GETTING ENGAGED

If engagement is this important, then your first question has to be how to engage your employees. There's a great story that answers this.

The Fighting Illini

After 13 years, the energy had run out of the very successful basketball program of University of Illinois head coach Lou Henson. From regular trips to the NCAA tournament throughout the 1980s and outstanding players who went on to great NBA careers, the Fighting Illini fell to ninth in the Big Ten in 1995–1996. Henson stepped down; long-time, popular assistant coach Jimmy Collins was passed over for the top job; and several players threatened to quit. This, and a lack of experienced big men, was the tough situation facing new coach Lon Kruger when he joined the program from the University of Florida.

Yet in his first year Kruger succeeded beyond all expectations. The Illini won more than 20 games, finished third in the conference,

FIGURE 10-2

Alignment from the Employee's Perspective

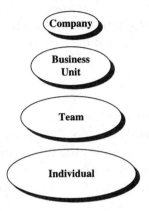

and won their first-round game in the NCAA tournament. How did Kruger do it? He attributes his success to helping the players develop an "ownership interest" in the team.

At the start of the season, he didn't tell the players what style of basketball they were going to play. Instead, he asked them what they wanted to do—play up-tempo or slow it down. Once they decided, he asked them what they thought they needed to do to make it work, and they helped him design an extraordinarily rigorous training program. This was unheard-of in big-time college sports. On a Chicago radio sports show the hosts spent their whole program expressing disbelief after an Illini player told them of Kruger's methods.

> If you want engagement, enthusiasm, and energy from your employees, show these things to them.

Kruger's ownership interest went beyond the gym. He paid attention not only to the players' basketball activities, but also helped them with academics, social issues, nutrition, mental attitude, and general health. He kept the lines of communication so open to players and their parents that one parent was quoted as saying, "The whole staff is interested in the kids' whole well-being," not exactly a common sentiment in the high-pressure, exploitative world of college basketball.

What happened here? Is there a lesson for business? Clearly there is (and I am not a U of I alum or fan), and it's as old as the Golden Rule—you get in life what you give. When you show genuine interest in people, that's what you get back. If you want engagement, enthusiasm, and energy from your employees, show these things to them. They'll show it back to you and your customers.

HOW TO ENGAGE

Excited employees, like the members of Lon Kruger's basketball team, give rise to extraordinary results and tight emotional bonds to their organizations. This enables them to keep producing and helping each other during bad times and good. Excited and engaged employees are one necessary outcome if you seek great long-term success.

How can you generate these kinds of behaviors? What can you do to establish the levels of engagement that will build enduring and exceptional value?

The answers to these questions remind me of a story I once heard about the shortest management article ever written. The whole

FIGURE 10-3

True Alignment and Engagement

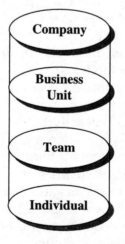

article consisted of two sentences that went something close to this: *Researchers have finally, definitively determined how to figure out what motivates your employees. The method: ask them.*

This stands out in Lon Kruger's approach. He didn't come in and tell his players what style he wanted them to play, though he had some ideas about what they should do. He asked and listened to them so they would become committed to a plan and own it.

Long-term engagement is more difficult, but the underlying principles are the same. They are:

- Explain
- Ask
- Involve

Explain

Explain means helping people see the big picture so they know where you are going, what you are trying to do to get there, how they can contribute, and what's in it for them to help. These are the four things I said earlier that every employee wants to know. You need to capture people's attention, define what you need from them, and help them understand the outcomes. There are different ways to do this, depending on what fits your style and the style of the different people to whom you are communicating.

Bob Creviston, senior vice president at Kellogg, uses the one-to-one or small group approach. According to Bob, "Just sit down with your people and start talking. There's always enough time for these kinds of meetings—fifteen minutes here, an hour there. Let people interact and see both sides. People get a lot more value out of this than big, once- or twice-a-year formal sessions."

Kent Norby, vice president at Cargill, says, "You have to help people understand more about the business, the big picture as well as operations. Help them understand how to get close to the customer and what the business needs them to do about it."

Ask

This is where many companies go wrong. They still tell people what to do. Far better to ask them how they can contribute. Asking is the start of participating, and participating leads to involvement, which leads to commitment.

I used to demonstrate this very simply in training programs with this little example. If I tell you it's a nice day outside, you can nod, grunt, look up, or just keep walking away if you want. My comment, as innocuous as it is, probably didn't even register with you. However, if I ask you what's the weather like today, you have to stop and think, if only for a second. The power of asking is that it requires thinking. That is the prerequisite for thoughtful participation.

Gaurdie Banister, president of Shell Continental Companies, says this is how Shell is bringing its business transformation to employees. "We are conducting workshops at all levels where we explain basic directions. Then managers stop talking and start listening. We ask about the assumptions people are making in developing their thinking so we get a greater depth of understanding. This helps us suspend our assumptions or preconceived ideas about where people are coming from."

Ed Dunn, senior vice president at Whirlpool, uses a similar approach. In the Whirlpool High-Performance Culture Initiative, 45,000 employees worldwide have attended a workshop designed to engage them in lifting the company to a higher level of performance. Dunn notes that the workshop asks employees to answer questions like, "What makes Whirlpool special?" "What can we do to make it more special?" According to Dunn, the important thing is to tap into employee pride, and you can only do that by asking what makes them proud.

Of course, it's absolutely essential that if you are going to ask, you have to listen. It's far worse to ask and not listen than not to have asked at all. This is where a lot of engagement processes run into trouble. Employees are skeptical about whether the company really cares what they think. I have worked on many of client task forces where members were absolutely convinced the answer to what they were charged to do had been preordained by management. It's extremely difficult to motivate a team under those circumstances. You have to convince them management has an open mind.

You cannot possibly use all employee suggestions, but you can let all employees know they have been heard. David Grainger ran W.W. Grainger for years as CEO and chairman. He made it a practice to respond to every employee letter, phone call, or e-mail with a letter, call, or visit. Employees were astounded the chairman took the time, but the commitment it built was legendary.

Involve

When your direction is explained, questions asked, and answers out on the table, then you need to involve people in moving things forward. The level of involvement will vary with the issue at hand. Involvement carries risks and concerns.

Nancy Siska, Cargill vice president, says, "People need to own the problems they bring to you and help to solve them. It sounds basic but it works to reduce cynicism. The hard part for management is to be open to their solutions."

At Amoco, Wayne Anderson, senior vice president, says people want involvement in key parts of changing work processes and solving problems, but not all parts. "People want to know they are making a difference. This is a big psychological motivator and source of meaning. But not everyone wants the responsibility of making decisions. Still, just telling people what to do doesn't get buy-in."

Bob Creviston puts it this way, "Employees want a boss, but not to tell them what to do all the time. The boss needs to be a resource to help them, make big decisions, and resolve big problems. The questions employees ask are how much influence do I have in the process and how much freedom do I have to implement. You have to get that clear early on in your relationship so you don't have to review it every time."

The levels of autonomy and influence people have will be different depending on the type of company they are in, and the specific decision-making processes. Products and customers companies generally provide more freedom than do operations companies, but this also will vary by issue. For instance, in its speed and convenience distribution business, Grainger tries to let each distribution center run like its own small business, with a lot of freedom but the advantage of centralized logistics and information systems.

> Command-and-control companies have a hard time getting and keeping creative people.

The one thing that's absolutely clear is that telling people what to do all the time deadens their initiative and commitment. With today's workforce, command-and-control companies have a hard time getting and keeping creative people. Mistakes always will be made in involvement processes, but it's essential to keep doing and improving them to get closer to customers and create more results.

THE SEARCH FOR MEANING

The engagement I have been describing creates a psychological bond between employees and your company. This attachment is essential for you to execute your desired business and workforce strategies. Evidence suggests establishing this bond is even more critical to your success today.

- North American companies have gotten about all they can out of downsizing and reengineering. The order of the day is growth, for many on a global scale.
- The downsizing and restructuring of large companies that occurred may have been painfully necessary, but it broke the bond that existed between companies and their employees. Even at companies that didn't downsize, there is less faith in the employer than there used to be.
- Growth requires people, and there is a shrinking pool of available talent. To attract skilled people, you are going to need to be seen as a great place to work.
- Not just growth, but profitability, increasingly is a function of the quality of human talent you can attract and retain. The economic value of intangible assets is increasing quickly relative to tangible ones, and the root source of all intangible assets is people.

Beyond these issues, there's something else. The baby boom, the largest and most influential part of the North American and European working population, is entering middle-age and the last phase of its working career. This is the era of life psychologist Erik Erikson called "generativity," a time when people start to look back and ask, "Was it all worthwhile?", "Did what I do mean anything?"

In earlier generations, except for the self-employed, much of people's sense of meaning at work was derived from the identity of their companies. That was another reward—perhaps the ultimate psychological reward—that employees got for the 40 (or so) years of life they gave to one employer. With that bond broken, something else has to take its place. The demanding generation of baby boomers is starting to insist upon it.

What's left as a source of meaning is the work itself. The job tasks, or the environment surrounding those tasks, has to be engaging enough to make up for the lost employee-company bond. Even if the company-employee bond is still strong, engaging work or an appealing workplace may be required to make up for the greater number of hours companies are demanding.

When it comes to creating meaningful work, there are two essentials:

- A sense of ownership
- A feeling of intimacy in the workplace

Ownership

A sense of ownership is a function of three things: 1) employee information about how the company operates; 2) employee influence over their work; and 3) a financial stake in the business. According to Judy Lindquist, who leads Hewitt's global consulting in employee ownership, none of these items by itself is as strong as all three together.

Judy says, "The most powerful aspects of engagement don't just happen by plunking in financial ownership or providing more business education and participation. Financial ownership should be a platform for communicating more about the business, how you measure performance, and how employees can contribute. More information and impact should carry a financial stake." These bring you back again to the things employees need to know and companies need them to know to be successful.

Actually, companies seem to be doing a better job of putting a financial stake in employees' hands. In 1997, employees owned more than 6 percent of all corporate equity—well over $500 billion. This ownership takes many forms, including ESOPs, stock bonuses, investment options in 401(k) plans, stock options, and stock purchase plans. The trend also is to keep putting more stock in employees' hands. Many companies in the last several years have provided larger ownership opportunities to broad groups of employees, among them Amoco, Boeing, Cargill, DuPont, PepsiCo, Microsoft, NCR, Tellabs, and Whirlpool.

In addition to equity participation, a financial stake also can be offered through variable pay opportunities. Hewitt data show that about two-thirds of U.S. companies offer broad-based incentive or bonus opportunities to nonexecutive, nonsales employees. After a steady increase in the number of these plans from the mid-1980s through the early 1990s, the number of employers offering them has not grown much in the last few years. However, companies who provide them continue to increase the size of the award possibilities and expand the numbers of employees who are eligible.

These financial plans by themselves are valuable. Wayne Anderson of Amoco says, "Something magical happens when you put stock in someone's hands." An incentive plan may drive specific goal achievement, while stock ownership and cash profit-sharing plans have more effect on attitudes. I compare the two as illustrated in Figure 10-4.

You can get a more direct, immediate impact from an incentive plan, but you may get a more long-term and broader company perspective from equity or cash profit-sharing. Equity and profit-sharing put a bigger burden on your company to explain what employees should be doing to improve financial and operating results because this won't be immediately obvious from the reward vehicle. It will be in a well-designed incentive plan.

Hewitt information and data from the National Center for Employee Ownership show improved performance does not magically occur with stock participation alone. You must have other complementary efforts towards greater information and influence. Effective performance management is a must, but it may not be enough to build a truly engaged workforce. You need more ongoing efforts at participation and involvement.

FIGURE 10-4

Impact of Incentive Plans versus Equity or Profit-Sharing

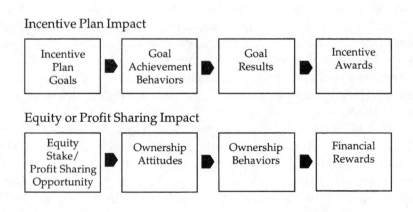

Intimacy

This leads me to intimacy, the need to feel close to the work and the workplace. Like engagement, this may not be a word you are used to seeing in business. Yet people who "love" their work are excited by it and engaged by it—exactly the outcomes you need to deliver lasting results. It's intimacy in terms of feelings of closeness, familiarity, and maybe a little passion. It only comes when people are informed, involved, and have some worthwhile influence over what they do.

So far, you have seen several ways companies can build engagement, leading to intimacy and meaning in work. Two other ideas are worth taking up briefly: 1) shrinking organization size, and 2) reducing hierarchy, especially moving to self-organization.

Size

Large organizations can make intimacy impossible. Intimacy is born of immediacy and involvement, and you can't get those two things in a large work group. At Levi Strauss, experience with work teams on the production floor showed the appropriate team size was from 8 to 12 people. Beyond that, it was too difficult to coordinate a highly interdependent sewing process.

It has been said that after 20 people, a business no longer feels like a sole proprietorship. I experienced this in the growth of the practice I lead at Hewitt. Once we got past 20, it was impossible to know everyone well and be as closely involved with people as I once was.

Microsoft often limits development teams to 35 people, and even then, splits them into smaller subteams. This is a product of the company's past when it was smaller and more intimate. Bill Gates turned this into a management practice so people on development teams get to know each other and take personal responsibility.

W.L. Gore has found the absolute limit to a business unit is 150 people. Bigger than that and the leadership team cannot know everyone personally. As soon as a business unit gets much larger than 150, Gore splits it into a new unit. The Gore environment, especially the sponsorship relationship, quality culture, and reward and recognition practices, demands that everyone know each other in the business unit.

I think Gore is really onto something wise. Keeping a limit of 150 and then breaking off new units enables Gore to manage in ways that help build tight bonds between Gore associates and the company. Personal associations grow, and an informal management style reigns. People know each other and expect one another to take responsibility for quality work. Recognition practices mean something because they can be personalized. It's possible to get meaningful, yet consistent, feedback and rewards because people are known quantities, but there are enough of them to look across a good-sized group. Also, Gore's preferred "lattice" style organization can take hold because people can work the multiple connection points face-to-face. Finally, and perhaps most importantly, business units stay flat so people can remain close to their customers, and nobody can get too removed from the day-to-day work.

Certainly your structure must follow from your strategy, but keeping units small makes possible the kind of intimacy that helps people find meaning in work. If you use teams or smaller workgroups, or continually subdivide business units, you will put pressure on your talent management practices to be effective. At the same time, it will give them some powerful, natural advantages that should help them work better. Small size also has the benefit of reducing hierarchy, another inherent opponent of intimacy.

Hierarchy

Hierarchy reduces intimacy because it takes people out of adult-to-adult relationships and increases the power distance between them. As soon as that happens, people in power start trying hard to keep it by protecting their turf and separating themselves from others. This distance is the opposite of intimacy and commonly leads to behaviors that are counterproductive to the business.

A short story to illustrate: A friend is an insurance broker for a division of a large company. His division specializes in big cases and a sister division focuses on smaller, higher risk cases. My friend was referred to a smaller case by a salesman he serves. He knew the sister division would be interested because it was a chance to take some business away from its bitter rival, so he called the vice president of sales at the sister division to give him the lead. Within an hour, he was called by the executive vice president who oversees both divisions. The executive was livid because my friend broke the chain of command by going across divisions, rather than going up all the way to the EVP first. To the EVP, protecting turf and control was more important than a good new piece of business.

More on hierarchy: Another friend worked in communications for a big consumer goods company. She was the third new communications specialist in three years at this company because a supervisor who had a reputation for micromanaging, wild mood swings, and erratic behavior kept running off good people. My friend knew there had been problems with her predecessors, but she was returning to the workforce after taking a break for childrearing, really needed the job, and her new boss seemed reasonable enough during the interviews.

This friend's long prior experience and talent enabled her to quickly establish herself as a valuable contributor, earning raves from her internal clients. However, the better she did, the more threatened her boss became and restarted her pattern of constant changes, petty criticism, and emotional volatility. My friend tried to work it out with her boss, and when that didn't work, with the second-level supervisor. The second-level acknowledged that her boss had problems, even told her the company was paying for counseling for the boss, but said nothing could be done about it.

Then came time for my friend's performance review. She received glowing written comments from her internal clients as part of a peer feedback process, but the worst rating possible from her boss. When she went to the HR department to ask about it, the HR representative told her that, despite the peer feedback, her boss had final say, and if she complained any more, she would appear to be insubordinate. Of course by now she was despondent and confided her problems to one of her internal clients, the supervisor of a large product development area. He offered her a job on the spot.

Now there was a real quandary: Should she stay? Should she go? Should she try for the transfer? Her answer came when she made one last attempt to work it out with her boss and the second-level supervisor. The second-level told her it didn't matter what the quality was of her work or the fact that her boss was still "learning" to be a supervisor (after four years). She was insubordinate for someone who only had been there a year. She couldn't transfer, and she couldn't work for anyone else in the department. She had to learn to work things out with the boss, and that it would be a good "growth" experience for her. She quit on the spot.

What is it about hierarchy that makes some people willing to sacrifice new customers or talented employees just to maintain a sense—usually false—of control? There are many reasons, but one simple explanation is that these people, like many others, are confused about what a hierarchical structure should provide for a company. Your structure should not be about power, especially when you are managing smart people who want to do well. As Bob Creviston of Kellogg says, "The more structure, the more problems you create. More layers mean more people carving up smaller and smaller decisions, or pieces of them, because they think it's their job to control things."

> **Your structure should not be about power, especially when you are managing smart people who want to do well.**

Structure can be about accountability, but there are other, more efficient ways for you to achieve accountability, primarily through values and effective performance measurement and consequences. Strongly shared values will provide a more powerful guide to positive behavior than any structure you could build. Well-crafted incentives will get more achieved for your company than any hierarchy or set of controls.

If creating meaning in work is your goal, structure should be used to provide opportunity, identification and support for your people. Opportunity should mean engaging in useful work and seeing what possibilities might exist for rewards and future development. Identification should enable your people to create a bond with a workteam, type of work, or location. Support should ensure that your employees get necessary resources to get things done.

Self-Organization

This leads us to a concept some people have referred to as "self-organization," or organizing from the bottom up, with as little structure as possible. In self-organization, your key unit becomes the individual or small team. The person (or team) governs him- or herself to the greatest extent possible, not the power structure. Given clear accountabilities, opportunity, identification, and support, self-organization can help your people become their own bosses, which we know for most people is the optimal condition for ownership, intimacy, and meaning.

It may be difficult, if not impossible, for every company to become fully self-organizing, but your company can move in this direction and will benefit from it. Just about every time you throw out the trappings of hierarchy—dress, reserved parking, different pay systems, fancy offices, executive dining rooms, and so forth—your employees will feel much better and productivity will stay the same or will go up. When you push accountability down, if you are careful to provide clear goals, information systems, tools, and safeguards, you will unleash more creativity and performance. You may need to calibrate, clarify, or coordinate after you delegate, but these issues get worked all the time. Even in many operations companies, where the need for consistency and structure may be the greatest, there is much greater room for self-determination in serving customers.

Some of the most positive, engaged, and productive work environments appear to operate with the least amount of management possible. In the end it will not only be your formal management practices that get your talent to perform and work together effectively. Your informal environment—your shared values, clarity of purpose, leadership skills, quality of people and workplace, clear goals and performance measures, availability of resources, and willingness to work together—also creates high performance and meaning in work.

CREATING THE TALENT SOLUTION

1. How engaged are your employees? Could you really use words like *eager*, *enthusiastic*, or *excited* to describe most of them?

2. Do your managers have the skills and confidence to explain, ask, and involve? What would it take to get a large number of them to be able to do this?

3. What's your employees' financial stake in your company? How much opportunity do they have to get information and exercise influence?

4. Think about your structure. Is it set up to create a more "intimate" work environment through smaller-sized units and flatter hierarchies? Is self-organization a possibility?

Innovative Practices that Engage Talent

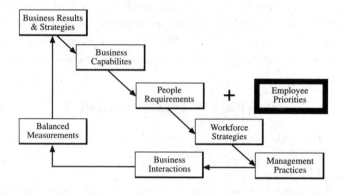

Smart companies engage their talent in a number of ways. There's no limit to the creative practices companies are adopting that are good for people and engage them in the business. In this chapter, you'll learn more about:

- Factors that contribute to engagement and ways to increase it
- The psychology of people going through change in the workplace
- The three factors—connections, choice, and coping— that enable people to change with you
- What some innovative companies are doing to help people cope with change and become more engaged

CONTRIBUTORS TO ENGAGEMENT

Explaining, asking, and involving are at the heart of engaging people in your business, but the causes of, and contributors to, engagement go deeper than that. Ultimately you engage to get performance, and performance is a more complicated topic.

As part of a study on rewards and recognition I was leading for Shell, another consultant conducted focus groups on the topic of engagement. The consultant found engaged attitudes could be explained mostly by three factors: 1) equitable treatment—fair treatment on pay and performance issues; 2) appreciation—largely determined by supervisory skills; and 3) alignment—people's understanding and agreement with Shell's values and business directions.

You probably recognize these three issues from earlier chapters in this book. Fairness is part of a positive employment relationship, and performance and rewards are key talent management practices. Appreciation and alignment are parts of the leadership characteristics of empathy and competence. This sample tended to be somewhat lower in the salary ranks at Shell, so it's intriguing that this group of employees was more interested in appreciation than alignment.

At Hewitt we are studying the root causes of engagement with larger groups of employees and more quantitative research methods. This research is uncovering fascinating things. According to Ray Baumruk, who helps lead this effort, the definition and correlates of engagement change somewhat with every client. However, there are some common lessons companies can learn to increase engagement.

Baumruk says, "Creating engagement is not about driving a particular set of behaviors, though managers would like that to be the case. It's much more about creating an environment in which people feel energized to do the best work of their careers."

If all you needed to do to achieve engagement is to drive behaviors, you could do it through performance management and incentive plans. Creating an environment to enable engagement feels much more amorphous, and that's why it's such hard work. Fortunately, some of the approaches I have been describing will help you build this kind of environment.

You should look to your workforce strategy and resulting employment relationship as your primary vehicles for determining how to engage employees. These will enable you to take a planned, business-driven approach. The mutual expectations you have for each other and the talent management practices you use to support these expectations offer you ways to define and build an engaged workplace.

Seven Factors in Engagement

Our research shows seven factors that stand out above the others in creating an employment relationship and environment that foster engagement. These seven factors are identified and defined in Table 11-1.

The good news is you can work on each of these seven factors to increase engagement. You can create engagement processes that align to your strategic style and use the explain-ask-involve process as the way to make changes. These two perspectives will tell you both content and process for designing or revising these factors. The outcome will be the dynamic employment relationship and engaged employees you need.

As you work on these things to improve engagement, Baumruk advises measuring at least three things. You should see increases in:

- Employee support and buy-in for your business goals
- Employee willingness to exert additional effort to accomplish these goals
- Employee desire to stay with your company

Additionally, your employees will be able to say they can see these things among their coworkers, are encouraged in these directions by their managers, and feel them themselves.

W. W. Grainger

Grainger is trying to both transform its businesses and increase engagement among its employees. It has taken a comprehensive approach to these two issues as a way of improving already excellent business results. The distribution business is changing rapidly, and Grainger is changing with it. With a strong history and an exceptional workforce, the company needs to maintain the best of its past to stay in close connection with employees and make some bold moves to stay ahead of the competition.

TABLE 11-1

Definitions of Factors in Employee Engagement

Shared values/sense of purpose	How well employees' values match the values of the company and the extent to which this enables them to derive a sense of purpose from work
Quality of work life	Satisfaction with the work environment, including physical environment, participation, and other employee programs
Job tasks	The extent to which work is challenging and interesting
Relationships	Satisfaction with relationships with managers, coworkers, and customers
Total compensation	Satisfaction with pay, benefits, and financial recognition
Opportunities for growth	Opportunities for learning, additional responsibility, and advancement
Leadership	Trust in and credibility of the organizations leaders

From a business perspective, Grainger is evolving from one highly centralized business into two different businesses. One business is its traditional speed and convenience business with over 550 industrial product distribution centers in North America. These centers offer a large, standardized set of products for customers. The other business is the integrated supply business, where Grainger employees go on-site and do other consulting to manage industrial purchasing and inventory for clients. In this business, they provide customized solutions.

Grainger is decentralizing following the alignment model. According to Vice President Gary Goberville, "We want to have a common set of values and key processes for reliability, speed, quality, and teamwork. We call this the Grainger Advantage. We also will be held together by our profit-sharing trust and employee benefits. Beyond that, we expect supporting management practices and delivery of them will be very different because the businesses are evolving that way."

To increase engagement and performance, Grainger has been working on all factors in the engagement model simultaneously. It has been using the explain-ask-involve process with all levels of the organization, including senior management. Grainger has accomplished the following.

- Defined a set of values and guiding behaviors. Some of these were always present in the company. Others are newer and designed to move things forward. The values are agility, empowerment and accountability, ethics and integrity, having fun, learning, and teamwork. Each value has a list of key behaviors that defines what it should look like.

- Created top-management understanding and alignment around these values so that leadership could demonstrate them every day.

- Conducted a variety of large group meetings and asked departments and teams to have their own small-group processes to gain employee understanding and a sense of purpose about the values and the new ways to do business.

- Embarked on major efforts to reduce cycle time in all its businesses; improve work tasks and processes like logistics, product movement, and electronic commerce; save money; and provide better customer service.

- Created and taught new approaches to teamwork to improve working relationships within and across the businesses.

- Revised almost all supporting practices to align more closely to the businesses, including competencies, rewards and recognition, performance management, selection, training, communication, knowledge sharing, and employee development.

- Used process-improvement teams, cross-functional teams, and lead breakthrough agents comprised of employees at all levels to create, design, and implement many of these changes. This was their broad-based involvement approach.

Gary Goberville says if the company is successful, and the early returns on this multiyear transformation are very positive, then it will have gone from being conservative, risk- and mistake-avoidant, top-down, and serious, to being "swing for the fences" risk-takers, learners, more diverse in thought and behavior, more fun, and significantly faster. This will create greater customer satisfaction and bigger business results, plus a different employment relationship. This relationship still will be long-term and much better suited to the directions the industry is taking.

THE PSYCHOLOGY OF CHANGE AND ENGAGEMENT

The Grainger example is helpful, because like Continental, Sears, Shell, Whirlpool, and others, the company has found it cannot transform its business without ensuring its talent is fully engaged. Grainger employees have to change if the business is going to improve.

This is a fundamental principle: there is no business transformation without behavioral transformation. You absolutely must engage people if you want them to change their behaviors to deliver more value to your customers. There is no substitute for this.

> There is no business transformation without behavioral transformation.

This principle is reinforced when you understand the psychology of change, alignment, and engagement. There is an ongoing debate over whether people really can change. Statistics often cited by those in the anti-change argument include how many people fail to lose weight in diet programs, start smoking again after quitting, or return to jail after probation. These "recidivists," as the argument goes, demonstrate that people can't or won't change.

It's ironic, or maybe just foolish, that this debate is going on all the while people and companies are making huge changes on a constant basis. Some people are thriving. Some are just getting by. Most are doing some of each. Just look at how people are living with the daily changes in communications, work processes, customer contacts, information management, and competitive conditions in your business, and you can see how much change people can handle. Clearly it's a lot.

It's evident people can deal with a great deal of change in the workplace. They just don't want to feel they are being made to change all the time—that someone else is in control. They want to deal with change the way they think they do when they initiate change outside of work. They want to feel like they have some control. That's why engagement and involvement processes are so crucial. They enable people to feel some level of control over changes occurring at work. Self-organization, which I described earlier as a way to increase meaning in work, is another way to give people more control over what they do.

In fact, feeling like you have some control over your environment may be more important than previously believed. Psychologists have known for a long time that these feelings were crucial for mental health. Now a large-scale study of British civil servants from 1985 to 1993 shows that feelings of little or no control at work is the biggest risk factor in heart disease, more powerful than low economic status, smoking, inactivity, or high blood pressure. The research suggests a rigid organization likely is the chief villain, more so than any bad boss.

HELPING PEOPLE GO THROUGH CHANGE

There are three things you need to understand and do to help your people keep up and implement the changes you have to make in your business. This is how you will get the behavioral transformation you must have to create business transformation. The three are connections, choice, and coping.

Connections

Making connections means helping people understand the changes you are introducing. Whether the understanding is deep or more on the surface, connecting is being able to put the changes into some type of pattern, to perceive how they fit with the other changes going on. Since we are in a period of rapid, simultaneous, and complex change, and we probably will never leave this stage—only see it accelerate—your people have a great and growing need to fit things together.

What is the change? Why are we doing it? How does this change fit the overall scheme? How does it affect the other changes? Is this one I need to pay a lot of attention to, or should I be putting more energy into other things? What's in it for me? What might hurt me? When you can help your employees answer these questions, you help them understand the change from intellectual and emotional perspectives.

Additionally, connecting means linking to other people in your work environment and how they are handling the change. What about my friends or my coworkers? How does this affect them? Should I be concerned for them? Do I need to make some new relationships to get through this or to get things done? This is the social side of change and will have extreme influence on your employees' intellectual and emotional understandings.

These connections enable your people to understand your change and put it in context. The only way to make this connection is through communication. In general, companies don't do nearly enough to keep communication flowing about which changes are happening.

Let me return to my golf analogy to make this point. The only way to get good at golf is to hit a lot of golf balls with a lot of different clubs and shots. You have to hit thousands of them, over and over, until your hands, arms, back, and legs hurt. And then you have to do it again, over and over. Most of us don't do this, and that is why, despite all the new technology and equipment in golf, the average score doesn't drop.

Communicating change to help make connections and build engagement is exactly like that. You have to communicate over and over, using lots of different media—large group, small group, electronic, video, face-to-face, written word, one-on-one—until it feels like it hurts to communicate so much. Then you have to start over. Few companies do this. I only can think of a very select number of companies that get told by their employees on their attitude surveys the level of information they have is "just right."

When you communicate change, you are, of course, trying to realign things to enhance the direction you want to go. Sometimes this is big change; most of the time it's fine tuning. I have found as a manager that employee understanding of alignment lasts about four months. Then people want to know the direction again, even if it hasn't changed. This is another big reason to keep communicating.

This need to communicate never stops. For example, we work very hard every October to communicate the firm's and our practice's directions for the coming year, which often is just a refinement of what we've been doing. If we don't recommunicate it in January, then by March, I start getting questions and complaints. "What's our direction?" "Where are we going?" "What's our vision?" Every few months this process repeats itself. That's why communication must be so constant.

In addition to a continuing dose of communication, using your strategic style helps too. Aligning to change is more effective when you are communicating those things that matter most to people. In the three different kinds of companies populated with different kinds of people, focus your change messages on different issues. Tell people what they need to know, but frame it in a context that fits their natural inclinations.

Type of Company	People Are Interested In	Primary Alignment To
Operations	Making things	Goals and results
Products	Ideas	Technical activities and resources
Customers	People	Values

For example, at Whirlpool, Dave Whitwam and Ed Dunn can communicate the High Performance Culture Initiative around the world, but until Whirlpool people see the scoreboard—the goals and measures—that will determine how the initiative will be judged, there will not be full buy-in. Similarly at Glaxo Wellcome, when leadership attempts to communicate change, people have to see how it will lead to better pharmaceutical discovery and development processes, or else employees won't see the connection.

Choice

You already have seen how important control is—both mentally and physically. Help people feel in control by giving them opportunities to feel they can shape how the business change will affect them—that they have some choice over how to behave. This could be something as everyday as how they use the output from a new system, to something as major as coping with a reorganization. Even in something mandatory such as adhering to a newly articulated set of company values, people need to feel some freedom to interpret and incorporate them in a way that makes personal sense. This contributes to getting them engaged in the change.

For example, teamwork is introduced as a value quite often these days. Employees need to internalize the meaning of your particular version of teamwork as it affects their jobs, their personal styles, and the people on their team. Particularly in the individualistic U.S. society, you need to allow people the choice to come to an independent decision about how to live the new value. This means giving them time to think it over, discuss it, come to terms with your parameters, and decide how to behave within them. Anything short of that starts to feel coercive, which reduces motivation.

The concept of the "side bet" illustrates this. This idea goes back to sociological studies done at the University of Chicago in the 1950s. To feel in control of change, people need to choose to make a side bet, a small psychological wager that gets them involved and aligns their interests with yours. When they choose to "bet" on you, they have decided your direction is correct, and they will participate in it.

The power of the side bet shouldn't be underestimated. Think about it. You may not care about the outcome of an election or a sporting event. However, if someone offers you a $1 bet, and you take it because you want the action, you'll become very interested in the outcome. You still may think it makes no real difference to your life who wins, but you've committed to the contest by making the bet. You'll start cheering your favorite on to victory—you may even start campaigning for someone or wear the team's T-shirt. In the best of possible worlds, employees bet on you to be successful and work to make it so.

There are two ways to increase the likelihood of getting employees to make their side bets on you. The first is to increase their range of choices. The more choices they have, the more employees will deal with your company in a free will, adult-to-adult relationship.

This is the great value of the market-based employment relationship I described earlier. If people have more free choices about whether to stay with you or go, they will stay with you when they think you offer the best opportunities for them. This will motivate them to work their hardest to make you successful because they feel it's their choice, they are not being forced to stay. When their choices are very limited, and they feel coerced into staying, their motivation and engagement will be much lower. This is when change avoidance, complaining, resistance, and low performance are most likely to occur.

This is why I think most of the compensation restrictions and "handcuffs" we put on employees to get them to stay are a waste of money and often counterproductive. I can see the value of protecting people from an unwarranted takeover. However, building up lots of restricted stock, or back-end loaded pensions to keep people from going defeats the purpose of achieving high engagement. It makes them feel tied to you by external forces, forces outside their control. If that's your primary hold on people, instead of their belief you will succeed as a business, you probably have a weak position in your marketplace and poor prospects for improvement.

Instead, give people compensation vehicles with lots of upside potential tied to performance, enabling them to take present value whenever they want to go. Then they'll stay voluntarily if they like your chances, and they'll work hard to improve them. If they don't like your chances, then competition in the labor market for talent will do to you what external competition does, force you to get better. This will improve your competitive abilities.

We took this approach with a Hong Kong investment bank. Hong Kong is a hot investment marketplace, with severe talent shortages and considerable job-hopping among employees at all levels. The bank, much to its credit, realized the only way to keep talented people and be a successful business was to create challenging work, provide autonomy and learning on the job, and offer lots of performance feedback. The compensation design included no handcuffs, immediate vesting for retirement even though competitive practice was five years, and rich rewards for people who performed. The bank has thrived on the strength of being a great employer and a beacon of free choice.

The second way to increase the probability that employees will make a side bet on you is to increase their feelings of being valued by you. Recall that Shell people said appreciation was one of their big three issues in feeling engaged in the Shell transformation. I already have discussed how to do this throughout the book: build the right culture and workplace, align to what interests your people, have competent and empathetic leadership, create a meaningful employment relationship, use the explain-ask-involve approach, and communicate until it hurts.

Maybe Bob Creviston of Kellogg expressed it most simply when he said you have to "bring people inside the loop." People need to feel they belong so they can feel valued. The more they can identify and feel they belong, the more likely it is they will bet on you.

Coping

Coping is the third thing you need people to do to commit to change. It's also a huge opportunity for your company to help people feel valued. Many people think coping means just getting by or being too stressed, like the popular phrase, "I just can't cope with this." However, the meaning of coping really is much more positive. The dictionary defines *coping* as "to contend with successfully," and the thesaurus uses "strive," "manage," and "handle" as synonyms for coping. Think about coping as a positive.

With this in mind, making connections and choices are part of coping with change. They enable employees to "get on top" of it and become engaged. In addition to what I have described you can do to increase connections and choices, many companies are helping employees cope by attacking it programmatically.

Some of these are big, all-for-one programs. However, many are directed at meeting specific individual needs within the context of a large-scale, flexible, workforce practice. My colleague Jack Bruner uses the term *mass customization* for this. This term has been applied previously to serving customers. According to Jack, it's time to use this approach for employees too, by recognizing their individual needs and helping them cope with new workplace demands.

You can begin to understand how to apply mass customization to employees by looking at data from Hewitt's LifePlan Resources database. This database represents responses of over 1 million employees to questions about their current needs, short-term fears and concerns, and long-term goals. There are differences by company, age of employees, gender, income, family status, part-time versus full-time, and people who plan versus people who don't. These differences mean that helping people cope so they can build engagement requires much more targeting of company responses to individual needs than ever before.

For example, Table 11-2 shows differences in employees' top 10 priorities in three different companies in three different industries.

You can see things that register high with one company's employees, like furthering education at the bank, don't even register with the other two. Similarly, financial security is on the minds of the telecommunications and oil employees but not a priority for the bank employees. They probably don't have that long-term of a view. Simply copying a best practice or borrowing approaches from other companies based on what's hot now misses the specific needs of individuals in different workforces.

Now look at the differences in financial priorities within the oil company based on the age of respondents (see Figure 11-1).

TABLE 11-2

Top Employee Priorities in Three Companies (1 = Highest, 10 = Lowest)

Employee Priority Areas	Ranking by Bank Employees	Ranking by Telecommunications Employees	Ranking by Oil Company Employees
Feeling secure in my job	1	1	3
Preparing for retirement	2	2	1
Saving for a home	3	5	7
Making more money	4	7	6
Furthering my education	5	—	—
Saving for child's education	6	4	4
Appropriate job opportunities	7	10	—
Affordable, quality health care	8	—	10
Staying healthy	9	8	8
Being recognized for my work	10	—	—
Financial security	—	3	2
Retiring early	—	6	5
Furthering my education outside of work	—	9	9

Figure 11-2 shows the significant differences across various priority areas within the oil company by gender.

You can see the only organization-wide programs that would make sense to meet peoples' needs would have lots of options. Financial priorities clearly differ by age, and women bring a very different set of needs and concerns to the workplace than men. This approach to understanding priorities and goals says you have to listen carefully to employees and respond with more tailored opportunities. This should be done in the context and support of your business strategy and strategic style.

Helping Employees Cope

There are some terrific examples of what smart companies are doing to help people cope with change. They respond to what employees say they need about career security, financial security, and time/work/life balance issues.

FIGURE 11-1

Predicted Financial Priorities by Age Within an Oil Company

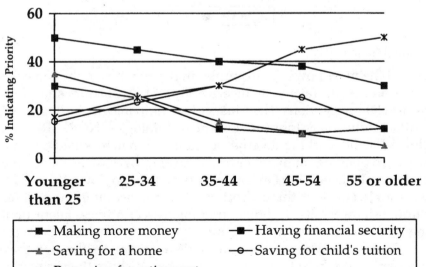

FIGURE 11-2

Predicted Priorities by Gender Within an Oil Company

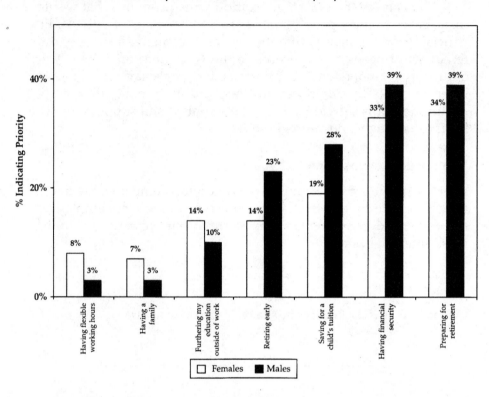

Talent Alliance

One of the most powerful examples in recent years in the career security area is the Talent Alliance, a nonprofit consortium sponsored by over 50 corporations. The Alliance has companies including AT&T, DuPont, Johnson & Johnson, Lucent Technologies, NCR, TRW, and Union Pacific working together to train and match skilled employees to job openings at member firms. An employee whose skills may no longer be needed at DuPont may be able to go down the road to work for J&J through this consortium. The Alliance offers job postings through its web site, technical training, career advice, talent pooling, and relocation counseling, among its many services.

This is a way to keep cycling skilled employees through these companies to where they are needed most. It shifts the focus from job security to career security, and maximizes employees' opportunities for meaningful work at leading companies as long as employee skills are current and useful. Some of these companies see them-selves as career employers, like TRW, and are more interested in temporary pooling of talent or loaning employees. Others, like AT&T, use this more as an avenue of opportunity for displaced employees, while it continues to downsize and adjust to deregulation.

From Figure 11-2 it's clear the definition of financial security changes with age. This is true for the oil company and most companies. Early on, saving for a home and making more money are key. Saving for a child's tuition takes on greatest significance in the middle years and then fades. Retirement planning takes on more importance beginning in a person's 40s and increases from there.

A significant value gap that occurs in financial security is that companies spend lots of money to provide total compensation, but employees don't always perceive the real economic worth. Incentive plans often are too complicated to understand. My own experience of 20 years of incentive design is that any plan that has more than two factors determining your payout won't be well-understood. Yet companies persist in creating complicated plans with too many objectives and measures.

In the retirement area about 80 percent of companies offer defined benefit pension plans to their employees. These are generally the most cost-effective for the company and provide the best, most secure retirement income. Still, their detailed and somewhat arcane formulas make them hard to understand for anyone but a pension actuary.

Glaxo Wellcome Inc.

Glaxo Wellcome is responding to these financial security concerns by providing a more comprehensive approach to total compensation with new opportunities to make more money and a new approach to value and flexibility in savings plans. The company set a BHAG (big hairy audacious goal) for itself for company revenues in 1997 and 1998. For employees it offered a BHAR (big hairy audacious reward) to "show them the money." If Glaxo Wellcome hits its revenue target—just one measure—in 1997, everyone gets a week's pay. If it does it again in 1998, everyone gets a month's pay. This is as simple and as powerful as it gets. Levi Strauss did a similar thing, offering everyone a year's pay if it meets its cash flow goals between now and 2001.

On the savings side, Glaxo Wellcome has moved to an enhanced 401(k) plan, a Life Cycle account and a cash balance plan, all at no extra expense to the company. The increase in cash balance plans is the most significant trend in retirement income in the U.S. Hewitt data show the prevalence of cash balance plans for salaried employees has grown from 3 percent in 1990 to 12 percent in 1996, a veritable sprint considering retirement plans are very slow to change. Glaxo Wellcome's cash balance plans offer the same advantages of a traditional pension plan regarding expense, economic value, and security. As HR Vice President Don Cashion says, "It has the additional advantages of immediate and full vesting, portability, an "account" that shows the cash balance of the plan, and quarterly statements to show how the account continues to increase."

Since people at different ages do have different needs and priorities about saving and expenses, the company took a small portion of the money that funded the pension and used it to enhance the match on the 401(k) plan. The advantages to employees are the 401(k) is voluntary, and it's possible to take loans from it, which can't be done from the cash balance account. Loans must be repaid, but employees can get access to their money in case of hardship, housing, or education needs. Employees also have more control over their money in the 401(k) because of their ability to direct it into different investments.

The Glaxo Wellcome Life Cycle account is an after-tax, payroll deduction savings plan, designed to help employees save for more immediate needs. The financial incentives to save are not as strong as in the matched 401(k), but the convenience factor is very positive. The Life Cycle account also offers the opportunity to invest in no-load mutual funds. Additionally, there is some limited matching by the company if the money is used for home purchase, elder-care, college education, and financial planning.

Employees still need considerable help balancing the increasing time demands of work and home life.

Nowhere is the move to help employees cope more noticeable than in the time/work/life area. Even though successful people appear to like working long hours, employees still need considerable help balancing the increasing time demands of work and home life. Additionally, as diversity in this country moves from being a compliance issue to a business issue, more companies are folding their diversity efforts into the time/ work/life umbrella of concerns. This enables them to tailor specific programs and responses to individual employees by promoting diversity of behavior and thought at the individual level, beyond race and gender.

At Amoco and Shell the 9/80 compressed work schedule is offered to most employees. This enables them to work 80 hours over 9 days and take the 10th day off. This 10th day is a Friday and gives employees a three-day weekend every other week. This is a no-cost benefit to the company and a boon to employees who love having the extra time for family and other pursuits. There appears to be no decline in productivity or customer service, just an increase in morale.

Ralston Purina

Ralston Purina has gone even further in making work time more flexible. It shifted its perspective from paying attention to the time its employees work to the results they produce. A 1995 survey of employees showed 81 percent wanted greater control over their personal life/work life balance. In response, the company introduced a major work/life initiative focused on providing more options for people to get their jobs done.

Ralston used the alignment model to define its business needs and people requirements as: 1) the best people, 2) with focus and energy, 3) being productive, and 4) showing measurable results. Using results from the employee survey and focus groups, it identified employee needs as: 1) greater work/life balance, 2) providing more time in the day, 3) with greater flexibility, and 4) manager support for this flexibility. In addition, Ralston was interested in enhancing its image as an employer so it could improve its recruiting opportunities and have a stronger image in its consumer and labor marketplaces.

The outcome was the creation of a comprehensive set of work/ life options people could choose to cope with increasing work demands and establish more control over their lives. Options included paid time off, short-term disability, work-at-home, flextime, voluntary reduced hours from 40 to 32 hours per week, job sharing, and sabbaticals. Providing options recognizes the same solution does not work for everyone. Individuals need to tailor their own answers to their own needs. The keys to using most of these options are developing a sense of shared responsibility between employees and the company for their proper use and the shift in perspective about measuring performance from hours and effort to results.

Increasing flexibility about work schedules is both a response to employee needs for greater control over their time and a way to become a more attractive workplace in a talent shortage. Hewitt data from a national survey show that 68 percent of employers offer flexible scheduling, up from 53 percent in 1991. Smart companies are learning that helping people cope with change by offering new approaches to work/life balance, as well as career and financial security, is part of the talent solution.

CREATING THE TALENT SOLUTION

1.   Rate your company on the seven factors that increase engagement. Which are high? Which are low? What problems do you have that you know need fixing?

2.   When you go through business change do you think about helping your people through it? How much do you do to help them make connections, give them some choices, or help them cope?

3.   What do you do that is innovative in the areas of careers, financial security or work/life balance? What should you do?

PART THREE

MEASURE

CHAPTER 12

Measure What Matters

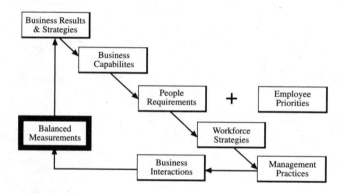

You have read about alignment and engagement. Now it's time to discuss measurement. I begin this section on measurement by discussing the right things to measure at the business level. In this chapter you will see:

- How and why you should create a balanced portfolio of business measures
- New measures of value, including a basis for measuring employee value
- Criteria you should use to determine whether your measures are good ones

MEASUREMENT CHANGES EVERYTHING

Measurement is the last of the three processes you need to connect talent to strategy to deliver outstanding results. Effective measurement will make alignment and engagement real for people and ensure your business is pursuing the right outcomes. If businesses "manage what they measure," then you need to measure the outcomes of alignment and engagement to be certain you are aligning and engaging in the right ways.

Measurement ties everything together. All elements of alignment and engagement become more urgent and useful when you start to measure their outcomes. If you aren't prepared to measure the results of these processes, they may not be worth doing. If you don't measure, you won't know or understand the results you are achieving.

Measurement changes everything. It has the potential to transform. The purpose of aligning and engaging is to improve the way you deliver value so you can increase your results. As soon as you have a baseline, you can and will try to beat it. Without measurement, behavior tends to be undirected. There is an old business saying, "without numbers, a goal is just a dream."

American businesses are focusing on measurement now more than ever. As a result, they are learning more about it and doing a better job at it. This new attention started with Total Quality Management and its process control/error variance approaches to improving quality. Now it is moving through new ways to assess value creation and intangible assets, as well as creating balanced portfolios.

Your company will reach the ultimate in measurement when an aligned set of measures drives the behaviors and results you want, from the corporate level to the individual or the work team. Despite much progress, most companies are a long way from that. In many cases, businesses still aren't measuring the right things or are measuring things that don't matter.

A BALANCED PORTFOLIO FOR MEASURING RESULTS

The Problem with Numbers

When people think about measuring business results, they start with profit and continue on to other financial measures. This is the appropriate starting point. Otherwise you can't stay in business.

The problem is many companies—even very good ones—stop there. Profit, both operating and in some form of return (return on sales, return on equity, and so forth), is all they measure. As Wayne Anderson says about Amoco, a very smart company, "Ninety-five percent of our strategic and quarterly reviews are about financial and finance-driven operating measures." Most other companies I know do the same thing.

There are a lot of reasons for this. Chief among these is numbers are what people are comfortable using. There is a certainty in "hard numbers," even numbers built on soft assumptions. Accountants have been developing financial ratios for hundreds, if not thousands, of years. For just as long, executives have been running their businesses with them. Familiarity breeds contentment when people are so used to doing things the same ways for so many years. This is what boards of directors are accustomed to seeing too.

In truth, financial numbers have been our only common language of performance, especially in U.S. businesses. Until now there have not been any recognized alternatives or additions to them. It's difficult to criticize this tradition when there has been nothing else to offer in its place.

Additionally, financial measures alone probably are good enough to assess results in both agrarian and industrial economies. Financial measures do a good job of capturing physical assets and the returns on them. These are the main source of wealth in those types of economies.

However, economists from the Brookings Institute and elsewhere estimate in information economies tangible assets only account for about 33 to 40 percent of the assets of the modern company. This percentage seems to be dropping quickly. Intangible assets—primarily people, knowledge, information systems, brand strength, and customer relationships—appear to count for a fast-rising proportion of the wealth of companies. This means companies cannot account for a majority of their assets or abilities to create value today if they rely solely on financial measures. As Vicki Chvala, vice president at American Family Mutual Insurance, notes, "The customer is talked about a little bit, and employees are an afterthought in measurement."

Authors Robert Kaplan and David Norton in their book *The Balanced Scorecard* offer another compelling reason why financial measures are inadequate by themselves to track business performance. According to Kaplan and Norton, customary financial measures are lagging indicators—they tell what you have just accomplished, where you have been as a company. They cannot tell you where you are going, except for the very short-term.

Using financial measures to predict your short-term directions leads to short-term thinking to "get the numbers up." This suggests the future will be like the present, which is seldom the case anymore. It also will prevent you from making long-term investments that will strengthen your value proposition to customers or your capabilities, because these typically cost money in the short-term and pay back over a much longer time period.

Moreover, in the information economy, many of the investments you make to increase long-term results must be in intangible assets: new information systems and databases, increased product or service quality, operating process improvements, enhancements to distribution and other logistics, customer service, organization change, and leadership and workforce development, among many others. A reliance on financial measures alone will show these as expenses, not investments, and prevent you from determining your return on them.

A more comprehensive approach, much better suited to the information economy, is to use a balanced portfolio of measures. A balanced portfolio will include your financials, but go beyond them to consider customer, operational, and employee measures. These are measures you can use to track your investments and progress on building intangible assets. Some of these will be lagging indicators, but many more will be leading indicators, designed to tell you where you are going. Leading indicators help you set goals for building and measuring improvements in your infrastructure and capabilities to deliver greater customer value. This helps you grow greater shareholder results over time.

Four- versus Three-Perspective Models

Kaplan and Norton depict a balanced scorecard as a strategic management process, relying on four categories of measurement. They liken the scorecard to the dashboard of an airplane, where you are flying by looking at all of the indicators, not just the altimeter of financial results. Their scorecard is shown in Figure 12-1.

FIGURE 12-1

The Balanced Scorecard

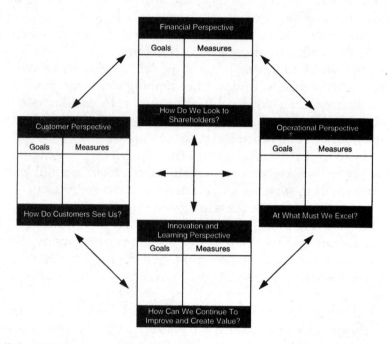

Source: Kaplan and Norton

Each of these four perspectives should be derived from your business strategy. In each perspective only the most important goals and measures are listed. Financial goals are straightforward. Customer measures include measures of satisfaction, quality, and customer results. The internal process perspective includes areas for operational improvements. Innovation and learning includes goals and measures for people development, information systems, and organizational processes.

While this is a very comprehensive approach to measurement, some companies find this to be "bulky," too cumbersome to understand and use easily. This has led me to a simplified alternative to the four-perspective model. This easier model is shown in Figure 12-2.

Going from four perspectives to three is fairly simple. Your financial measures go to shareholder value, and your customer measures go to customer value. Measures of operating improvement can be parceled out, depending on who will benefit from the improvement. Usually this is the customer, but sometimes it's the other two stakeholders. Some improvements are strictly financial plays so they go to the shareholder. Learning and innovation measures can be directed to employee or customer, with the majority of them ending up with the employee.

A most important part of developing this three-category portfolio is to remember to focus on leading indicators, not just lagging indicators. This is a little more obvious in the four-perspectives scorecard. The three-sided portfolio also accommodates them, but you have to be mindful to include them. They are absolutely crucial because this is where you commit to building capability to increase value.

In addition to being less complicated, this three-sided approach:

- Makes the intuitive explicit—Many executives intuitively understand that they have three primary stakeholders to satisfy: shareholders, customers, and employees. This approach makes this explicit by establishing measures in each area. It also contributes to being externally focused and adaptable because employee and customer needs keep changing.

FIGURE 12-2

Three-Perspective Balanced Portfolio

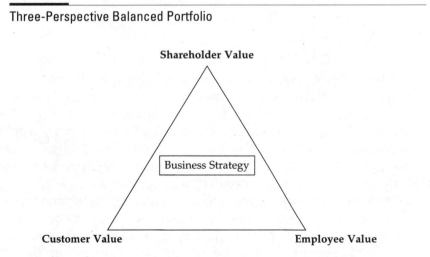

- Is easier to communicate—There are fewer elements to explain, the terms are more familiar to employees, there are likely to be fewer measures because of three categories instead of four, and employees see their interests in the measures. This tells them they are an important part of the business process and goals, so they are more motivated to listen and can engage more readily in accomplishing them.
- Is research-based—Data from other studies (see the Appendix) show quite clearly that companies that attend to all three stakeholders—customers, employee, and shareholders do much better financially in the long term than those that don't.

Arguments For and Against

Whether you use three buckets or four, further support for taking this balanced approach comes from the Conference Board Report, *Case Studies in Strategic Performance Measurement*. The report included data that showed companies using balanced measurement systems were much more likely than others to:

- Be perceived as industry leaders
- Rank in the top one-third in financial performance in their industries
- Judge that their last major change effort was successful
- Report better teamwork among management
- Experience more self-monitoring of performance by employees
- See more risk-taking by employees

These data suggest many business and organizational goals, including financial ones, are enhanced by using a balanced portfolio of performance measures. Ed Dunn of Whirlpool said employees found it "thrilling" as the company rolled out its balanced portfolio to replace its financial-only goals. They immediately saw the connection between the results demanded by the scorecard and Whirlpool's High Performance Culture Initiative.

If using a balanced approach to measuring performance is so powerful, why are companies just slowly adopting it now? There are several reasons. First, it's new. People aren't used to it, and there is not much history to many of the measures, especially on the employee value side. John Anderson is Hewitt's global practice leader for compensation consulting and deals with boards of directors on this issue. According to John, "Boards today are uncomfortable with nonfinancial numbers. They still don't trust them, don't see them as real. Only a small minority of boards are paying attention to them now, and that will persist until we create more believers."

Second is the issue of accountability. Using a balanced approach means leaders will be held accountable for a much broader range of outcomes than ever before. Broader accountabilities require people to reduce their personal control over things they're used to doing and take more risk, something many managers are loath to do. Wayne Anderson of Amoco notes that everybody seems to want to be empowered today, but very few people want true accountability and consequences for outcomes.

> **Leaders will be held accountable for a much broader range of outcomes than ever before.**

A third major reason is that many companies don't yet understand the value of leading indicators or how to develop them. Knowing where you are going is hard enough. Measuring it, attaching value to it, and holding people accountable for achievement seems nearly impossible to many who haven't tried it.

Rob Weinberg leads Hewitt's human capital measurement efforts and has been helping companies develop new, leading performance indicators for some years. Rob says, "Lead / lag concepts are hard because companies still don't have a clear concept of what drives value in their businesses—what their leading indicators should be. They need to understand this first and then try to manage it. You can't measure something until you know what you want to manage."

Despite issues of newness, accountability, and difficulty in setting leading indicators, a balanced portfolio of business measures is absolutely essential to you in an information economy. Otherwise, it's impossible to measure the return and value of a majority of your company's assets. To help you begin to create a balanced approach, let's look at some critical things that determine measures of value.

MEASURES OF VALUE

The simplest definition of *value* is the benefits outweigh the costs. From a customer perspective, this probably is still a good way to think about value. Remember the earlier discussion that says customers look for three types of value—leading-edge products, best total cost, or customized solutions or service. In each case, the specific benefits must be greater than the price they pay.

For business measurement, the current definition of value is more complex. It not only means that benefits outweigh the costs, it also means the benefits of an investment outweigh the possible benefits of alternative investments with the money.

Business Value

Companies just started taking this perspective on business value in the late 1980s, and it has changed the way value is regarded. No longer are simple return measures like return on assets or return on sales deemed adequate to assess performance. They still may be useful to track, but now those returns are judged on whether they also exceed the cost of capital used to obtain them. This is a higher and harder hurdle rate. The bar has been raised on company performance.

Cost of capital, very simply, is the cost of obtaining that capital on the open market, usually assumed to be the cost of borrowing the money. As an example, if I borrow $10 from you at 10 percent, I only create value if I can make more than a 10 percent return on the $10. If I make anything less than $11, I am destroying the value of the money I borrowed. The same thing holds true for a vice president or general manager of a company. When he or she gets allocated $100 million in assets, and the assumed cost of capital is 10 percent, then to create value is to return more than $110 million.

Understanding value creation is part of the way companies are getting better at measurement. Thinking about value creation has led to a new emphasis and, in some cases, "discovery" of new measures of financial performance, including economic value added (EVA), cash value added (CVA), total shareholder return (TSR), and others. These measures definitely improve the way companies measure financial performance because they track more closely to real value creation and stock performance. Managing to EVA or CVA has a closer correlation to stock price performance than using more traditional return measures. TSR is a direct measure of market value because it measures growth in stock price and the payout of dividends, divided by the starting stock price for the period.

These measures are a real step forward, but by themselves they are not enough to measure total value. There are other, significant sources of value—especially customers and employees. EVA and CVA will pick up the financial outcomes of delivering customer value, but they can't account for the enduring value of consumer awareness, brand loyalty, and goodwill. Moreover, EVA and CVA do nothing to track employee value creation, other than its ultimate return to shareholders. They are lagging indicators, just like other financial measures.

Additionally, EVA and CVA are measures of return. They do not measure growth. Yet a successful, long-term company needs to grow. In fact a singular focus on current EVA or CVA may cause a company to do things that destroy value in the long run. A company may be tempted to live with worn-out plants and machinery to maximize current EVA or CVA, rather than invest to keep growing. These measures have to be looked at both on a current basis and over time to measure return and growth. At least investments in tangible assets can be amortized and tracked for their paybacks over time.

This investment issue is particularly acute regarding intangible assets and improvements to business capabilities. The expenditures you make to increase them will be treated as expenses on the income statement, not investments, thus decreasing net income and EVA or CVA. According to Accounting Professor David M. Smith, "Accounting standards persist in ignoring investments in the most valuable resources of a company—its workforce, knowledge, and customer relationships— because of the difficulty of measuring the returns on these investments. Accountants by nature are afraid to make subjective judgments." Managers may see themselves as destroying EVA or CVA by spending on staffing or learning and may be reluctant to do it, rather than favoring them as long-term investments.

Employee Value

Thinking about employee value creation from the standpoint of EVA, CVA, or value above some set cost may be the wrong way to value people and other intangibles. Professor Abbie Smith of the University of Chicago notes that using EVA or CVA as an evaluation model for thinking about people won't work because it's impossible to justify the payoffs, short- or long-term. Instead, Abbie Smith suggests the right evaluation model for people is more like the one used for stock options.

According to Abbie Smith, "Investing in people is like an option grant. There's a very low downside, you don't really lose much on any one person, and a huge upside potential. The right people can make you rich. Plus, it's an uncertain investment. Like options, some people will pay off big, and some won't. Finally, it's definitely long-term and volatile. There will be times when people's skills put you 'in the money,' and sometimes when they will seem 'underwater,' unable to meet market demands."

This is a very unique way of regarding employee value creation and one that offers lots of possibilities. Most importantly, it supports the idea that employee value is about creating individual competencies and business capabilities that serve customers. Some people look at employee value as the value of services delivered to employees and how satisfied they are with them. This is too internally focused. Employee value is about the value your employees can deliver to your customers.

Viewing people as options to hold, grow, and harvest at relatively little cost per person, while understanding that some will pay off big and justify the total expense, is quite similar to what pharmaceutical companies do with drug discovery or what oil companies do with drilling wells. These industries take a long-term view to creating resources that has served them and their customers very well. Not coincidentally, the oil industry generally believes that EVA and CVA are not good valuation models for its upstream operations. These measures don't do an adequate job of capturing the value of proven or potential reserves that are still in the ground.

CRITERIA FOR GOOD MEASURES

So what criteria can you use to judge whether a particular measure is a good indicator of business performance? Mark Gordon of Hewitt suggests the following criteria for good measures:

- They show a close relationship to shareholder value—return is above the cost of investment, including nonfinancial measures.
- The time frame for measurement is right—the current period for return and longer-term for growth.
- They are as simple as possible, given their strategic importance.

- There should be multiple measures to reflect the complexity of the environment—single measures can lead to overfocus and "blind spots."
- They are meaningful to the business and where it is at a given point in time, and can be widely understood.
- There is consistency among measures over time and across business units.
- There has to be a rational context for assessment. This could be relative to a competitor group or historical performance, or absolute against a standard or goal, or both, depending on the context.

To this list, I add the point raised by Abbie Smith. The same model of value creation used for the shareholder may not be right for the customer or employee perspective.

WHY YOU MEASURE

To build good measures it's also necessary to understand why you are measuring. Being clear about your purposes becomes part of your criteria. You can distinguish among five types of measures. They are:

- Valuation—to assess the worth of what's measured
- Navigation—to help set and stay the course of business direction
- Diagnosis—to determine what needs attention, what problems exist
- Monitoring—to assess progress or performance against a standard
- Accountability—to evaluate whether commitments are met

In particular, customer and employee measures may have other purposes than just valuation, especially when you are constructing leading measures to track your investments in intangibles. When you are establishing these measures for improvement, you probably are setting navigational or diagnostic measures because the payoffs and evaluation of return are so far out in the future. An example is if you are launching a large new initiative and need to set a baseline because you don't have historical data.

Monitoring and accountability deal as much with managing through measures as they do with the measures themselves. Monitoring relates to both the content of your measures and the process of how you use them. Increased accountability for performance should be an outcome of any measurement effort.

Using this framework, one client, a financial institution, set these criteria for their portfolio measures:

Measures Should Be....	So That They...
Focused	Measure what matters
Balanced	Integrate multiple perspectives
Strategic	Center on achieving vision versus maintaining control
Simple	Can be easily understood by all
Implementable	Are based on available and accessible information
Trackable	Can be evaluated to manage performance

Establishing a portfolio of measures, particularly when they include navigational and diagnostic measures, will get you into the debate of activities versus outcomes. It's easy to agree that outcomes are what really matters, what you should be tracking. However, in the early stages of an effort to increase employee or customer value, you may have to track activities.

For instance, in the first year of Whirlpool's High Performance Culture Initiative, one of the measures in the company's balanced portfolio was the deployment of the initiative through training and communication. It was the best first-year measure of the initiative, and there was no way to measure real outcomes because of the long-term nature of the expected payoffs. As our team tried to get to outcome measures, Chairman Dave Whitwam, a bottom-line, results-focused leader if ever there was one, reminded us, "You have to have activities before you get to outcomes."

Whitwam's comments highlight what I think is the first rule of measurement. Measures have to be meaningful to the situation and the people using them to guide you to create real value.

CREATING THE TALENT SOLUTION

1. Do you use a balanced portfolio of performance measures or do you track only financial results? If you are financial only, what possible measures of employee or customer value could you consider?

2. Have you started to measure value, or are you still measuring return?

3. How do your measures stack up against the criteria for good measures listed in this chapter? Which measures make the grade? Which need to be improved?

How to Balance and Cascade Measures

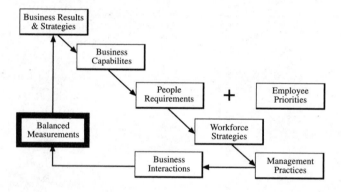

In this chapter, you will see examples that will enable you to set balanced performance measures and cascade goals through your company. In particular, you will see:

- Examples of balanced scorecards for three companies
- A process for cascading goals and measures from the business to the employee
- Some new and better ways to measure employee value

EXAMPLES OF BALANCED PORTFOLIOS AND MEASURES

The recent balanced portfolios of some smart companies show you clear linkages to strategy and customer value; measures of return and growth; and leading and lagging indicators, including employee value and business capability. Moreover, you can see how both the content and process of putting together these scorecards align with company strategic styles. These examples come from products company Glaxo Wellcome, operations company Whirlpool, and customers company Hewitt.

Glaxo Wellcome Inc.

Glaxo Wellcome Inc. (GWI) is a products company, the U.S. arm of Glaxo Wellcome PLC. It does not yet use emerging measures of shareholder value like EVA or CVA, but takes a broad view of shareholder value in the measures it uses (see Figure 13-1). In addition to measures of revenues and profits, GWI also measures growth in sales of new products; a key, leading measure for a products company. The entrepreneurial process is a navigational measure of how effectively the company is implementing a way to get to market faster, a leading indicator of improvement in business capability.

Similarly, GWI's customer measures are both process improvements, leading indicators of getting products approved more quickly and answering customer calls faster and at lower cost. The employee value measures are navigational and focused on building infrastructure, including clarity around cultural and leadership values and behaviors, a reward system more closely aligned to these new values and behaviors, and improving diversity so it more closely reflects GWI's consumers. Each of these is an investment in GWI's abilities to grow in the future. Returns won't be known for some time.

GWI's broad view of shareholder value may reflect its European heritage. Shareholder value and measures of it are seen in many European countries and companies as a distinctly American obsession. Even in England, home of GWI's parent, and a country that has restructured its economy to emphasize free markets, shareholder value does not carry the same passion it does in the U.S.

The broad European view is to achieve global competitiveness while maintaining social cohesion within communities and countries. Many companies, particularly on the Continent, are run by foundations that have social obligations, and very little or no obligations to shareholders. Instead, alignment with strategy is a potent driver, seen as crucial to being a strong competitor. Balancing strategic alignment is another driver, maintaining the worth and value of workers. This driver is particularly powerful in these heavily unionized countries.

FIGURE 13-1

Scorecard of Glaxo Wellcome Inc.

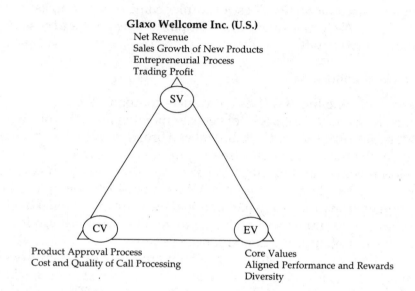

Glaxo Wellcome Inc. (U.S.)
Net Revenue
Sales Growth of New Products
Entrepreneurial Process
Trading Profit

SV

CV

EV

Product Approval Process
Cost and Quality of Call Processing

Core Values
Aligned Performance and Rewards
Diversity

Whirlpool

Whirlpool, in contrast, pushes hard toward shareholder value around the world. Its measures reflect that. It uses both EVA and cash flow as value measures. Earnings per share is retained as a lagging outcome measure because stock analysts and investors still pay close attention to it. Total cost productivity measures the company's never-ending need to keep reducing costs because products are so price sensitive. These measures all focus on current returns. Whirlpool measures growth in its long-term incentive plans.

Whirlpool's customer measures are hard numbers as befits its product offerings and emphasis on operations. Quality means product reliability and is measured by service incidents. In a way, this starts to get at customer results, because a goal of a customer buying a Whirlpool appliance is no breakdowns or down time. Market share shows volume, brand strength, and acceptance by consumers in key product categories. It can be viewed as both a lagging and a leading indicator. Customer satisfaction is the other indicator that has elements of lag and lead to it.

Employee measures for Whirlpool refer to the deployment of the culture initiative and its perceived acceptance and implementation. It is measured both by completion of deployment activities and perception by managers and employees through an attitude survey. These are leading indicators. Another way the company measures deployment is whether management practices have been realigned to support the values of the initiative. This is a navigational and diagnostic activity measure.

Other employee measures address training and development and diversity. Training and development is measured by hours per employee, cost, and quality, using a combination of hard and soft measures. Diversity in this instance is something of a cross between a return measure and a growth measure because it tracks both compliance (return) and increase in diversity of management staff (growth). The breadth of employee measures was one of the elements that helped employees embrace the balanced scorecard concept at the company (see Figure 13-2).

Hewitt Associates LLC

At Hewitt we have had the same three long-term goals for most of our history—quality work for clients, satisfying work experience for associates, and financial growth (see Figure 13-3). Our annual objectives fit neatly into this balanced view of performance. Since we have no outside shareholders, just active owners, our view of financial performance reflects our goals and budgeting process. Revenue growth is key since we set our budget to handle our investments and share profits at the end of the year. In consulting, where ideas and systems have short shelf lives, most investments really are sunk costs to keep competitive. Longer-term views of discounted cash flows and alternative investments are not quite as meaningful.

Profitability and productivity track quite closely since most of our expense is people. The other source of productivity is machine time, and we are able to assign that to people through client work. If we know our productivity, we know how profitable we will be, and this is our return measure.

The preponderance of goals for customer value is not surprising, given we are a customers company. Client satisfaction is hard to track through surveys because there is a lot of wobble in the numbers. Our client goals tend to be activities and outcomes we can track.

FIGURE 13-2

Scorecard of Whirlpool Corporation

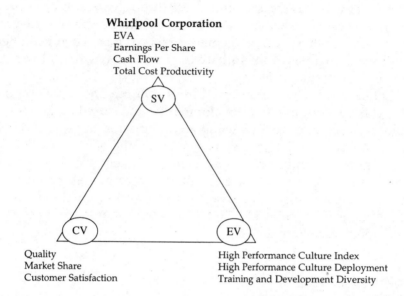

Whirlpool Corporation
EVA
Earnings Per Share
Cash Flow
Total Cost Productivity

Quality
Market Share
Customer Satisfaction

High Performance Culture Index
High Performance Culture Deployment
Training and Development Diversity

Our best indicator of whether we are serving clients well is if we are capturing a growing percentage of their work, particularly from clients where we make the largest investments in time, thought leadership, and client service. Measuring growth in service to these clients is a leading measure of our success. Growth in globalization and outsourcing reflect two major thrusts of current strategy. Integration is a leading navigational measure that tracks how well we are bringing diverse services together to serve clients in coordinated ways.

We keep people goals simple because we know we need to keep associates satisfied so they will satisfy clients. We measure satisfaction through an associate survey. Since learning is so critical to our clients and our people, we monitor whether associates have, and are accomplishing, development plans. This is a leading measure of competency development and a useful diagnosis for improvement.

DIFFERENT STYLES, DIFFERENT MEASURES

Business performance measurement is an inexact science at best. There is no one right way to do it. Performance measurement also takes me back to my beloved golf analogies because, like golf, no-one is perfect at it, and almost everyone struggles to get better. Just like golf, it takes a positive attitude, constant hard work, and some experimentation to get better. Technology helps too, as more things can be tracked more easily and accurately now.

Of the three companies, GWI, Whirlpool, and Hewitt, none is where it wants to be in measurement. Each works hard every year to get better. You can see some big differences in how each company does it. These variations mirror real differences in industries, ownership structures, value propositions, strategies, and practices. You should expect to see these kinds of differences because of different strategies and strategic styles. Be suspicious of anyone claiming to have the "one" right measure for business performance.

What each company does well is align measures to strategic style and goals so they can be used as a management tool. Using measures this way directs talent to its most useful and profitable purposes. These measures give "teeth" to what the companies are trying to accomplish and enable them to hold people accountable for results. Measures communicate to all levels the seriousness of

FIGURE 13-3

Scorecard of Hewitt Associates LLC

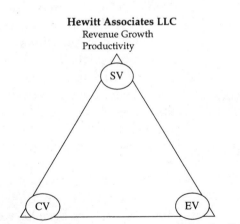

the business plans. They create a platform for communicating business direction, monitoring progress, and discussing results on an ongoing basis. Each company is adept at frequent communication to employees about results.

CASCADING GOALS AND SCORECARDS

The three companies also share something else of vital importance. They all go through an active cascade process, pushing down budgets, goals, and measures to successive levels for annual planning. The framework of the balanced portfolio provides a useful and easy-to-communicate structure for forming budgets, goals, and measures at each level. It can be motivating too.

Hewitt Cascade Process

A cascade needs to reflect the organizational structure of the company. Hewitt is a matrixed organization, with geographical regions interacting with practices to manage both client relationships and consulting content. Practices are like lines of business. Some are global and some are national. Additionally, some associates are assigned to client teams on a full-time basis, and some work on multiple teams on an assignment-by-assignment basis. This means a good deal of complexity even with our flat organization and somewhat limited range of products and services.

In a cascade, the key point of interaction is where the matrix comes together. The only way to work this is through a series of back-and-forth conversations. Practices often formulate goals first, using teams of region practice managers and others who reflect client needs. These are reviewed and revised in conjunction with regional managers who do budgeting and planning based on clients and markets in their regions. Next, regional practice managers establish goals based on these directions. This is where things come together into operations. Then because we are a flat organization, we go from the regional practice level to the individual or client team. Obviously, more layers would make things more complicated. The cascade is illustrated in Figure 13-4.

> Cascaded measures usually are of two kinds. Some are aggregated and some are aligned.

Cascaded measures usually are of two kinds. Some are aggregated and some are aligned. Usually, financial measures and many

FIGURE 13-4

Hewitt's Cascade Process

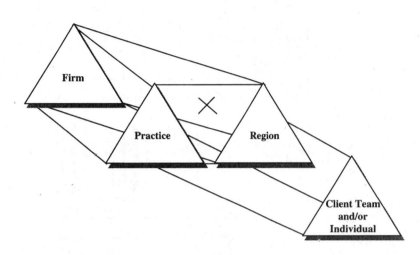

other types of numerical measures aggregate—they add up to a whole, like a budget. Other measures, some that may be region- or practice-specific, and most activity-oriented measures, align but don't aggregate. This means they can't be added, but the presence of a set of indicators at one level signify that the results are occurring and should relate to results at the next level.

When we are successful, the scorecard cascade process flows as shown in Figure 13-5.

A scorecard process must begin with mission or vision, long-term goals or business intent, and values. These should reflect your value proposition and strategic style, which are ongoing. Next comes your planning and budgeting process that should be structured to align and engage for performance. Finally comes the balanced portfolio of measures, first at the firm, region, and practice levels, followed by individual or client team measures. In ideal cases the individual or team measures are allocated into the same balanced categories as the organizational ones.

Monitoring and accountability come next. This occurs as the firm, regions, and practices monitor and communicate progress. Team or individual coaching should follow the same path and reflect complementary messages. The end-of-the-year assessment of business results should be in harmony with end-of-year performance evaluation of teams and individuals.

FIGURE 13-5

Hewitt Scorecard Process

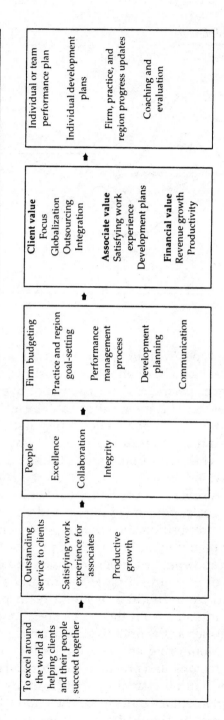

QUALITY OF CUSTOMER AND EMPLOYEE MEASURES

Balancing and cascading are evolving approaches to measurement so there are several issues companies still are learning to manage. I discussed some of these in Chapter 12, including simplicity of the portfolio, how to value employees, and activity versus outcome measures. The quality of measures and the relative importance of weights assigned to portfolio categories are other key areas to address.

The quality of financial measures is getting much better with the new emphasis on value creation. There is a great deal of momentum occurring in using and learning about EVA, CVA, TSR, and other measures of value creation; their strengths, limitations, and appropriateness to specific situations. The speed at which these measures are replacing or supplementing traditional measures of return and earnings really is remarkable, given how long and how widely traditional measures have been used.

Companies haven't made the same progress with customer and employee measures. As I indicated before, companies still are trying to determine how to measure value for these two key constituencies. It probably will take a long time to improve measurement in these areas, but there are things you should be aware of now.

Customer measures still focus on satisfaction, retention, and loyalty, or on processes designed to improve them. In time, customer measures need to measure customer results—how you are affecting your customers' business or individual results.

> **Customer measures need to measure customer results.**

Perhaps a pharmaceutical company should evaluate not how satisfied its customers are with its product, but how many people the product cures, how quickly, and with what side effects. A chemical company might want to measure what profits its customers make by using its compounds in their products. Professional services companies should measure how clients create more value or improve business capabilities using their services.

This requires committing to appropriate use or implementation of the product or service by your customer and agreed-upon measures of performance between you and your customer. This is starting to happen in a few isolated incidences, but it is still a long way off for most companies. Most of the examples I have seen deal with cost savings because of one-time process improvements or cost reductions. Still, the more your company moves in this direction, the stronger your value offerings will become.

Employee Value Measurement

Employee measures seem almost prehistoric compared to financial value measures, and they lag well behind customer value measures too. Survey measures, activity measures from new initiatives, compliance, and cost reduction goals dominate. Survey measures of satisfaction probably are used most frequently. It's important to have satisfied employees, but that misses the definition of employee value I suggested earlier. Employee value is about creating capabilities and competencies that can be used to serve customers.

A few companies measure employee productivity, usually on a gross basis. This is a reasonable return or lagging measure, when you cannot create a more specific measure. You should do it by looking at revenue or operating income divided by total compensation expense. Some companies use number of full-time employees as the denominator, but this tends to distort the measure, depending on the mix of pay levels you have in your workforce.

An innovative way to establish leading measures of employee value is to try to assess the tangible ways you are trying to increase the value of your human assets, often referred to as *increasing human capital*. Based on his extensive work in this area, Rob Weinberg of Hewitt highlights at least four areas you could target for leading measures:

- Leadership development
- Level and development of workforce competencies
- Ability of companies to share and apply information
- Adaptability and readiness to change

These are key areas to manage and measure as you try to grow your business capabilities to compete. Unfortunately, creating and using these measures is difficult, and you are pioneering new territory. For instance, with one financial services client, Weinberg defined a measure of leadership development as the supply of unique, viable candidates for management jobs. This measure gets at both quantity and quality and is central to the client's aggressive, global growth strategy. It cannot grow without an adequate supply of new leaders.

Yet even with a good and straightforward measure like this, there were difficulties. We found even after the measure was defined, identifying the correct data and extracting it from information systems were huge problems. Few companies have the data and systems they need to measure employee value.

In the long run, identifying, defining, and collecting data on a handful of key outcome measures supporting business capabilities should prove much more useful than the current practice of gathering satisfaction measures. I am often asked how to evaluate training or learning beyond how satisfied people are with a specific workshop. To me, cycle time reduction in new product development or process improvement is the ultimate business outcome of learning. If you can do something faster at a high quality level, clearly you are learning.

Even activity measures, which in time will lead to outcome measures, are more useful in measuring real employee value than satisfaction surveys. For instance, measuring participation in a workshop designed to teach new software may be a forerunner of measuring productivity improvements from the software. Companies need to think through what outcomes they really want from their talent management practices to begin determining how to measure them. At American Family Mutual Insurance, senior management is most concerned with how the company will staff jobs that are growing in number and skill demands and what it will do to retool people whose jobs are at risk because they no longer are needed. This has become a focus of employee measurement there.

A place for you to start in creating employee value measures is to understand the concepts of return and growth. You need both. Then you can look at measures that track your current results, like safety or retention, and growth areas where you need to build capability, like leadership or knowledge in an identifiable topic. Growth measures may be more likely to be activities rather than outcomes, but then turn into outcomes later. Key areas for measurement are highlighted in Table 13-1.

HOW BALANCED IS YOUR PORTFOLIO?

Another major issue is the relative importance of the three perspectives: shareholders, customers, and employees. Perhaps in an ideal world you would weight them equally—33 percent, 33 percent, and 33 percent. Unfortunately, the world is not yet ideal. This issue is biggest when the scorecard is used to determine incentive awards, which usually happens at the executive level. Only a very few courageous companies, like Whirlpool, use it for broad-based incentive plans too.

TABLE 13-1

Key Areas for Measurement

Employee Return Measures	Employee Growth Measures
• Productivity	• Innovation
• Safety	• Training
• Staffing	• Job formation
• Retention	• Adaptability to change
• Engagement	• Diversity
• Learning/cycle time	• Leadership development
• Compliance	• Knowledge/human assets

This really gets at the heart of the issue—who is the most important stakeholder? Who comes first? The predominant view in the U.S. is it's the shareholder. Most compensation plans weigh financial measures tied to shareholder value creation at 50 to 60 percent, with customer and employee measures splitting what's left. Both Sears and Whirlpool place 50 percent on financial measures and 25 percent each on customer and employee. I also have seen some 50 percent financial, 30 percent customer, and 20 percent employee splits.

Some of this comes from management's and the board's desire to ensure the financial results are there to "fund" the plan. Yet I think most of it comes from our mania with satisfying shareholders and putting them first. Management and boards don't want shareholders to see significant incentive payouts when current financial returns aren't there, even if the company worked very hard to build new capabilities that will pay off in future years.

Current thinking is those efforts will be rewarded when they show a return in the future. On the other hand, a good argument could be made that managers and employees should be given incentives to continue building capability to protect the assets and viability of the company, even when current financial returns are lower. I also would suggest that creating incentives based primarily on financial measures misses most of the value creation activities of a company, given our inability to know and measure the true worth of our intangible assets.

There are a few heretics out there. Some years ago, Hal

Rosenbluth, the head of Rosenbluth Travel, wrote a book called *The Customer Comes Second*. His point was that employees come first and have to be satisfied if they are going to deliver great service. This is the same theme found in the workforce strategy of successful customers companies.

Stan Shih, the founder, chairman, and CEO of Taiwan-based Acer Group, the $6 billion computer company, has argued for his "1–2–3" philosophy. He says, "The customer is number 1, the employee is number 2, and the shareholder is number 3." Shih believes this is the only way to protect shareholder returns, and as one of the company's biggest shareholders, his self-interest is clear. Shih's point is focusing on the customer and enabling employees to contribute is the way to lasting value, a familiar point in this book.

John Kay, the director-designate of Oxford University's School of Management Studies, as quoted in *Fortune*, suggests it is not a matter of putting one set of interests—namely the shareholder—first, but balancing a broad variety of stakeholder interests that makes a successful long-term company. Kay believes the mantra of maximizing shareholder value would be more compelling if a company consisted only of physical assets the shareholders owned through their equity. However, this is only a small part of company value. Kay adds it's ridiculous to think shareholders own most of the intangible assets, like employees, brand strength, or company reputation. In fact, Kay agrees successful, long-term companies don't even act as if enriching shareholders is their primary goal. Instead they focus on building a thriving enterprise that balances the needs of customers, employees, vendors, communities, and society, as well as shareholders.

Balanced performance measures are so new perhaps it's all right for now if weighting for incentive plans is skewed toward the shareholder. After all, it is "their" physical assets that are being divided. Whirlpool employees who were thrilled at seeing the balanced portfolio probably are typical of employees everywhere today who would just be happy to know their value finally is being discussed and measured. However, as we move further into the information economy and the era of intangible and intellectual assets, it's quite likely this skewing won't be good enough. Managing and measuring the workforce to increase value will demand more equal weighting and balancing of interests.

CREATING THE TALENT SOLUTION

1. If you were going to construct a balanced scorecard today, what would it include? Are you able to measure both return and growth?

2. How would you assess the quality of your measures? Do you have both lagging and leading indicators? What measures would you want to improve?

3. Do you have a cascading process to inform and engage everyone in your business goals and measures? Where are the key points of interaction in your organization?

4. How would you weight the three categories of measures—shareholders, customers, and employees?

Manage What You Measure

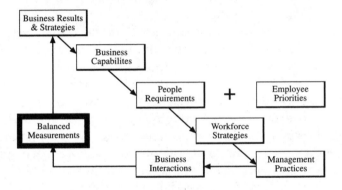

In this chapter you will see that the last, and most critical, piece of the alignment-engagement-measurement process is performance management. It's the talent management practice that brings this entire process home to your people on a personal level. You'll learn:

- Why you should use performance management as an engagement building tool and how to do it
- What mistakes companies make in performance management and what you should do right
- How you should construct performance management and pay tools to improve performance and motivation

THE DRIVE TO EXCEL

I have made an assumption throughout this book—talented people want to excel. Businessperson-turned-psychologist Robert White suggested many years ago the one universal motivator is the drive to master one's environment, the need to show competence. This is how skilled people around the world behave in achievement-oriented or competitive situations. They want to do well, to be the best they can be.

Your talented employees have this drive. They want to know what determines success in your business and what they have to do to excel. When they know the rules of your game—what matters and what they need to do—they get it done. The problem in so many companies is people don't feel they have clear expectations of what to do and how they fit with the business. Yet knowing this is the essence of the talent solution.

To make sure your people can excel, you need a straightforward, complete, and aligned performance management process. A full performance management process includes setting expectations for individual or team performance tied to business plans, offering feedback and coaching about performance and development, providing regular performance evaluations, and tying performance evaluations in an appropriate way to decisions about rewards, promotions, and other people decisions. It is not just end-of-year performance appraisal, though many companies and managers still think it is. In the Hewitt study, *The Impact of Performance Management on Organization Success*, Danielle McDonald and her team found more than half the companies they surveyed did not have a complete performance management process. Yet they need to—there's no substitute.

THE OVERWHELMING IMPORTANCE OF PERFORMANCE MANAGEMENT

Getting the right talent into your company and getting them trained is the prerequisite for success. Once you do that, the essential talent management practice is performance management. It is the single-most meaningful thing you can do to align, engage, and measure peoples' contribution to your business.

Effective performance management ties all of the activities and processes I have described so far together. It makes them real for employees and enables them to perform in the ways you need. It's how employees deliver value. Without it, you can't serve your customers well, and you will have lower productivity and financial performance.

Total performance management starts with the measurement cascade processes described in Chapter 13, and takes business goals and measures and turns them into individual and team scorecards (see Figure 14-1). It is not a separate process from managing your business; it should be how you manage your business.

It doesn't matter what your business strategy and customer value proposition is, you need to do this. What and how you measure and manage these steps and linkages will differ depending on whether you're an operations, products, or customers company. Regardless of how you do it, performance management should be how you get work done and execute strategy through talent.

It's no coincidence that of all the management practices Scott Adams' *Dilbert* cartoon lampoons, year-end performance appraisals top his list. He dislikes the same things I do—performance appraisals that are divorced from business plans and employee realities, that force Dilbert's pointy-haired manager to select from ridiculous categories to rate or rank people, and that appear to exist only to justify

FIGURE 14-1

Total Performance Management

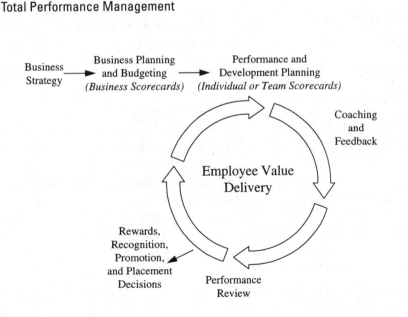

some mind-bending pay scheme. If your company is doing these things, you should stop doing them—now. You're doing more harm than good to your business and your people.

Personal Energy

When done right, performance management should be tremendously liberating, freeing up personal energy and ambition to get good things done. A performance plan should be a road map to achievement, helping the individual or team understand what is needed to demonstrate mastery. It should be a performance contract that helps people understand how they can successfully deliver value. Who wouldn't find clear expectations energizing?

If you think about human nature, people keep score on themselves voluntarily in all sorts of ways and activities. They do it in their sports or recreation, how good a deal they got when they bought something, how many miles they've driven, how long it takes to get somewhere, what their weight is, how many interesting places they've visited, how many friends or relatives attended a wedding or reunion, and so forth. A solid performance management process will enable them to keep score on themselves at work and monitor their most important activities.

> **Much of performance management goes wrong because companies continue to see it as a way to control people.**

In addition to these links to personal mastery and self-monitoring, performance management speaks directly to the four things employees keep telling us they want to know: 1) Where are we going as a company? 2) How are we getting there? 3) What can I do to contribute? and 4) What's in it for me when I do? Backward-looking performance appraisal systems don't really tell people any of that. Effective, forward-looking performance management should tell people all of that. This is a key reason why performance management has to be part of the business planning and scorecard process.

Control versus Commitment

Enabling... liberating... personal mastery... self-monitoring... essential communications... very few companies and employees would describe their performance management processes with words like these. Why is there such a big gap between what is and what should be? Much of performance management goes wrong because companies continue to see it as a way to control people through appraisal, pay, and other mechanisms. They really should see it as a self-control tool, something people can use to increase their own performance.

For the last 15 years, I have been describing performance management as an opportunity to move from control to commitment. I contrast those two approaches as shown in Table 14-1.

SELF-MANAGEMENT

The navigational purpose of measurement can help you understand this approach to commitment. Performance management should help people understand where they need to go and enable them to get there on their own as much as possible, checking their course along the way, and making midcourse adjustments to get back on track or accelerate their trip whenever they can. Above all, it should be a self-management tool. This is the best kind of talent management.

Performance management as self-management suits the market-based, person-centered, changing employment relationship that will dominate developed economies for the foreseeable future. It is the best vehicle to help people understand what they need to do to

TABLE 14-1

The Move from Control to Commitment

Control	Commitment
Once-a-year "report cards" of personal achievements	Ongoing cycle of business-driven planning and progress reviews
Backward-looking appraisal	Looking ahead to what's needed
Management by exception— "the squeaky wheel gets the grease"	Frequent coaching feedback and constructive problem-solving
Subjective supervisor assessment of personal characteristics, and minimum standards	Multisource feedback and mutual evaluation of results and how they were achieved
Little employee participation	Employee involvement and open dialogue at every step

align their individual goals to business goals and how to perform to create value. It addresses the person, not the job, can be changed as often as needed to capture changing business conditions, and can be tailored to fit specific situations.

For employees, it enables them to assess their opportunities for gaining a viable return from the company—how can I contribute, and what's in it for me when I do? It should speak to them as unique individuals or as active members of a small team, rather than as interchangeable job holders. This will help people decide whether and how to commit to maximize their performance.

This market-based performance contract is an adult-to-adult vehicle. It lays out terms of agreement clearly and can be modified as needed. It eliminates dependencies, particularly the kinds of company-employee dependencies that create entitlement mindsets, while encouraging more realistic and mature employment relationships.

Performance management as self-management also is the vehicle for self-organization. Earlier I described self-organization as organization from the bottom up, getting work done as individuals or teams with as little organization and management as necessary. Self-organization can work only when talent knows clearly what it needs to do—the performance plan—and what resources are available to help—through coaching and feedback.

In his book, *JobShift*, William Bridges states the concept of the job is no longer a useful way to think about organizing work. Jobs are too static and inflexible to match the dynamic way work is being done today. Instead, for a growing number of people, work is a series of tasks, and careers are a series of assignments, perhaps with the same employer, perhaps with a series of employers.

Wayne Anderson of Amoco agrees jobs don't work as well today as they did years ago. According to Wayne, "We have been too structured in big corporations. We need to do without the structure of jobs, though people still need direction and some organization to utilize their skills properly."

To me this is another argument for performance management as self-management and self-organization. It's becoming easier to imagine a world of work where many people don't have fixed jobs and job titles. However, it's increasingly impossible to imagine these people without performance plans that align their tasks and outcomes to business needs. In a market-based employment relationship you are your skills and outcomes. Performance management lets you know how to use your skills and what the necessary outcomes are.

PERFORMANCE MANAGEMENT FOCUS

Earlier I said many companies do performance management wrong because they see it as a control tool. This overemphasis on control comes because they see it as a way to restrain pay and to manage people through money. I have heard dozens, if not hundreds, of executives say while money doesn't motivate them (I'm sure it's because they have more than enough), it's the main motivator for their people. If it's the main motivator, then it must be the best way to exercise control. As long as executives think this way, you can be sure they'll never get commitment right.

This focus on the tie to pay is absolutely backwards. There's no point in getting into the long and laborious debate of whether money motivates. Research and real-life evidence is clear and incontestable that for most employees who work in other peoples' companies, pay is about third, fourth, or fifth on their list of motivators. It only becomes more important when they think they are being treated unfairly. If it was the only or prime motivator, most people wouldn't go to work for companies, they would work for themselves—that's where fortunes are made.

What should be the focus of performance management? It should be about creating conversations about the work people need to do that's vital to your business. Concentrate performance management on talking about what you need to get done to be successful. You need it, and it's what employees consistently say is important to them: doing challenging, useful work. This is another situation where the needs of companies and the needs of employees mesh together perfectly, but somehow management has become distracted with other issues.

Danielle McDonald of Hewitt puts it this way; "Performance management should be limited only to things absolutely crucial to the business. Focus on conversations that matter so performance management becomes the way you speak about work. Don't get distracted with administrative or trivial issues. Ask yourself, is this worth talking about for our customers?"

CHANGING PERFORMANCE MANAGEMENT

There's another reason why some companies get performance management wrong. They either keep changing the process too often, or they let it go so long it falls out of sync with the business. If performance management is tied closely to what employees need to do to contribute to your business, then how often you change it must be linked closely to significant business changes.

Another golf analogy: There is a clever and insightful advertisement for a very popular putter that says, "A person buys a new driver, on average, every three years. A person buys a new set of irons, on average, every five years. If it weren't such a long walk to the pro shop, a person would buy a new putter, on average, every four holes."

It's not unusual for some companies to treat their performance management processes like people who want to keep changing putters. They make visible changes to their performance management processes every year, and substantial redos or complete revisions every two or three years. Some of these changes might actually be real improvements but, like buying new golf equipment constantly, they probably don't help much. It's not changing the process that helps so much as it is getting people to talk to each other about performance.

On the other hand, there are companies who let things go for seven or eight years or more without making changes. If they have the basics down really well, they probably can get away with this and not miss much. After all, a golfer with a great swing and an old wooden driver can beat a golfer with a lousy swing and the latest graphite and titanium booster rocket. However, most companies' performance management processes are not that good and managers lack sufficient skills, so this is too long. What is really happening is that companies just neglect it. This avoidance means they have that much farther to go to be competitive.

> It's valid to make significant changes to your processes every four to five years.

Every company is different, but with the current pace of business change, it's probably valid to make significant changes, or complete redos, to your processes every four to five years. When Whirlpool redid its 1989-built processes in 1996, Chairman and CEO Dave Whitwam remarked the company probably had waited two years too long. Cargill built a new process and began worldwide rollout in 1992. By 1997 it was beginning to make major modifications to the behavioral competencies aspect of the process, incorporating different behaviors new senior management thought were more valuable. At the same time, it's probably all right to make a few small modifications to your process once or twice within that four- or five-year span. However, tinkering every year drives managers and employees crazy and causes the process to lose credibility.

One reason why companies wait too long to change is they make too big a deal out of the change. They approach the project as if they are creating something meaningful and permanent, when it's only meaningful. They appoint taskforces and steering committees; gather lots of input; do all sorts of benchmarking; manage long, involved design processes; conduct extensive pilot testing; get layers and layers of approval—all before rolling it out to people. This may have worked when the world moved more slowly, but not anymore.

Instead of this, in many situations we use a rapid design team that builds a new performance management process in five to seven consecutive working days, including gaining input and approval. This puts a dedicated group of six to eight people together for an extensive and efficient redesign effort. The emphasis is improving the quality of the conversations about the work that needs to get done, and how to express it in a performance language that fits the company. This works because team members focus on the task, stay with it till it's complete, and recognize this performance management process won't last forever. This means it has to be effective, but it doesn't have to be perfect, so companies don't obsess about it.

The moral of the story is to keep it simple. In the 1980s and early 1990s, there was a tendency to build lengthy, involved forms that cataloged all sorts or duties, activities, results, and behaviors shown by people. By the time everything was written down, forms could be four to eight pages in length. That's too much administrivia. No one reads long forms, no one wants to write them, and no one gets much from them.

Instead, you should concentrate on the few key results people need to achieve and the small number of meaningful behaviors or competencies they need to display or learn. This is what needs to get done and how it's supposed to be done. Moreover, how you think about performance and describe it probably will change every four or five years because you will change the way you think about your markets and the results by then. The whole written tool should be a page or two of key items to complete, at most. If you can't do it briefly and simply, you probably can't do it well.

HOW TO DO PERFORMANCE MANAGEMENT RIGHT

As you consider whether your performance management process is an effective employee scorecard, remember there are two key reasons for it:

- To align employees' contributions to your business plans
- To improve performance, largely through developing people or solving problems about getting results accomplished

Everything else is secondary and adds complexity. You really ought to ask whether some other purpose is needed to serve your customers better before adding anything to your list.

The research Danielle McDonald and others did on the impact of performance management on organizational success looked at purposes and practices of effective performance management. They asked senior line managers and human resource executives about their goals for their processes. Line management and HR agreed on these six goals:

- Improve customer satisfaction
- Increase profits
- Increase sales
- Create a high-performance culture
- Achieve business plan objectives (in addition to those already mentioned)
- Increase employee productivity

As you can see, these are business necessities, not nice-to-haves or even workforce goals. The single-most important thing you can do is align your performance management process to your business plans and customer value proposition. This is the mindset you need as you review and improve your process.

McDonald and her team also studied the most important practices that were part of effective performance management. They found the singular difference between companies who executed performance management well and those who didn't use it to align, engage, and measure was action. Executives at effective companies put a lot of time, effort, and brains into making it work. In fact, at these companies, executive management used the same performance management process as salaried employees to set business goals for themselves, monitor progress, and evaluate performance. As a result, they were linked to the rest of the workforce and had a lot of self-interest in making the process work well.

In addition, McDonald and team confirmed performance management is a line management responsibility when it's done successfully. It is not delegated to or owned by staff. Finally, companies who are good at performance management are never satisfied with it. They change it, but tie process changes to real business changes, not administrative tinkering.

FOUR CORNERSTONES

A very practical framework for understanding exactly what to do to make performance management work for you comes from a model developed by a Hewitt team led by Bob Campbell called "The Four Cornerstones." The cornerstones are the four *outcomes* of effective performance management. The model is illustrated in Figure 14-2.

FIGURE 14-2

The Four Cornerstones

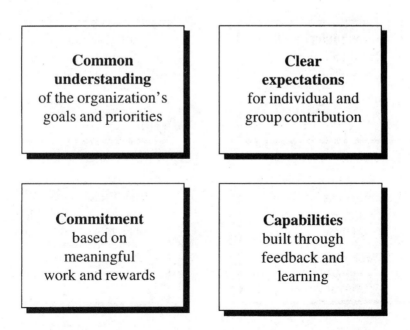

As you can see, the cornerstones speak directly to alignment, engagement, and measurement. They tell employees just what they need to know to be successful and what they want to know. High levels of common understanding, clear expectations, capabilities, and commitment translate to delivering value and creating results through your workforce.

The great thing about using the cornerstones is you don't need to build a process, policy, or forms to use them. You simply ask yourself what outcomes you need to increase to be more successful. Perhaps you have a highly committed workforce, but they're not properly directed. Then you try to increase understanding and clear expectations, probably through communication and goal-setting, without redoing everything. Or, you may feel of all the issues, capability is the one most in need of improving. You can address this through feedback, skills assessment, training, and coaching.

Taking what we know from research and experience, we can fill in the cornerstones with the practices most likely to get you these outcomes. These are depicted in Figure 14-3.

FIGURE 14-3

Sample Practices to Achieve Outcomes

Common understanding
- Communicate mission, goals, and values
- Cascade key scorecard measures

Clear expectations
- Individual and team goal-setting and scorecards
- Defined competencies and behaviors

Commitment
- Challenging work assignments
- Performance feedback
- Career development
- Meaningful rewards and recognition

Capabilities
- Development planning and opportunities
- Multirater feedback
- Performance coaching

Examples of companies with successful performance management will show you how to use this kind of outcome thinking. You also will see clear linkages to the company's strategic style because performance management is a direct expression of it in smart companies.

COMMON UNDERSTANDING AND CLEAR EXPECTATIONS

Levi Strauss & Co.

A great illustration of building common understanding and clear expectations is the Levi's "Partners in Performance" plan. It was born partly from CEO Bob Haas' desire to incorporate Levi's powerful value statement, known as its "Aspirations" into everyday company and employee performance. As a customers company, values are critical to Levi's to support the customer, it's culture, and decision-making. The Aspiration statement talks about what kind of company Levi's wants to be. It also lists the leadership behaviors everyone should demonstrate to make the Aspirations a reality. These include new behaviors, diversity, recognition, ethical management practices, communications, and empowerment.

The company built a common understanding of business mission and aspirations through extensive training and communication. Then to make sure people would live it, it incorporated these things into performance management. Employee performance expectations are based on four areas that link directly to business plans and values:

- What people accomplish on basic job responsibilities and annual business objectives
- What people contribute to longer-term strategic objectives in their departments
- How people show aspirational behaviors
- What people do to keep learning and improving skills

These performance criteria ensure everything everyone does should align to business direction and values. Additionally, the criteria make explicit Levi's value that everyone must continuously improve their skills and abilities.

Cargill

When Cargill rolled out its performance management process (PMP) in 1992, its emphasis also was on building common understanding and aligning to clear expectations. As a very decentralized company, Cargill had many different business planning processes. Cargill wanted to use PMP to put some order into business planning across its businesses.

To do this, Cargill defined five areas of performance focus: 1) financial results, 2) strategic advantage, 3) work process improvement/innovation, 4) customer/partner satisfaction, and 5) positive work environment. The company then used these five areas to help organize business unit and individual performance planning. Business units, like Cargill Salt and the Financial Markets Group, changed their operating planning processes to establish goals and initiatives in these five areas. As part of PMP, individual key results areas were linked to business plans in one of the five areas.

According to Kent Norby of Cargill, "Our alignment chain starts with our corporate vision and mission, goes to business unit missions and plans, and reaches employees through PMP. With PMP our business plans have become more open. In our decentralized environment, we find, not surprisingly, some business units do a great job of PMP and others don't. How effective they are depends on how much they use PMP for business planning and communications."

As an operations company, Cargill is outstanding at measurement. Its PMP asks employees to define each key results area at three levels of performance: below expectations, meets expectations, and exceeds expectations. It is very difficult to do this for some goals, but the intent is for people to have a very exacting view of what kinds of performance will earn them what levels of evaluation and recognition.

Cargill also wanted to create very clear expectations about the behaviors it needed to ensure jobs got done right. For the PMP, Cargill described in great detail eight behavioral competencies. True to its measurement focus, it scaled these behaviors into below expectations, meets expectations, and exceeds expectations. Each area has several examples of behavior at each of the three levels of performance. The eight areas are communication, continuous improvement, decision-making/problem-solving, giving/taking responsibility, managing change, teamwork, risk management, and managing people (supervisors only).

Five years later, and with new senior management, Cargill is changing the behavioral competencies to reflect a new leadership and learning model. The new approach uses four areas of leadership: personal, workforce, interpersonal, and business. Within each leadership area are several specific competencies, like thinking globally, inspiring people to excellence, and modeling organization values. True to its operations nature, Cargill is scaling these into levels of below, meeting, and exceeding expectations. In addition to performance management, the company will use these competencies to link career development and learning to its alignment chain. This will strengthen Cargill's focus on the capabilities cornerstone.

BUILDING CAPABILITIES

Development Planning

Individual development planning is key to both capability building and personal motivation. It's the heart of talent development. A study at Kodak found employees with individual development plans were 15 percent more satisfied than those who had no plan. Development planning puts a large burden on managers to become coaches for growth and learning, something for which most of them have no preparation and very little aptitude.

Individual development planning is key to both capability building and personal motivation.

Smart companies build support for managers in this role by providing tools and training, and making sure employees know they share equal or more responsibility for their own learning. Amoco's career management program announces this shared responsibility right from the start. Then a variety of print and electronic tools are available for employees to gather information about themselves and their potential futures.

At Hewitt, we ask associates who want to have an in-depth career discussion to put themselves through a self-guided self-assessment, using a tool called "Looking Inward," and scan the environment for opportunities, using a tool called "Looking Outward," before having a discussion with their unit managers, called "Looking Forward." At the same time, all associates have more immediate development goals for learning and performance improvement every year as part of their performance management plans.

Whirlpool requires that personal development objectives also be set when business objectives are set, and they must link directly to business balanced scorecard objectives.

360° Feedback

Capabilities cannot be built without feedback. The strongest tool for giving feedback is multirater or 360° feedback. This means gathering feedback from a variety of people—coworkers, other supervisors who know the employee, subordinates, vendors and other business partners, customers, and so forth. *360°* is meant to describe full circle, but in practice it means getting comments on the person from a variety of people.

How broad the sweep for feedback goes depends on the company, as does the complexity of the system. You can ask many people to comment, but experience suggests after about five people, you have captured all you can practically use to provide meaningful and actionable performance feedback. A person only can work on improving a few things at a time anyway.

For data gathering in multisource feedback, some companies use sophisticated electronic systems with lots of people inputting comments on long lists of behaviors. Others use short forms to capture behavior on their lists of aligned competencies. Still others use open-ended questions, like "What is the person doing well?" and "What could they improve?" Regardless of how you collect feedback, from an alignment perspective you should develop a set of competencies aligned to your customer value and use them in an integrated way across your talent management practices, especially for feedback.

The great advantages of multirater feedback are it helps managers by providing them with information from many sources, and employees think it is more valid because it doesn't just reflect one point of view. This relieves managers of the burden of having to develop all the feedback themselves, as well as gives them some fresh information and perspectives on their people. Done right, it can actually make an onerous job much easier. Very few people like to give feedback, though almost everyone wants to get it. Multirater feedback can take managers out of the bad guy role and make them a much more helpful messenger.

This is the essence of the coaching role, helping people see themselves as their performance really is and the way the rest of the organization sees them, so they can develop a realistic picture of themselves. Once they get it, reasonable employees will do what they can to enhance their performance and prospects according to their desires and abilities. People who refuse to accept a fairly constructed picture of how others see their performance and behaviors are destined to cause you problems.

Employees find multirater approaches valuable if they have a say in picking who will comment on them. Picking the five or so people should be a negotiation between employees and their managers, with a little give and take on both sides. If the people are picked for you, instead of with you, you will be less likely to believe what you hear, and probably think the system has been rigged. My personal experience has been that most people are able to come to agreement on a balanced list.

In many cases, the power of these approaches quickly surpasses companies' estimation of them. Some of my clients have been very cautious in installing multirater feedback, starting from the top and going very slowly down through their organizations over several years. They also start out by announcing they will use multirater feedback for employee development only, not for evaluation for pay and other decisions. They think this will placate people because it is just for their advantage and can't be used against them. This comes from the old control mentality about pay.

Actual experience is very different in many companies. After going through the process once so they can see it's fair, employees want to expand the process and use the information as part of their overall performance assessment for all sorts of purposes—pay, promotion, and so on. Multirater feedback seems much more impartial and aboveboard to most people, as opposed to their managers making all the decisions by themselves. This is another instance of more openness satisfying both company and employee needs, but you have to be willing to shed your old attitudes about control to get it.

I suggest to companies they move as quickly as possible with these multirater approaches since they have very little to lose—they can't be worse than what they are doing now—and a lot to gain. It really isn't worth trying to introduce new behaviors in a company without expanding use of multirater feedback as much as possible.

Along with a balanced scorecard and effective goal-setting, it's the most powerful thing you can do to transform behavior to improve performance.

COMMITMENT

This brings us to our last cornerstone—commitment. I already covered a lot about engagement and commitment in previous chapters, so here I will discuss just appraisal and pay. I have been working in this area for 20 years, and most of what I have seen is so bad there are more negative examples than positive ones.

Performance Appraisal

After all these years, I find myself in league with Dilbert. I just don't believe much in year-end performance appraisal, the awful ritual of managers sitting down once a year to evaluate employee performance. There's no evidence anywhere that a formal appraisal process improves motivation or performance. Even when they are part of a comprehensive performance management process, appraisals clearly are the weak link and should be completely recast.

Most performance rating scales—telling people they are "outstanding," "great," "good," "needs improvement," or "failing," or any of the countless variations on them, are useless, insulting, and should be junked. Even worse are forced rating scales that require managers to classify some number of their employees into prescribed classifications. Companies create these things, and I confess I have done this for them in the past, to force discipline onto their managers—to make the tough call about performance. All this does is to admit the company hasn't done a good job training managers how to manage performance, tell employees their opportunities are artificially limited by bureaucratic weaknesses, and build a lack of trust in the workforce. On the other hand, if you want to create a fearful workforce, this is the second-best technique. It's the runner-up to announcing layoffs well in advance of doing them.

Fortunately, a small but growing number of smart companies, like Amoco and Levi Strauss, have gotten rid of performance rating scales. Instead, they have insisted on open and honest conversations about performance with employees. This is the right way to do things.

What does improve performance and engagement? Put simply, it's treating people like adults. If you build common understanding and clear expectations by sharing plans and aligning them to goal-setting, and you help build capabilities or competencies through regular coaching and feedback, then people can monitor their own performance and appraise themselves. At least 80 to 90 percent of your time in performance management should go into goal-setting and coaching.

Talented people who know what they are supposed to accomplish and have the tools and information to keep score on themselves, whether they come from a reporting system or come through conversations with managers and others, will exercise the self-management needed to know how well they did. They don't need another adult to sit in judgment of them on an annual basis. This is the exact opposite of treating people like adults.

The downside of this is it takes a lot of organizational and individual maturity, good communication and measurement systems, and regular conversations and feedback. Many companies don't have these elements. Yet I suggest you spend your time working on establishing these things, rather than building formal appraisals and other systems of control. Ultimately the only kind of control that works is self-control, and that's what you should be trying to build. When you create it, you will increase engagement and meaning for people and results for your company.

I use a tool with clients called CultureFit™ that looks at six dimensions of organizational culture and process. It provides companies with a great analysis of where they are and where they need to go. My favorite dimension is labeled "systems control vs. self-control." Does the company rely on formal systems, like performance appraisals, written policies, many approval levels, and so on to direct employee behavior, or does it enable people to rely more on their personal judgment to accomplish results?

Companies that rely more on self-control have infinitely more possibilities to unlock employee energy to accomplish breakthrough performance. In these companies, employees don't have to ask whether they can take action to solve a problem, they just solve the problem. Even operations companies that need to establish more detailed process controls to deliver standardized products and services can provide greater self-control within those processes. Contrast the behavior of two airline ticket counter agents, one who can't help you solve your problem because he or she is "just following the rules," and the other who goes above and beyond to help you get to your destination more comfortably, and you'll recognize the difference I am describing.

Pay and Promotions

In my ideal, managers work as business plan communicators, balanced scorecard keepers, goal-setters, and aligners who help employees set their own linked goals, and coaches who help employees get and understand feedback. Then employees make decisions about their own performance. There is one more thing managers need to do. They need to make decisions about pay and promotions.

Why? Managers' jobs have changed considerably in recent years and much of their control over information and other resources has been delegated to employees or has just disappeared. Still, someone must maintain responsibility for allocating scarce and valuable resources like pay and promotions to accomplish necessary business results.

Beyond that, pay and promotions are among your company's most powerful message givers about who you are and what you value. What gets rewarded and who gets ahead tells employees whether you have integrity about what you say is important to you and how much they can trust you. Managers should approach their decisions about pay and promotions from these perspectives—allocating resources to achieve results and delivering messages that impact trust—rather than trying to control people.

Unfortunately, for too many years human resource and compensation departments, following instructions from senior management, have built intricate systems treating pay as a control device, rather than as a way to reward outstanding achievements. In these approaches, the system design not only controls how employees get paid, it also controls how managers can make decisions. The emphasis clearly is on limiting what managers can do so the company gets compliance to its rules and limits mistakes. The message that really gets sent is managers can't be trusted to make these decisions.

The results usually are pay practices that spread dollars out pretty evenly to employees, like peanut butter on toast. Real star performance is not often rewarded. This is in contrast to executive compensation where big dollars often get delivered, sometimes for stalwart performance, sometimes just because of a favorable stock

market. Any concept of pay as a tool to achieve and recognize performance for broader groups of employees or to deliver critical cultural messages is lost in many companies.

Benchmark research I did a few years ago turned up an illumi-
nating finding. The fewer guidelines managers were given to make
decisions about pay and related personnel matters—meaning no
forced guidelines or decision-making matrices about pay increases,
but rather a pot of money they had to use to reward performance as
best they could and some principles to follow—the better managers
they became. It was explicit in these companies that managers had
to use their own judgments and not rely on tools provided by the
compensation department. They did it with the same business judgment they used in making other, much larger, financial and operating decisions. The longer they did it, the better they got at explaining
performance requirements, giving feedback, and justifying their decisions. In the absence of system controls, they managed themselves
and improved their own managerial behaviors.

KEEP IT SIMPLE

When control isn't the problem in pay systems, very often complexity is. There's an old saying that only three things in life are certain:
"death, taxes, and a new human resource fad." The recent attempt
by some compensation professionals to try to create competency-
based pay systems is the latest in a long line of faddish missteps.

A Bad Idea

Briefly, competency-based pay approaches argue if increasing individual competency and knowledge is crucial in the information age,
then companies should create pay systems that carefully manage
and directly reward the acquisition of competencies. Competency
pay is the successor to skill-based pay and other intricate schemes
that have been cooked up over the years. Lately I have seen organizations try to build skill- and competency-based pay plans so complicated that managers and employees had no chance to figure out
how to make them work.

Trying to capture competencies directly in your pay practices
just leads to unnecessary complexity. It's bureaucratic and stifling to
replace old point factor job evaluation plans with competencies or
to try to concoct exhaustive descriptions of role competencies and

skills to try to pay people. Pay plans should be as simple as possible, and tied to the marketplace and performance. If they are, by necessity they will reward competent behavior also.

> **Pay plans should be as simple as possible, and tied to the marketplace and performance.**

My French colleague, Eric Sarrazin, consults to European clients on these issues and says paying for competence actually is a very old idea. According to Eric, "Our grandfathers, great grandfathers, and most of our ancestors ultimately were paid for how competently they did their work, just like our grandsons and great granddaughters will be. Any pay plan that rewards you for performance, beyond just showing up and putting in another year, will pay you for how competent you are." It's completely unnecessary to build an elaborate competency-based plan.

In the U.S. over the last 20 years, almost all of the increase in real wages has gone to the most educated 20 percent of the population. This is general evidence that the most competent and knowledgeable get rewarded and promoted even in weak pay for performance plans. If your pay plan downplays seniority and doesn't pay you for just another year in the company or because the market moved, you probably are paying for competency and performance in some fashion. The real issues are how large are the rewards are for great performance and who gets them.

Lynn Snyder Bick, President of QualComp Research Company, an independent compensation consulting firm, agrees. Bick says, "Too many compensation professionals think you have to try to pay people directly for everything they do. What people really want is to feel they are keeping up with costs and with coworkers, and their contributions are being recognized."

I saw this in some research I did for Amoco many years ago. We asked hundreds of employees how managers should make decisions about their pay increases. People told us two things: 1) Help us keep up with rising costs (this was in a time of 4 to 5 percent inflation) and 2) Pay me for my performance. A pay plan that tries to be competitive with the marketplace and offers rewards for performance through incentives or bonuses can do this easily. You don't have to try to reward people for everything they do. That just creates an attitude of entitlement among employees.

Motorola recently rediscovered that trying to get too fancy with pay is a bad idea. Motorola has a high percentage of people working in teams so some compensation professionals thought they should create team-based pay, yet another "new" idea. Motorola employees told them resoundingly not to "mess up teams with pay." Employees said they wanted to be recognized for their individual contributions to team success. This is consistent with what I said earlier about how to measure and reward performance in products companies.

HOW TO MANAGE PERFORMANCE AND PAY

Successful performance and pay management treats people like adults and trusts them to do the right things. To summarize, here's what you should do to manage what you measure and build great results:

- Build a balanced scorecard to set goals and measure share-holder, customer, and employee value.
- Cascade these measures to all levels of your organization.
- Help employees, whether individually or in teams, set their own goals tightly aligned with the business scorecards for their areas.
- Specify the behaviors or competencies that should guide employee actions and tell people how results should be achieved; help people set development plans for their continued learning and improvement.
- Make sure managers are trained and supported to give people plenty of feedback; hold them accountable for doing this; hold employees accountable for asking for it.
- Use multirater feedback approaches and give employees the information they need to monitor their own performance.
- De-emphasize or eliminate supervisory performance appraisal and help people appraise their own performance—by all means, get rid of performance ratings now.
- Keep pay systems simple and understandable—avoid anything that seems like a fad; create pay plans that keep you competitive in your labor markets, enable you to pay bigger salaries to your high achievers, and provide large bonuses or incentives for star individual or team performance.

- Turn your pay plans over to your managers; train them and allow them to make their own decisions about how to reward performance—send the message you trust them to run your business, and in turn, they'll send a message to employees they trust them to do a great job.

CREATING THE TALENT SOLUTION

1. Do you treat your talented people like they have the drive to excel? What's your personal attitude—do you really think people want to do the best they can?

2. How effective is your performance management process? Does it reflect your strategic style? Do you manage the business and execute your strategy through it?

3. What could you do to improve performance management at your company? Are you clear about what results and behaviors you need for business success? Do managers have the skills and freedom they need to manage performance and pay?

4. What could you stop doing today in your performance management process that wouldn't affect the way you do business? If you can identify something, you probably can take it out.

PART FOUR

IMPLEMENT

Improving Strategy Implementation

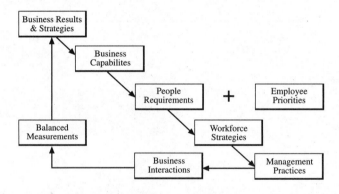

You've seen how to align, engage, and measure your organization and talent to deliver extraordinary business results. Now you need to make it happen. This chapter will give you some practical approaches, including:

- A process for determining what needs to change to implement strategy more effectively
- An understanding of the three areas you need to address to implement strategy
- A model that will help you know how to change
- The absolute necessity of communication to help employees accept the changes and improvements you want to make

GETTING STARTED WITH IMPLEMENTATION

Connecting strategy to talent is how you implement and execute your business strategy. You can sharpen your execution by improving the ways talent is aligned, engaged, and measured. The better you get at execution, the better your business results will become.

Before you get started, remember something I said earlier. *There is no business change without behavioral change.* You can line up all your capabilities, requirements, and practices to fit your aligned business and workforce strategies, but you won't improve unless you engage people and measure performance. That's where implementation really occurs. You have to touch people personally, help them understand why and how they need to change, and then hold them accountable for new behaviors if you're going to do something different and big. Otherwise, you'll look good on paper, but you won't win anything.

When clients want to improve their strategy execution or their talent management practices, I take them through a straightforward, three-step process to determine what needs to change.

- Assess who you really are and what you need to become.
- Determine the gaps between today and tomorrow.
- Decide where it hurts the most.

WHO ARE YOU, REALLY?

It's always hard to come to grips with your basic character—whether it's your personality or your company. Your strategic style is as much about who you are as what your specific strategies are. You need to align/engage/measure to who you really are as a company, because that's how you enable your workforce to deliver the right customer value.

You only change who you really are as a company when you have to change your basic value proposition, the way Ford had to in the early 1980s or Chrysler in the early 1990s. By the time it comes to that, you're hemorrhaging badly and probably near death. In most cases, you probably are more like IBM or Sears who rediscovered their true selves and set out to make them better.

Getting to know who you really are as a company involves looking at your enduring value proposition, specific strategies and tactics, how you make decisions about customers and employees, and then coming to a judgment about what your style is or should be.

Sometimes it's obvious. Sometimes the clues are more subtle. Sometimes companies aren't even clear about their strategies. They're the ones in the most trouble.

Competition is so ferocious these days your company probably is working on all three areas—operations, products or services, and customers—at once. You need to separate your long-term, sustaining strengths from current areas of improvement. In particular, ask yourself which one of the three areas do you absolutely rely on to beat the competition, even to the point of sacrificing something in the other two areas if you had no choice. This will tell you what your essential character and strategic style is.

A team from a consumer goods company was working through this process, making the usual assertions that the company had to be unbeatable in all three areas. After hours of discussion, team members finally acknowledged that while continually reducing production costs was a necessity, the company was very unlikely to invest in information, logistics, distribution, and customer systems to make them significantly better than their competitors. It was enough just to keep up in these areas. What really mattered was investing to keep their products the best in their categories so they commanded premium prices and shelf space. This convinced team members they belonged to a products company and should act accordingly.

Once you know who you really are, ask yourself, "What would it look like if we were totally aligned/engaged/measured?" The information in this book will help you form that vision. I ask my clients to write a newspaper story about themselves five years into the future, describing what their business and workforce strategies and practices should be and how they should be aligned. We then compare stories among team members to get agreement on the picture of the future. Arthur Martinez used this technique to get Sears' management focused on its future at the start of its turnaround.

WHAT GAPS?

The next step is to compare your future with your present. This is a gap analysis. You need to determine:

- Strong alignments, engagements, and measures
- Misalignments
- Weak engagements
- Missing or wrong measures

Usually there's no lack of candidates for the three problem areas. Even companies that do a good job of align/engage/measure can do better. Most organizations don't do very well at all, and are more likely to feel overwhelmed by the number of issues. So it's not a question of whether there is anything to fix. It's how much and how soon.

It's also likely that gaps will be different in different business units or functions. Typically, the more decentralized you are, the more varied the issues will be. Alignment will vary by business unit or staff group. Some business units will be better at measurement or execution of key management practices than others. Functions and units will be at different points in how well they engage their workforces. Often, it's a result of the leadership team in that area. Whatever the variation or the causes, this step is not to solve problems, just to catalog them.

A strategy team made up of representatives from different areas usually can do a good job of a preliminary gap analysis. Their initial findings need to be tested with managers from their areas to be sure they are on target. Obviously, it's counterproductive to proceed to solutions until problems are identified accurately.

My colleague Lori Grubs likes to use a technique she calls reverse engineering in this step. Rather than start with a view of the future and compare the present to it, she starts with today and assesses the messages you are sending. She asks study teams to respond to these questions: "What do your talent management practices say about your people?", "Is this what you want them to say?", "What do you want to say differently?" This reveals the immediate areas of concern.

WHERE'S THE PAIN?

With gaps identified, you can begin to decide which problems should be addressed quickly, later, or not at all. Some issues will emerge from analysis and discussion as big priorities for change. Others will seem smaller. Some will be quick hits. Others will take more time.

The point is not everything can or should be done at once. Maybe some things are so small, you decide you can live with them. Maybe some issues will get resolved by solving the other concerns surrounding them.

I ask my clients to go through a brief exercise of separating the gaps by whether they are big or small, and whether they need to be addressed sooner or later. This produces a pretty good 2 x 2 chart that adds clarity to the discussion.

Then group members go through a priority-setting process. I tell them they have $100 to spend to solve these issues and ask them to allocate their money by where the company will get the biggest increase in customer performance and shareholder value. This produces a definitive set of high-impact, business-driven priorities.

WHAT SIZE CHANGE DO YOU NEED TO MAKE?

When you know where it hurts, how much pain you're in, and what you want to do about it, it's worthwhile to figure out how big these changes are. This will give you a sense of scale, and tell you what challenges you face in improving execution. This will help you create plans and tactics for going forward.

Size and type of change often go together. It's simplistic, but you can think of these as small, medium, or large. As the change gets bigger, focus and complexity become very different (see Table 15-1).

TABLE 15-1

Relationship of Size, Focus, and Complexity of Change

Size of Change	Focus of Change	Complexity and Type of Change
Small	Process or content	A fix or improvement to a few of the things you're already doing—one or two practices need realigning, or there are just a few gaps that need to be addressed. This is *organization development*.
Medium	Process and content	One huge practice or process needs a major overhaul and this will affect several other practices, or several practices and processes need change at the same time. This will be a lot of work. This is *whole systems change*.
Large	Process, content, and context	Your whole way of doing business needs to change. You either have to reconfirm and renew your basic business strategy and align almost every process and practice to it, or you have to change your value proposition and start over. This is *transformation*.

Small changes go on all the time. If they are directed toward greater alignment, engagement, or measurement, they probably can be considered corrections at worst and organization development at best. A planned approach will be optimal. Hopefully, this can be done quickly and with a minimum of disruption. Sometimes you can target your audience with these types of changes.

The focus in small changes is on content or process. Making changes to your performance management practice, refreshing your values statement or competencies, or clarifying some part of the employment relationship are examples. Cargill's updating of behavioral competencies in performance management is an example.

When process and content have to change at the same time, or multiple processes and contents have to change, you are dealing with whole systems change. Putting in competencies and applying them to several different management practices, developing new reward systems (including pay and performance), or creating a new company approach to learning are examples. Levi's Partners in Performance/Total Remuneration Plan or the enhancements to several compensation and benefits plans at Lincoln Electric in 1996–1997 are whole systems changes. So is the balanced scorecard cascade introduced at Glaxo Wellcome Inc.

Large-scale transformations occur when you change your whole way of doing business, typically in a relatively short time. The very way you see your markets and how you intend to pursue them strategically changes, so how you align/engage/measure must change drastically. Shell's and Continental Airlines' huge efforts are transformational.

> You'll know when you are in a transformation because it feels like the whole world is turning upside down.

You'll know when you are in a transformation because it feels like the whole world is turning upside down, and you have to change your own behavior dramatically. Transformation is made up of changes, not change. Complex, simultaneous, and radical are good words to describe these changes. Gaurdie Banister of Shell says everyone—you, your employees, your competitors, even your families—looks at you with amazement when you go through transformation. "If you go with it, it changes your very being."

WHAT TO CHANGE TO IMPROVE STRATEGY IMPLEMENTATION

I work with clients primarily on strategy alignment and implementation. They come to me when they are creating or clarifying business strategy and recognizing the need to change how their organizations and employees do business. My role is to help them identify and implement the organizational and individual behavioral changes required to make the business changes work. Otherwise the time, effort, and money they spent on business strategy development are wasted. To improve strategy implementation, you need to operate in three areas, often at once. These are shown in Figure 15-1.

Strategy and purpose refer to a clear statement of the business strategy or the particular change strategy, how it links to the business needs of your company, and how it will improve your business results. People need to see and understand the business need for change to get engaged in it. If they can understand the business need and how both your company and they will benefit, they will be more likely to enlist. This will not end all of their resistance to change, but it will help reduce it.

Moreover, it's not enough to say, "The culture isn't working," or "We need to do a better job of serving the customer." Unfortunately, that's what many companies do, and why their change efforts fail. When you state clearly and compellingly the business reasons for the strategic change and what you want to accomplish, it's much easier to create some outcome measures of whether the change worked.

FIGURE 15-1

Strategy Implementation

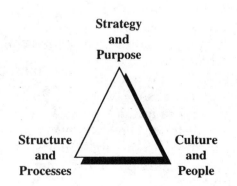

Structure and processes are some of the things you need to affect to activate change and improve execution. New structures are among the most powerful ways to start changes because they command so much attention. They can create new opportunities, identifications, support, and accountabilities for employees, even if they are *ad hoc* or informal. Changes in structure often begin new relationships or alter status. A move to less structure can be confusing at first, but ultimately it's extremely potent as it creates more freedom.

New processes will be pointed more directly at new behaviors than new structure is. Processes potentially can be as powerful as structure, but sometimes companies mistakenly put in processes that lag change, like new rewards, and expect them to initiate behavior change. This won't happen. Process changes have to address work expectations, performance measures, or work design to activate change.

Culture and people describe the organizational and individual levels of behavior. These are values, decision-making, how people treat each other or customers, leadership, employee development, teamwork, retention, and related performance issues. No implementation or change effort is complete without a thorough explanation and communication of how these things must shift and the consequences attached to changing them. Even more than process, it's hard to activate change here. These changes usually are more downstream, though this is where the new strategy becomes personal and where behavior change has to occur.

Complete transformation or whole systems change requires touching all the bases of the triangle. You have to describe how you want the new strategy and purpose, structure and process, and culture and people to operate and how these elements should interact with each other. Then you can use these descriptions as milestones and measures of how complete, integrated, and effective you've been at implementing strategy.

My personal observation of several failed reengineering efforts is they addressed structure and process quite completely, strategy and purpose somewhat, but left culture and people relatively untouched. That's precisely why they failed. On the other hand, many tries at changing culture and people fail because they don't connect with business strategy and purpose, or structure and process.

W.W. Grainger is an example of a company doing it all. It has declared a new strategy—to focus its speed and convenience business on standardized processes and product delivery and grow its new, more tailored consulting business. It is doing major process redesign, primarily working on cycle time reduction and work flow improvements in the speed and convenience business and then seeing what tools can be used by consulting. It also is revising its supporting talent management practices and letting them differ by line of business. Finally, it is working the culture and people side heavily. Grainger executives went through a values alignment process and communicated a revised set of values to its people. Then, through communication, the new management practices, and extensive teamwork training, it is trying to change the way people behave.

I recommend to clients they chart all three areas—strategy and purpose, structure and processes, and culture and people—and be sure they are doing enough of the right things in each. A lack of action in any of the three is major cause for worry.

HOW TO CHANGE TO IMPROVE STRATEGY IMPLEMENTATION

Strategy and purpose, structure and processes, and culture and people describe what to change. How to change describes the mechanisms you have at your disposal to improve implementation and execution. Again, I use three categories of things—activators, enablers, and reinforcers (see Figure 15-2).

FIGURE 15-2

Mechanisms for Change

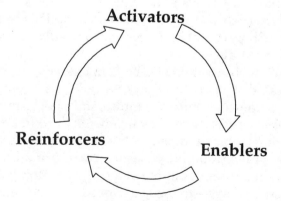

Activators start people behaving differently. They create new expectations. To some extent they force change. A new strategy and set of goals or performance measures can activate; so can new individual or team accountabilities. As I said earlier, structure can activate. In some companies, new values can begin change, but they are a hard sell without some accountability mechanism. Companies sometimes try to use training as an activator, but this is difficult because learning doesn't always transfer easily back to the day-to-day job. You have to pair training with new accountabilities or rewards to use it to begin change.

Enablers are tools that help people behave in new ways. Training, communication sessions, one-on-one conversations, development processes, 360° feedback, competency assessments, and feedback processes can be enablers. A new information system also may be an enabler. To return to my golf analogy, the first tee is the activator. Your golf clubs, tees, and golf balls are the enablers.

Reinforcers sustain the change once it is underway. Success is the best reinforcer because it maintains and strengthens new behaviors. Success, of course, demands measurement. Measures can be reinforcers. Many enablers also are reinforcers, particularly feedback and information processes. Knowledge of results is usually an internal or intrinsic reinforcer. Rewards and recognition are the external reinforcers most companies use. To complete the golf analogy, a good swing, golf hole, or score can be an internal reinforcer, while a medal or prize is an external or extrinsic reinforcer.

The key points to remember are: 1) you need all three types of change mechanisms to begin, continue, and sustain change (if any are missing or lacking, your efforts will fail) and 2) You need to use the right mechanisms for the right purposes. It's next to impossible to start change with an enabler or reinforcer. As much as I think 360° feedback is a tremendous change tool as an enabler and reinforcer, you're not likely to start change with it. You need the communication of strategy, goal-setting, new performance measures, structure change, or some other activator first.

Additionally, the three mechanisms interact with each other in a continuous fashion. They are not linear. You can implement and keep adding to them in simultaneous and interactive ways, as long as you have enough activation. That's why I show them in a cycle.

The thing to do when you are planning strategy implementation is to chart whether you have enough of all three. Then you should check to make sure you intend to use them the right way. Continental Airlines used all three during its transformation. Its declaration and explanation of running "a good on-time airline" was a strategic activator. Its town hall meetings and other communication vehicles were powerful enablers. The $65 on-time bonus was a visible and effective reinforcer.

If you work all of the areas for change and use the three mechanisms, you will have a complete and winning idea of what and how to change. Additionally, you should create a change management plan to describe and take you through this journey. It should list the activities, accountabilities, milestones, and time frames for change. You will revise it as you go, but without it, you are likely to stall, lose your way, or get waylaid all together.

Changing to Implement Strategy

An operations company client set a new strategy to improve the reliability of its service delivery and to increase its speed and reduce its costs by targeting its market on certain types of customers. Before, it had tried to be too many things to too many people; and its quality, timeliness, and costs were no longer meeting its performance hurdles. After setting its business strategy and identifying its revised business capabilities and people requirements, the client identified four heightened elements of its workforce strategy. These were the new behaviors and attitudes it needed from people to be successful. The client used the model illustrated in Figure 15-3 as part of its communication.

Alignment meant setting, lining up, and connecting company goals to team and individual goals. Competency was a new competency model that detailed the skills required by the new strategy. Accountability was improved performance management and increased consequences for results and behaviors. Ownership referred to the initiative, engagement, and pride the company wanted employees to demonstrate as they set out to execute the new strategy.

To accomplish these changes, the client used rapid design teams to create new talent management practices that would communicate, measure, and sustain the behaviors and interactions it wanted. They planned their activators, enablers, and reinforcers as shown in Figure 15-4.

FIGURE 15-3

New Behaviors to Drive New Strategies

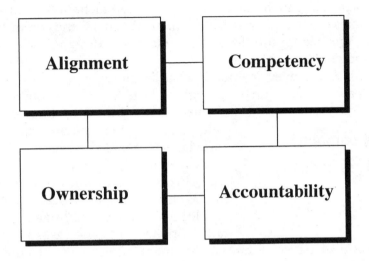

The client created an integration team to put all of these elements together in a consistent plan and to manage the overall change
process. Changes were introduced over the course of 18 months.

COMMUNICATE, COMMUNICATE, COMMUNICATE

Accompanying any change effort is the absolute requirement to communicate—on a regular basis and in a two-way fashion. Communication activities should be part of your change management plan.
This will help ensure that you inform and involve people so they
can engage with you.

Employees often go through an identifiable set of stages of their
own as you introduce change. These stages are shock > anger > resistance > acceptance (S > A > R > A), and correspond to the same
phases people go through when they are grieving. Elizabeth Kubler-
Ross first identified these in her work on bereavement. Experiences
trying to change organizations have validated these SARA phases
among employees.

Smart companies use countertactics to help move people
through these stages from shock to acceptance. Effective tactics are
based on communication in multiple media and from credible

sources. They also require you to ask broad groups of employees to participate in the changes—first by learning about them, next by understanding them, then by doing something with them, and finally by incorporating them into their work lives. A tactic almost all smart companies use to build participation, involvement, and commitment is to commission multiple employee teams to design specific practices and communications.

Still, I find every company changes in its own ways. Usually, there is a strong relation to strategic style. Like other customers companies, Levi's does it by appealing to values. That's often enough to get their associates to mobilize. Operations companies, especially the really big ones like the oil companies, do it by having top management compel critical masses of employees to move their huge organizations forward. In some cases it's absolutely critical that corporate management is perceived as leading the charge. In others, employees generally ignore what corporate says and wait for local management to show they're serious. In either case, it's top-down change. Products companies often implement new

> Every company changes in its own ways.

FIGURE 15-4

Change Elements

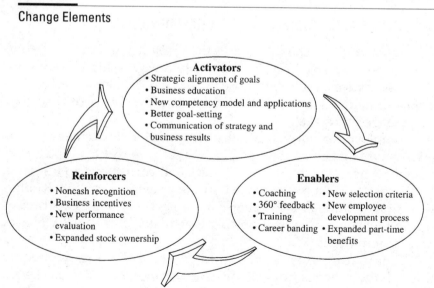

strategies by appealing to people on an intellectual or technical basis, like the rush to create a new product. You have to analyze what moves your people and what cues they look for to see if you are serious, and then execute against those.

In any case, you can expect employees to go through the SARA stages and resist your attempts to advance until they are sure you're sure. My colleague Bob Gandossy says, "If you're serious about change and your employees aren't anxious, they don't believe you."

Even if they get to acceptance, you are not done convincing them. Gary Goberville, who is leading many of the changes at Grainger, says once employees accepted the changes Grainger has been trying to make, they still were deeply concerned about keeping pace with how fast the company was moving. Additionally, Goberville heard employees "worry we would lose what made us a great place to work in the first place and wonder if we would stay with the new culture if times got tough."

This returns me to where I began this chapter. Ultimately, all change is personal. People have to feel it and do it for your business to advance. You have to reach them in their hearts to implement your strategy.

CREATING THE TALENT SOLUTION

1. What gaps exist between how you currently align/engage/measure your talent to implement strategy now and where you would like to be?

2. What changes need to be made to close gaps in strategy and purpose? Structure and processes? Culture and people?

3. Think about your most recent change effort. Did you pay proper attention to activators? Enablers? Reinforcers? What will you do differently the next time?

4. How effective are you at communicating your strategy and how and why people need to change to implement it fully?

CLOSE

THE ERA OF TALENT

The growing effects of the information economy, globablization, and changing demographics are coinciding to create a new era in business—the era of talent. Your ability to attract, manage, and retain talent will determine whether you succeed. This wasn't always true in the past. Before, you could succeed if you controlled enough physical resources. Today, talent is the fundamental resource in business.

This has shifted power to skilled employees. In an information and service economy, the upstream source of all value is talented people. As the world moves in this direction, talent will become as valuable on a global basis as it is in developed economies. With this power shift, talented people will be able to demand challenging work, a positive working environment, and competent and empathetic leadership.

This already is happening in the U.S. The almost exclusive emphasis on shareholder value we saw in the 1980s is starting to moderate somewhat. Companies already are beginning to return more to employees in higher salaries, wages, and benefits. In smart companies there will be a new and better balance among meeting the needs of customers, shareholders, and employees.

Yet competing for employees primarily through higher compensation never has been enough to attract and retain the best talent. After a while, the kinds of people you really want to employ look for more from their work than just pay. There are many great jobs available. There aren't many great organizations. Talented people demand the kind of satisfying and meaningful work experiences that require you to build a great work culture and manage people skillfully. If you do these things well, you will have the talent you need to succeed.

With this talent, you can satisfy customers and shareholders and create terrific results. Already, some stock analysts, investors, and pension fund managers are beginning to realize companies that manage people better are stronger investments. In the near future, market-makers will look first to the quality of a company's talent and talent management as the keys to their investment strategies. The knowledge and skills of your workforce and your abilities to enable them to contribute to the heights of their talents will be how your company gets its investment grade.

This means every one of your skilled employees owns a big piece of your future success, including your personal wealth. You need to value each person like a scarce resource and maximize your return on them by aligning, engaging, and measuring their performance in line with your strategic style. This is how you will get the most from their talent, and they will get the most from you.

APPENDIX

What's the Evidence that Managing Talent Makes a Difference?

THINKING ABOUT THE DATA

What hard evidence exists that aligning, engaging, and measuring your organization and workforce really builds your bottom line? No one has tested this proposition specifically. It would be hard to do because companies are so different and are in such different situations. However, there is a large and growing body of evidence from a variety of sources that shows being an employer that values its workforce, demonstrates it, and tries to improve talent management practices tied to business strategy pays off with better long-term financial performance.

As you review these data, please keep a few things in mind. This is not experimental data, collected under careful scientific conditions. It can't be—it's about real-life business situations with differing markets, customers, employees, leaders, work processes, financial situations, and so on. Under these circumstances it isn't possible to conduct laboratory experiments. Instead it's the work of careful thinkers and analysts doing their best to make reasonable assumptions and clean out "noise" in the data. It's also about putting measures to what many people call the "soft stuff" of organizations—values, people, and the ways they're treated and managed.

As a result, these data cannot be used to prove causality; I can't say definitely this caused that to happen. There are too many other things happening at the same time.

Also, many of the observations that generated these data are subjective. They are ratings or critiques given by people to soft phenomena and represent best efforts to measure things that generally haven't been measured previously. While they are sound attempts, they also show it's impossible to put a precise ruler to certain things.

TWO TYPES OF CONCLUSIONS

What can be concluded from this data? At least two conclusions can be drawn. The first is correlational. You can see what types of things happen together. If certain management practices keep occurring in successful companies, and aren't as prevalent in less successful companies, then it's safe to say these things occur together or *co-vary*. I can't say which came first or what caused something to happen, just they appear to go together.

There is one piece of research in this Appendix that goes beyond simple correlation and looks at before and after. It was conducted by my colleague Danielle McDonald and her team at Hewitt, along with Professor Abbie Smith of the University of Chicago. A before/after design helps move closer to asserting causality, but it cannot get all the way there.

The other type of conclusion comes from the weight of the evidence. If a number of researchers come to similar conclusions based on data from a number of settings, I think you have to use common sense and reasonableness, even if you don't have experimental or statistical purity. If a large number of different researchers find the same phenomena occurring in different situations, there may be similar things happening that are creating value, even if the value is different because situations are different. Repeated, subjective measurements can provide some objectivity, if they are done over time.

When the weight of many studies point to the same conclusions about good long-term talent management practices and their positive effects on financial results, it's worth the risk to assume there are some facts there. It should lead to some new ways to create financial value. There's certainly no evidence any of these practices detract from value creation.

THREE TYPES OF STUDIES

I am going to review a number of studies from different sources that say smart talent management practices, the kind you would find in companies that take a strategic view toward their people and organizations, at least correlate, if not contribute, to greater financial returns and shareholder value creation. By no means are these all of the studies. It has been estimated that more than 100 pieces of research have been conducted in the last 10–15 years trying to correlate management practices with financial success. I will present only a small set, classified into three types of studies:

1. Culture studies—Studies that show effective and adaptive cultures, including being good places to work, correlate to higher financial returns.

2. Management practices—Studies that show talent management practices, usually considered key parts of effective cultures, correlate with, and possibly contribute to, higher financial returns.

3. Downsizing studies—Studies that suggest the opposite style of management doesn't help financial results. Downsizing is not the opposite of strategic talent management, but repeated or careless downsizing could be symptomatic of it.

Culture Studies

I use the term *culture studies* to describe a group of studies—some intended as scholarly research, some not—that characterize types of organization cultures and show which are associated with better financial results. None of them test for what came first, the effective culture or the financial results. Additionally, the characterizations of culture are different from study-to-study but do point in fundamentally the same directions. None specifically cover talent management as I am describing it, but effective culture companies would be breeding grounds for that kind of management.

Adaptive Cultures

John Kotter and Jim Heskett, two Harvard professors, probably have done the most exacting study of these culture issues in their book, *Corporate Culture and Performance.* Theirs was the first academic study to examine empirically the issue of culture and its relation to financial performance. They used interviews, observations, written documentation, and financial analysts' ratings to study a large group of companies.

Kotter and Heskett found having a strong culture was not enough to indicate higher financial performance. Changes in the business can doom a strong culture that cannot change. They also found that having a culture that fit the business strategy was more powerful than just having a strong culture, but the issue of change was still there. Could a culture that fit the business at one time adapt fast enough when the business changed?

The answer to their ultimate question—which types of cultures were associated with the strongest financial performance—was cultures that could be described as strong, a good strategic fit, and adaptive were associated with the best business results. These cultures helped people coalesce around business goals and values, were appropriate for the company's strategy, and changed relatively quickly when business needs changed. They did this because from the start they balanced the needs of shareholders, customers, and employees. Their leadership directed them to be focused externally to keep changing to meet the needs of customers and labor markets. This balance, leadership, and external focus enabled them to reward shareholders very handsomely.

When Kotter and Heskett compared the 1977–1988 results of companies with strong, adaptive cultures with another group of well-known companies that lacked these types of cultures, they found some very dramatic results (see Table A-1).

The authors concluded the financial results of cultural strength, fit, and adaptation are overwhelming. Adaptation comes from a strong set of values that emphasizes paying equal attention to shareholders, customers, and employees; having management practices that fit the business strategy; being able to recognize quickly the need to change because leaders and others keep scanning the external environment; and having the leadership to change practices as needed. I think this is the direct opposite of managing with an exclusive, short-term view of generating returns to meet only shareholder needs.

TABLE A-1

Adaptive versus Nonadaptive Cultures

Performance Measures	Firms with Strong, Adaptive Cultures (12)	Firms with Less Adaptive Cultures (20)
Revenue growth	682%	166%
Employment growth	282%	36%
Stock price growth	901%	74%
Net income growth	756%	1%

Visionary Companies

Another set of cultural data come from the book *Built To Last*, written by James Collins and Jerry Porras of Stanford. Collins and Porras compared 18 pairs of companies matched for their industries, like Citicorp versus Chase Manhattan, Ford versus GM, and IBM versus Burroughs. Their purpose was to identify which habits made one set of pairs visionary, and the other set merely successful. They defined visionary as more than enduring success. *Visionary* was defined as the companies that are "role models for the practice of management around the globe."

Their financial barometer was stock returns. Visionary companies' cumulative stock returns outperformed the general stock market by more than 15 times since 1926, adjusted for when the companies started to be publicly traded. The comparison companies beat the market also, but only by a little more than 2:1.

Next, Collins and Porras derived a set of themes from their research findings about how these visionary companies construct their cultures to be so successful. What's more relevant here is some of the criteria they used to determine how visionary companies differed from the others. Many of the criteria are highly suggestive of aligned workforces and talent management practices.

The criteria are:

- Consistency between ideology (core values) and actions
- Significant orientation (indoctrination) of new employees to the core values
- Use of selection, rewards, and other processes to ensure a tight fit between new employees and company values
- Formal management development programs and processes
- Careful succession planning and CEO selection
- Investment in human capabilities (recruiting, training, and development)

On each of these criteria, the authors rated the companies *high, medium,* or *low*. Their evidence suggests strongly that visionary companies with their outstanding financial returns use many more of these strategic practices than do other successful companies. When you manage for long-term success, you must pay attention to people.

Let's look at the number of companies (out of a possible 18) they rated as high on each criterion (see Table A-2).

TABLE A-2

Scoring High on Each Criterion

Criteria	Visionary Companies	Comparison Companies
Consistency	13	0
Orientation	12	1
Tight fit	8	0
Management development	7	1
Succession planning	7	0
Investment in people	10	0

In every case, the differences between the two groups is striking. Comparison companies usually were rated a medium on these criteria.

Collins and Porras describe many other organizational characteristics that distinguish visionary companies, like the use of stretch goals, long-term investment, presence of change mechanisms, and so forth. I am making no claim these talent management practices are precisely what make these companies visionary. Still, it's clear these practices are found among the world's most successful, enduring organizations.

Could it be that in turning around a company, it might be more powerful to incorporate some of these changes, rather than just sell off or close down weaker operations or create massive layoffs? Obviously it would take longer and may be much more difficult, but perhaps the company would be alive and stronger when you are done.

Competitive Advantage

Another set of culture findings are not quite as rigorous, but come from a respected academic, Jeffrey Pfeffer, in his book *Competitive Advantage Through People*. Pfeffer started by looking at companies that had the highest total return to shareholders (stock price appreciation plus dividend yield) in the period from 1972–1992.

They are:

1. Southwest Airlines—21,775%
2. Wal Mart—18,970%

3. Tyson Foods—18,118%
4. Circuit City—16,410%
5. Plenum Publishing—15,689%

Next Pfeffer asked what could this disparate group of companies possibly have in common that could enable them to generate such great returns? As a checklist, he used Michael Porter's highly regarded criteria for strategic advantage. Pfeffer figured that for these companies to be this successful, they must possess some of these characteristics.

Porter said strategic superiority ultimately comes from innovation, which in turn comes from proprietary inventions or technology, capturing emerging new markets or industry segments, government regulations, or sustainable cost advantages. These things pose high barriers to entry for the competition. The purpose of developing strategy is to determine how to innovate so you can differentiate your company and then erect or take advantage of barriers to entry.

When Pfeffer looked closely, he saw none of these companies had these strategic advantages to any great degree. They tended to be late entrants in highly competitive industries, most with low margins; for instance, airlines, discount retailing, chicken processing, and so on. They just outsmarted or outexecuted the competition.

When Pfeffer tried to find what enabled these companies to do that, he saw the only sustained advantage each had was in the way they managed people. Each did some distinctive things in selection, training, labor relations, or staffing that reflected their organizational values and enabled them to win big. Each also was seen by employees as a very good place to work.

Pfeffer didn't really test alternative hypotheses. It could be, for instance, Porter's framework was wrong. Some recent business writers have claimed strategic planning is dead. However, as Mark Twain said about the rumors of his own death, reports of the demise of strategic planning are premature and inaccurate. Most business writers don't spend much time in company planning meetings.

Strategic planning looks different in the late 1990s than it did ten years earlier. It's less elaborate and quantifiable, but it's still how large companies approach their futures. Also many of Porter's concepts still guide companies in their planning processes.

Instead, it's more likely there is no real alternative hypothesis. Some of these companies, especially Wal Mart and Southwest Airlines, have been written about so much Pfeffer's explanation has a lot of face validity to it. They have aligned their organizations, processes, and people tightly to fit their plans, execute very well against these plans, and have distinctive and compelling management practices.

Southwest's hiring and training policies, for example, are well-known for selecting and educating people to bring fun back into flying. I was on a charter on another airline recently when the flight attendant perked up the safety and information speech with a lot of humor—so much that people actually listened attentively. Another flight attendant standing near me said, "He must have been trained by Southwest!"

Best Workplaces

A final set of cultural data come from Robert Levering. Levering and his colleague Milton Moskowitz have written the bestseller, *The 100 Best Companies to Work for in America*. Theirs is a bottom-up view; what makes a company great for employees. They have written two editions of the book, one in 1984 and the other in 1993. The authors visited all of the companies they considered for inclusion in their list, as well as many that didn't make it.

Their list of characteristics for a great company are high levels of:

- Pay/benefits
- Opportunities
- Job security
- Pride in work/company
- Openness/fairness
- Camaraderie/friendliness

After publishing these books, Levering went back to compare the financial performance of these companies to relevant indices. He has taken a backward look from the publication dates so that for the 1984 book, he looked at performance in the ten prior years (1975–1984), and for the 1993 edition he looked at performance from 1984–1993. These are not the same companies, though there are many repeats. Nor did he use the same financial measures. These differences weaken his conclusions, but the conclusions still are instructive.

Looking at the companies listed in the 1984 book and comparing their ten-year growth in earnings per share to the Standard & Poor's 500 index for the same time, Levering found the "best companies" return improved 380 percent, while the S&P 500 grew 169 percent, less than half. This is a powerful difference but just a suggestive finding, not conclusive.

For the 1993 edition, a much stronger analysis was done by BARRA, an investor research service. BARRA compared the performance of an equally weighted portfolio of publicly traded firms from the 1993 edition to an equally weighted portfolio invested in the Frank Russell 3,000 Index, a broad index of 3,000 stocks. Results again showed a dramatic difference (see Table A-3).

These results again show the value of strong management practices on financial results, though this time the companies were chosen from the employees' point of view. You could argue these companies can afford to be more generous with pay, opportunities, and security because they are more successful. However, remember the criteria also included some environmental or values-oriented issues, like openness and pride. It takes outstanding management to create and maintain that type of environment, particularly from the employees' view.

None of these studies taken alone makes a convincing argument. Taken together, they form a powerful picture suggesting strong, adaptive cultures that emphasize smart talent management practices make a very good long-term investment and are terrific places to work.

TABLE A-3

Returns of "Best Places to Work" versus Frank Russell 3,000 Index

	Portfolio from Frank Russell 3,000	Portfolio from 1993 Best Companies List
Annualized return 12/84–4/93	12.05%	19.47%
1993 value of a $100,000 investment done in 12/84	$260,000	$450,000

Management Practices Studies

Another type of research builds on the culture studies by trying to identify the specific management practices that contribute to bottom line results. You can think of this as drilling down deeper into what makes for effective talent management. It's likely companies that do these kinds of things well have the types of successful cultures I have just described.

Rutgers Studies

One of the most comprehensive of these studies was done by Mark Huselid, a researcher at Rutgers. Actually, Huselid's work resulted in a number of analyses over time.

Huselid was interested in management practices that increase employees' knowledge and skills such as recruitment, selection, training, and participation programs. He also was interested in those that deal with employee motivation, like performance appraisal and pay. His list of practices evolved from some earlier studies and are generally in line with the Department of Labor's list of what constitutes talent management practices. Some people have complained that many of the practices on his list are not sophisticated enough to describe high performance. Still, they do form a kind of baseline case that a wide range of small and large companies could consider. To an Amoco or Marriott, they may not seem so refined or progressive.

In a first analysis published in 1993, Huselid took 700 companies, ranked them, and clustered them into fourths, based on the number of practices they used. He didn't look at the quality or spread of practices. He then compared them on annual shareholder return and gross return on capital. He found a very consistent pattern (see Table A-4).

The data show a positive association between increasing these practices and increasing financial results The pattern is mostly linear and reasonably strong, probably as good as could be expected for this type of data. Remember he was simply counting practices and looking across a broad array of companies, and not comparing them to an index or within industries. At the ends of the spectrum, those are big differences.

Fortunately, Huselid went much further in his analysis. He expanded his sample to 986 companies, refined his list of management practices, and adjusted for many other variables such as firm size, industry, and unionization. He also began to look for the real effects of these practices, which he reasoned would not be directly on finan-

TABLE A-4

Management Practices and Financial Returns

	Number of Management Practices			
	Bottom 25%	Second 25%	Third 25%	Top 25%
Annual shareholder return	6.5%	6.8%	8.2%	9.4%
Gross return on capital	3.7%	1.5%	4.1%	11.3%

cial performance but instead would more likely be on employee productivity (sales per employee) and employee turnover. His questions became: Would using more of these practices increase productivity, which is generally related to profitability, and decrease the costs associated with turnover? If so, what would the dollar effects be on the bottom line? Huselid found every time a company increased the number of practices it used by a standard deviation increase (it's impossible to tell you from his research report how many practices this is or which ones they are, just that they used significantly more of them), it experienced a 7 percent decrease in turnover relative to average. Additionally, for every one standard deviation increase in these practices, sales per employee went up by $27,044. This is a 16 percent improvement over the average reported in the study, $171,099. It also accounts for only a one-year improvement. Companies should enjoy the cumulative effects of several years' improvement based on a one-time intervention.

Finally, Huselid wondered what these improvements would mean for market value and cash flow, because adopting these practices also costs money. His market value analysis suggests that an increase of one standard deviation in the number of practices yields an increase of $18,641 per employee. He estimates cash flow would increase by $3,814 per employee. Multiply these by the number of employees affected in a company, and they become powerful results from decreasing turnover and/or increasing productivity through smart management practices.

USC Studies

Ed Lawler, Susan Mohrman, and Gerry Ledford of USC conducted studies in 1987 and 1990 with *Fortune* 1000 companies on their use of employee involvement (EI) programs and methods. They defined EI as greater sharing of information, knowledge, rewards and power in a company. Many of the techniques they identified that increase involvement through knowledge and reward sharing areas are what I have labelled as talent management practices. For example, the USC team examined many aspects of training as part of knowledge sharing and different types of incentives, gainsharing and profit sharing, recognition awards, and employee ownership as part of reward sharing. In 1993 they extended their study to look at adoption of total quality management (TQM) by these companies.

As part of their research, the USC team did a sophisticated analysis of the effects of EI and TQM on company financial performance. The team controlled for industry type and capital intensity and looked at a number of return and productivity measures. Adopting EI and TQM were correlated—a majority of companies saw them as integrated or managed them on a coordinated basis—so the USC researchers had to look at their effects together. It was impossible to say whether EI or TQM, or which parts of EI or TQM, had the biggest effects.

The analysis demonstrated that EI and TQM showed a significant relationship to four return measures—return on sales, return on assets, return on investment, and return on equity. Increases in the use of EI and TQM showed meaningful increases in financial performance on these indicators. For instance, companies that were low users of EI and TQM (defined as one standard deviation below the mean) had average return on equity of 16.6%, while companies that were high users (one standard deviation above the mean) had average return on equity of 22.8%. These are big differences in usage of EI and TQM—it would be a stretch to go from low to high on the USC measures—but a more than 6% improvement in returns would be very strong gains.

Interestingly, the results revealed only modest impact on productivity and no impact on total return to investors. TQM usually is not intended to produce specific increases in productivity the way some other talent management practices are, and it could be that combining the impacts of EI and TQM obscured some of the effects of the talent management practices imbedded in the EI measure. Total return to investors can be impacted by external market forces well beyond internal initiatives like EI and TQM.

Hewitt Studies

My Hewitt colleague, Danielle McDonald, wanted to look at one practice and its bottom line effect in even greater depth. Danielle has a career-long interest in performance management and believes strongly it is the fundamental management practice by which a business aligns its employees to achieve its outcomes.

Danielle assembled a Hewitt team consisting of Sally Shield and Katherine Donohue and worked with Professor Abbie Smith of the Graduate School of Business at the University of Chicago. They studied the performance management processes and financial results of 437 publicly traded firms using a questionnaire and the Boston Consulting Group/HOLT financial database.

Of the sample, 232 companies said they did not have a formal performance management process—they either did simple year-end evaluations or nothing at all, and 205 used a formal process. This suggests companies were being realistic in describing their practices. The significant differences between the two groups are remarkable (see Table A-5).

The specific numbers themselves are telling. Danielle and the team looked at three-year financial performance (1990–1992), the results of which are illustrated in Figure A-1.

There are a number of interesting things about this study. Like Huselid and unlike the culture studies, the Hewitt team looked at average American companies. This was a recessionary period, and financial results reflected it. Performance management companies averaged 10.2 percent return on equity; nonperformance management companies averaged 4.4 percent. The companies that used performance management may not have been star companies, but the ones who didn't use it were laggards.

TABLE A-5

Comparison of Companies With and Without Formal Performance Management Processes

Companies with Performance Management	Companies without Performance Management
Higher profits	Lower profits
Better cash flows	Weaker cash flows
Stronger market performance	Weaker market performance
Greater stock values	Lower stock values

FIGURE A-1

Financial and Productivity Performance 1990–1992

Financial Measures

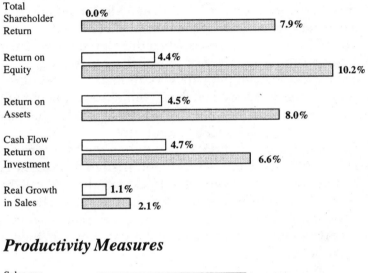

Productivity Measures

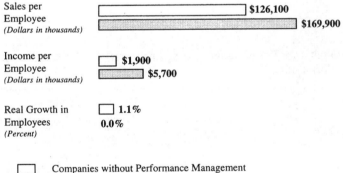

☐ Companies without Performance Management
▨ Companies with Performance Management

The other similarity to the Huselid study is most striking to me. The impact of performance management on the bottom line seems to occur through increased productivity. Companies with performance management not only had higher sales per employee, they also had no real increase in employment during this period of slow growth. Put simply, they were able to do more with the same number of employees. Companies without performance management had to keep hiring, despite lousy results. Unlike Huselid, we didn't study turnover.

Of course, these data in no way indicate whether using a performance management process caused these differences. Yet, here is where this study goes further than others. McDonald and her team were able to look at before-and-after implementation of performance management because they asked when these processes were implemented. Surprisingly, many were of recent vintage.

The before-and-after data are very dramatic (see Figure A-2).

Everything got better when these companies implemented performance management. All financial indices showed an increase and three of the five were statistically significant.

Since this before/after data spanned only a three-year period (1990–1992), McDonald and her team returned to the data in 1995 to take a longer look. They were able to extend the analysis by two years (1990–1994) to test for more definitive results. They found a strong association with wealth creation by companies after implementing performance management versus companies in their industries that did not.

FIGURE A-2

Before versus After Performance Management Implementation: Changes in Financial Performance

	Deviations From Industry Averages		
	Average Before	**Average After**	**Average Change**
Total Shareholder Return	–5.1%	19.7%	24.8%*
Stock Return Relative to Market Index	–0.13%	0.18	0.31%
Price/Book Value of Total Capital	0.03	0.26%	0.23%
Real Value/Cost	–0.06	0.13	0.19*
Sales per Employee ($ Thousands)	98.8	193.0*	94.2*

Significant at the .10 probability level or better.

The next three graphs show stock return relative to market index, price/book total capital, and real value/cost ratio all increased significantly after performance management implementation versus other companies (see Figures A-3, A-4, and A-5). These are sophisticated measures of a company's performance in creating real economic value. With results like these, perhaps companies should announce publicly when they are putting in a new performance management process so investors could know these are the stocks to buy.

Again, the data do not show causality. However, take a look at productivity as measured by sales volume per employee. It soars once employees participated in a process designed to help them understand better how to contribute. This probably wasn't the only thing employers were doing to increase productivity during this time. There could have been new technology and equipment, restructuring, or other new management practices, though I don't know that.

I do know performance management tells employees what they want to know about their expected contributions. Employers should be telling them these things. The way to drive real economic value with your workforce is to increase productivity. McDonald's work, along with Huselid's, shows how it can be done without downsizing and layoffs.

Service Quality

There is another stream of data that has relevance here, though it has not yet been converted to bottom line financial results. That should be coming soon, though. These studies deal with improving service quality and customer satisfaction. It is easier and more direct to see the effects of employee attitudes and behaviors in service businesses because employees are inseparable from the delivery of the service in many cases. The conversion to bottom line results is occurring as companies begin to put a dollar value on having and keeping satisfied customers.

Service quality research looks at customer satisfaction or perceptions of quality as a function of service capability, which is the employee's perception of his or her ability to deliver good service, and service passion, the employee's willingness to give good service. This research demonstrates how service capability and service passion are related to management practices. Some of these practices are straightforward—having the tools, information, policies, and

FIGURE A-3

Stock Return Relative to Market Index*

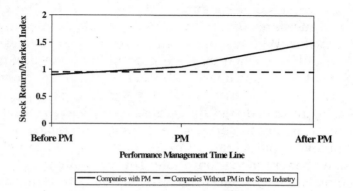

FIGURE A-4

Price/Book Total Capital*

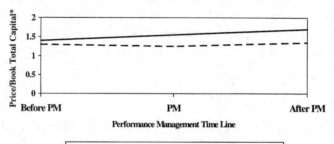

FIGURE A-5

Real Value/Cost Ratio*

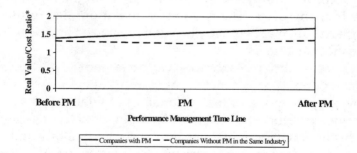

*Increase is significantly higher than industry average at the .10 probability level or better.

processes to do the job. Other correlates are talent management practices.

In a study of three financial services organizations, researchers from the University of Maryland looked at which organizational characteristics and management practices correlated with service passion. In addition to items directly connected to delivering the service and interacting with customers, the next most important things employees talked about were hiring procedures, performance feedback, internal equity of pay, and training. These items all correlated positively with service passion and accounted for much of the desire to provide great service.

A different study done by professors at the Harvard Business School surveyed 9,475 front-line employees and managers working in three divisions of two U.S. insurance companies. The professors found six components of internal service quality were related statistically to service capability. Two of these were having the right tools to do the job and having policies that helped to get the job done. Four were management practices: teamwork, management support, goal alignment, and training. Goal alignment also had the most powerful relationship to job satisfaction. Goal alignment is the starting point of performance management.

These studies, and others like them, suggest a company can improve its service capability and employee service attitudes through strategic talent management practices. These, in turn, are related to customer perceptions of quality and satisfaction. If this can be done, it won't be long before you will be able to tell how much change is needed in each management practice to bring about a change in customer satisfaction.

Some companies like Xerox, Sears, and Chrysler already are starting to calculate how much a satisfied customer is worth to them. If a company knows this and how management practices relate to customer satisfaction, it should be able to do a cost/benefit analysis to determine the value of each management practice.

To summarize this group of studies, it's becoming clearer how management practices contribute to employee productivity and turnover, and how these contribute directly to profitability and economic value. Soon you also will be able to see how these management practices lead to customer satisfaction and retention. In the not-too-distant future, research will be able to tell with some certainty exactly how much you will be able to increase profitability, cash flow, and market value by adopting specific talent management practices. Right now, it's no stretch for you to conclude that developing and using these practices will improve shareholder value and make your company a better place to work.

Downsizing Studies

If effective talent management is a key to improving financial results, then not using these practices should lead to deteriorating results, or at least they should not have a positive impact. It's hard to study the effects of bad management in a carefully controlled environment. It's like trying to force people to smoke, or maybe exposing them to a virus, and trying to study the effects. Downsizing *per se* may not be a sign of bad management, but I think repeated or careless downsizing is. A good deal of data has been collected on the topic, and a few things can be concluded from it.

Anecdotal data here is spotty and inconclusive. For every AT&T that keeps going through repeated downsizings but still doesn't seem to be improving results, there's an IBM who has shrunk a lot and now seems to have turned its business right again. AT&T hasn't created any real economic value for years, but its regulated history is a millstone that may take generations to discard.

There is helpful survey data to review from the American Management Association (AMA) annual survey of downsizing. The AMA has been collecting data from a broad group of companies since 1990. The results point to some intriguing ideas. Studies done by other researchers help confirm and expand the AMA findings.

Looking at the AMA data, it's clear downsizing has changed. When companies started engaging in it heavily during the 1980s and very early 1990s, it was focused on cutting costs to increase profits. In general it didn't work. Only about one-third of companies increased their productivity from downsizing and less than one-half increased operating profits. Stock price tended to go up immediately following the announcement, but then fell back down to where it was before, or even lower. One study followed 16 large downsizings in the 1980s and showed the stock price of downsizers was 26 percent lower than competitors three years later.

There are several reasons for this. Then, companies often weren't very thoughtful or lacked planning for how they cut. Across-the-board layoffs and broad voluntary severance plans meant a lot of good people left, including some of the best. When companies did start to pick and choose who should go, sometimes the criteria were poorly defined or based on seniority or organizational level. This meant energetic new employees, or the people doing day-to-day operations often left, again robbing the organization of valuable resources. In many companies it seemed better to be a leaver than a survivor.

By the mid-1990s, downsizing had become more surgical. Companies were better able to target where to make reductions. Still, the AMA data is pretty constant over a seven-year period. Downsizing doesn't lead to increased profits or productivity right away for the majority of companies. It appears to take about two to three years to recover.

Why? Downsizing leads to a huge decrease in morale, a substantial increase in turnover, and increases in absenteeism and disability claims. Absenteeism and insurance claims are direct costs to the company. Also, consider the data we have just seen on turnover. Huselid showed *decreasing* turnover led to better financial results.

Turnover has a bigger cost than just replacing employees who leave. For instance, Chrysler found that while it only costs $7,000 to bring on a new salesperson, the difference between a veteran salesperson and a new hire is more than $175,000 in gross profits over a two-year period. Fred Reichheld demonstrated in *The Loyalty Effect* that employee retention, provided they're the right employees, leads to customer retention. Small increases in customer retention lead to big increases in operating profits and customer share, and the value of customer retention grows every year. Perhaps the two- to three-year period to recover from downsizing is no coincidence. Like the Chrysler information, Reichheld's data from several industries demonstrate it takes about three years before new employees start to create real economic value for their companies.

Decreases in morale do not lead to better service or quality. That's fairly obvious. Have you ever received good service from a demoralized employee? Only 26 percent of the firms in the AMA survey said quality increased after downsizing. A 1996 survey by Olsten Corporation of 640 firms reported that 48 percent said their downsized companies were having a harder time meeting deadlines, and 38 percent said customer service levels had declined.

Downsizing in the late 1990s in the U.S. is going on at the same time that steady job growth is occurring, often at the same companies. In fact, hiring started to increase much faster than firing in 1996, and the quality of jobs was very good—higher-paying technical and managerial jobs. The reasons for downsizing also have changed, away from cost cutting to reengineering, restructuring, better staff utilization, automation, and outsourcing. It appears that companies are not getting smaller, so much as they are changing shapes—what they do and who does it. This is likely to continue as long as the economy stays strong.

The last issues to consider from downsizing data in many ways are the most fascinating. They provide the strongest support for my contention that smart talent management is key to value creation, and training is absolutely essential for every company. For the last few years, the AMA has reported companies that increased their training budgets after downsizing are far more likely to experience increased productivity and profitability, both short-term and long-term. In fact, companies that increased training after downsizing are twice as likely to report increased long-term productivity. Employees who get trained in new work processes and automation after downsizing are much more likely to increase their productivity. Increasing training budgets appears to be as correlated with increasing long-term profitability as is cutting headcount and expenses. Unfortunately, only about one-quarter to one-third of companies reported increasing training budgets after job cuts.

What conclusions can you draw from this downsizing data? Downsizing is a game of chance when it comes to getting what you want from a productivity and profit perspective. The AMA data suggest companies that reported being profitable after downsizing probably were profitable before they downsized. A recent study by Indiana University reports only about half of the companies that downsize become more profitable.

Additionally, it's clear that staff reductions and turnover have costs far beyond what were ever considered. Above all, companies that want to get leaner need to do more training, so employees have the skills they need to be successful in their new environments. Finally, companies had better make sure before they cut that the right people are leaving and customers will stay.

A PERFECT WORLD

I have shown you a large amount of data regarding talent management and its effects on the bottom line. This includes data on culture, management practices, and downsizing. All of it suggests the smarter and more strategic you are about managing people the more likely you are to create higher profits, cash flows, and stock returns.

You also have seen that the effects of talent management on economic value come largely from higher productivity, reduced turnover (as long as high performers stay and low performers go), and improved service quality. I didn't show data on how talent management raises manufacturing quality and how that increases the bottom line, though there are several studies from the automotive and steel industries on this. You also have not seen any studies that show that strategic talent management has a negative impact on financial results—because there aren't any studies that demonstrate this.

So, in a perfect world, with a great product or service, how could you apply this data to your company? Here's what you should do:

- Start with a good set of values, ones that really appeal to peoples' sense of pride in serving customers or building great products. Stay with them for the long run but keep refreshing them.
- Weave those values into an organizational culture that balances the needs of customers, shareholders, and employees. Maintain the balance, even when times get tough.
- Stay focused on the outside world, especially your customers and labor markets. Anticipate changes in these constituencies and lead change quickly when the need arises.
- Manage your workforce strategically. Build in the right management practices. This book tells you which ones. It should be clear that performance management has to be a foundation.
- Manage your workforce for productivity, retention of strong performers, and quality. Remember you get what you measure, so determine how to measure these things.
- Avoid downsizing, other than eliminating poor performers. Keep training people so they can stay up with the changes you keep making in work processes, technology, service quality, organization, and other areas.

If you do these good things and have a good value proposition for your customers, you will be successful over the long-term, and make plenty of money for you, your employees, and your shareholders.

REFERENCES

American Compensation Association. *Raising the Bar: Using Competencies to Enhance Employee Performance*, May, 1996.

American Management Association. *Corporate Downsizing, Job Elimination, and Job Creation*, 1995.

American Management Association. *Downsizing, Job Elimination, and Job Creation*, 1996.

Bridges, William. *JobShift*. Reading, MA: Addison-Wesley, 1994.

Collins, James C. and Jerry I. Porras. *Built To Last*. New York: Harper Business, 1994.

Erikson, Erik H. *Childhood and Society*. New York: W.W. Norton, 1950.

Granitsas, Alkman, and Trish Saywell. "Managing, Barely." *Far Eastern Economic Review* (August 28, 1997): 52-58.

Gubman, Edward L. "Aligning People Strategies with Customer Value." *Compensation & Benefits Review*, American Management Association (1995): 15-23.

Gubman, Edward L. "People Are More Valuable than Ever." *Compensation & Benefits Review*, American Management Association (1995): 7-14.

Gubman, Edward L., ed. "What Employers Want, What Employees Need." *Compensation & Benefits Review*, American Management Association (1995).

Heskett, James L., W. Earl Sasser, Jr., and Leonard A. Schlesinger. *The Service Profit Chain*. New York: Free Press, 1997.

Hewitt Associates. *HR's Strategic Role in Building Competitiveness*, 1992.

Hewitt Associates. *The Impact of Performance Management on Organizational Success*, 1995.

Hewitt Associates. *The Impact of Performance Management on Organizational Success: Additional Research*, 1996.

Hexter, Ellen S., ed. *Case Studies in Strategic Performance Measurement*. The Conference Board, 1997.

Hochschild, Arlie R. *The Time Bind*. New York: Henry Holt & Co., 1997.

Huselid, Mark A. "The Impact of Human Resource Management Practices on Turnover, Productivity, and Corporate Financial Performance." *Academy of Management Journal* 38(3) (1995): 635-672.

Jackson, Phil. *Sacred Hoops*. New York: Hyperion, 1995.

Kaplan, Robert S. and David P. Norton. *The Balanced Scorecard.* Boston, MA: Harvard Business School Press, 1996.

Kirkpatrick, David. "This Tough Guy Wants to Give You a Hug." *Fortune* (October 14, 1996): 170-178.

Kotter, John P. and James L. Heskett. *Corporate Culture and Performance.* New York: Free Press, 1992.

Kubler-Ross, Elizabeth. *On Death and Dying.* New York: Macmillan, 1991.

Lawler, Edward E. III, Susan A. Mohrman, and Gerald E. Ledford Jr. *Creating High Performance Organizations.* San Francisco: Josey-Bass, 1995.

Levering, Robert and Milton Moskowitz. *The 100 Best Companies To Work For in America.* New York: Currency Doubleday, 1993.

Morris, Betsy. "He's Smart. He's Not Nice. He's Saving Big Blue." *Fortune* (April 14, 1997): 68-83.

Pfeffer, Jeffrey. *Competitive Advantage.* Boston, MA: Harvard Business School Press, 1994.

Porter, Michael E. *Competitive Strategy.* New York: The Free Press, 1980.

Porter, Michael E. "What Is Strategy?" *Harvard Business Review* , vol. 74 (November-December, 1996): 61-78.

Reichheld, Frederick F. *The Loyalty Effect.* Boston, MA: Harvard Business School Press, 1996.

Risher, Howard. "Behind the Big Picture: Employment Trends in the 1990s." *Compensation & Benefits Review,* American Management Association 29(1): 8-18.

Robinson, John P. and Geoffrey Godfrey. *Time For Life.* University Park: Penn State University Press, 1997.

Rosenbluth, Hal F. and Diane McFerrin Peters. *The Customer Comes Second.* New York: Morrow Quill, 1992.

Rousseau, Denise M. *Psychological Contracts in Organizations.* Thousand Oaks, CA: Sage Publications, 1995.

Schlesinger, Leonard A. and Jeffrey Zorintsky. "Job Satisfaction, Service Capability, and Customer Satisfaction: An Examination of Linkages and Management Implications." *Human Resource Planning* 14(2): 141-149.

Schneider, Benjamin and David E. Bowen. "Human Resource Management is Critical." *Organizational Dynamics* (1993): 39-52.

Sellers, Patricia. "Can Home Depot Fix Its Sagging Stock?" *Fortune* (March 4, 1996): 139-149.

Sellars, Patricia. "Sears: The Turnaround Is Ending, the Revolution's Begun." *Fortune* (April 28, 1997): 106-121.

Stratford, Sherman. " Levi's: As Ye Sew, So Shall Ye Reap." *Fortune* (May 12, 1997): 104-118.

Stross, Randall E. *The Microsoft Way*. Reading MA: Addison-Wesley, 1996.

Tetzeli, Rick, "And Now for Motorola's Next Trick." *Fortune* (April 28, 1997): 122-133.

"The Fast Food Computer Strategy—An Interview with ACER'S Stah Shih." *Strategy & Business*, Fourth Quarter (1996): 52-57.

Treacy, Michael and Fred Wiersema. *The Discipline of Market Leaders*. Reading, MA: Addison-Wesley, 1995.

Ulrich, David and Dale Lake. *Organizational Capability*. New York: John Wiley & Sons, 1990.

Wells, Susan J. "Honey, They've Shrunk the Workweek." *The New York Times* (June 15, 1997): 9F.

White, Robert W. *The Enterprise of Living*. New York: Holt, Rinehart and Winston, 1972.

Wiersema, Fred. *Customer Intimacy*. Santa Monica, CA: Knowledge Exchange, 1996.

Wolfe, Thomas. *The Right Stuff*. New York: Farrar, Strauss, Giroux, 1979.

INDEX